Optimization and Applications of Modern Wireless Networks and Symmetry

Optimization and Applications of Modern Wireless Networks and Symmetry

Editors

Pingping Chen
Long Shi
Yi Fang

MDPI • Basel • Beijing • Wuhan • Barcelona • Belgrade • Manchester • Tokyo • Cluj • Tianjin

Editors
Pingping Chen
Fuzhou University
China

Long Shi
Nanjing University of Science and Technology
China

Yi Fang
Guangdong University of Technology
China

Editorial Office
MDPI
St. Alban-Anlage 66
4052 Basel, Switzerland

This is a reprint of articles from the Special Issue published online in the open access journal *Symmetry* (ISSN 2073-8994) (available at: https://www.mdpi.com/journal/symmetry/special_issues/Wireless_Networks_and_Symmetry).

For citation purposes, cite each article independently as indicated on the article page online and as indicated below:

LastName, A.A.; LastName, B.B.; LastName, C.C. Article Title. *Journal Name* **Year**, *Volume Number*, Page Range.

ISBN 978-3-0365-5345-0 (Hbk)
ISBN 978-3-0365-5346-7 (PDF)

© 2022 by the authors. Articles in this book are Open Access and distributed under the Creative Commons Attribution (CC BY) license, which allows users to download, copy and build upon published articles, as long as the author and publisher are properly credited, which ensures maximum dissemination and a wider impact of our publications.

The book as a whole is distributed by MDPI under the terms and conditions of the Creative Commons license CC BY-NC-ND.

Contents

About the Editors . . . . **vii**

Pingping Chen, Long Shi and Yi Fang
Editorial of Special Issue "Optimization and Applications of Modern Wireless Networks and Symmetry"
Reprinted from: *Symmetry* **2022**, *14*, 1825, doi:10.3390/sym14091825 1

Lianghong Zhu, Huaikun Xiang and Kai Zhang
A Light and Anonymous Three-Factor Authentication Protocol for Wireless Sensor Networks
Reprinted from: *Symmetry* **2022**, *14*, 46, doi:10.3390/sym14010046 3

Bingrui Wang, Zhijian Lin and Xingang Zhang
A CNN-MPSK Demodulation Architecture with Ultra-Light Weight and Low-Complexity for Communications
Reprinted from: *Symmetry* **2022**, *14*, 873, doi:10.3390/sym14050873 23

Lingjun Kong, Haiyang Liu, Wentao Hou and Bin Dai
Improving Decodability of Polar Codes by Adding Noise
Reprinted from: *Symmetry* **2022**, *14*, 1156, doi:10.3390/sym14061156 35

Eduardo Michel Vieira Gomes, Edson Donizete De Carvalho, Carlos Alexandre Ribeiro Martins, Evandro Mazetto Brizola and Eduardo Brandani Da Silva
A General Framework for Geometrically Uniform Codes and Signal Sets Matched to Groups
Reprinted from: *Symmetry* **2022**, *14*, 1214, doi:10.3390/sym14061214 53

Wei Kuang Lai, Chin-Shiuh Shieh, Yuh-Chung Lin, Chun-Yi Tsai and Yu-Dai Yan
Unlicensed Spectrum Allocation for LTE and Wi-Fi Coexistence with HAP
Reprinted from: *Symmetry* **2022**, *14*, 1650, doi:10.3390/sym14081650 69

Tian Gao, Min Xiao, Pingping Chen and Diyan Gao
New Unequal Error Protection Strategy for Image Transmission Based on Bilayer-Lengthened PLDPC Code in Half-Duplex Relay System
Reprinted from: *Symmetry* **2022**, *14*, 1662, doi:10.3390/sym14081662 91

About the Editors

Pingping Chen

Pingping Chen (Senior Member, IEEE) received his Ph.D. degree in electronic engineering from Xiamen University, China, in 2013. In 2012, he was a research assistant in electronic and information engineering with The Hong Kong Polytechnic University, Hong Kong. From 2013 to 2015, he was a postdoctoral fellow at the Institute of Network Coding, The Chinese University of Hong Kong, Hong Kong, and from 2016 to 2017 at Singapore University of Technology and Design (SUTD), Singapore. Chen is currently a full professor at Fuzhou University, China. His primary research interests include channel coding, joint source and channel coding, network coding, and UWB communications.

Long Shi

Long Shi (Senior Member, IEEE) received his Ph.D. degree in electrical engineering from the University of New South Wales, Sydney, Australia, in 2012. From 2013 to 2016, he was a postdoctoral fellow at the Institute of Network Coding, Chinese University of Hong Kong, China. From 2014 to 2017, he was a lecturer at Nanjing University of Aeronautics and Astronautics, Nanjing, China. From 2017 to 2020, he was a research fellow at Singapore University of Technology and Design. Currently, Shi is a professor at the School of Electronic and Optical Engineering, Nanjing University of Science and Technology, Nanjing, China. His research interests include blockchain networks, mobile edge computing, and wireless network coding.

Yi Fang

Yi Fang (Senior Member, IEEE) received his Ph.D. degree in communication engineering at Xiamen University, China, in 2013. From May 2012 to July 2012, He was a research assistant in electronic and information engineering, Hong Kong Polytechnic University, Hong Kong. From September 2012 to September 2013, he was a visiting scholar in electronic and electrical engineering, University College London, UK. From February 2014 to February 2015, he was a research fellow at the School of Electrical and Electronic Engineering, Nanyang Technological University, Singapore. Fang is currently a full professor and Vice Dean at the School of Information Engineering, Guangdong University of Technology, China. He served as the Publicity Co-Chair of the International Symposium on Turbo Codes and Iterative Information Processing 2018. His current research interests include information and coding theory, spread-spectrum modulation, and cooperative communications.

Editorial

Editorial of Special Issue "Optimization and Applications of Modern Wireless Networks and Symmetry"

Pingping Chen [1,*], Long Shi [2] and Yi Fang [3]

[1] Department of Electronic Information, Fuzhou University, Fuzhou 350116, China
[2] School of Electronic and Optical Engineering, Nanjing University of Science and Technology, Nanjing 210094, China
[3] School of Information Engineering, Guangdong University of Technology, Guangzhou 510006, China
* Correspondence: ppchen.xm@gmail.com

This book contains the successfully published submissions [1–6] to a Special Issue of *Symmetry* on the subject area of "Optimization and Applications of Modern Wireless Networks and Symmetry".

Due to the future demands of IoT/5G communications, channel coding techniques are widely used in modern wireless communications to enhance reliability and spectral efficiency. In particular, channel coding and network protocol are being optimized for the next wireless standard and wireless sensor networks. This invokes a great deal of attention on the modern symmetry or asymmetry wireless communications.

This Special Issue covers channel coding, modulation, and network protocol of the recent advances in modern communications. The volume contains six published papers, with authors from areas throughout the world (Brazil, China, Taiwan).

In the first paper of this Special Issue, entitled "A Light and Anonymous Three-Factor Authentication Protocol for Wireless Sensor Networks", L. Zhu et al. propose a new lightweight and anonymous three-factor authentication based on symmetric cryptographic primitives for WSNs. By using the automated security verification tool ProVerif, BAN-logic verification, and an informal security analysis, the proposed scheme is proven to be secure and can achieve all known security features in WSNs. Moreover, the proposed scheme is shown to be practical and efficient through the comparison of security features and performance [1].

In the second paper, entitled "A CNN-MPSK Demodulation Architecture with Ultra-Light Weight and Low-Complexity for Communications", B. Wang et al. propose a generic architecture for MPSK demodulation, referred to as CNN-MPSK, from convolutional neural networks (CNNs). The architecture utilizes a single-layer CNN and a pooling trick to crop network parameters. In comparison with conventional coherent demodulation, the CNN-MPSK can avoid using three modules, carrier multiplication, bandpass filter, and sampling decision. Experimental results reveal that CNN-MPSK has almost the same performance as the conventional coherent demodulation, with much-reduced complexity. Additionally, the proposed scheme can be readily applied for demodulation of non-symmetric MPSK constellations that maybe distorted by linear and nonlinear impairments in communications [2].

In the paper entitled "Improving Decodability of Polar Codes by Adding Noise", L. Kong et al. present an online perturbed and directed neural-evolutionary (Online-PDNE) decoding algorithm for polar codes. This decoding algorithm converts uncorrectable received sequences into error-correcting regions of the decoding space by adding specific noises. Moreover, PDNE decoding and sole neural-evolutionary (SNE) decoding for polar codes are further proposed to provide a considerable tradeoff between the decoding performance and complexity. Numerical results suggest that the proposed decoding outperforms other conventional decoding algorithms, such as simplified successive cancellation (SSC) decoding [3].

In the next paper, entitled "A General Framework for Geometrically Uniform Codes and Signal Sets Matched to Groups", E. Gomes et al. propose a general treatment of the metric, providing a necessary and sufficient condition for an isometry between a group G and a signal set S to be considered a matched labeling. The definition of the G-isometric signal set is presented to connect the various concepts discussed in this work. Despite emphasizing the hyperbolic case because of its rich properties and Euclidean cases for historical reasons and applications, the results are valid for any metric space. Additionally, the article opens up new possibilities for applying discrete metrics that come from the group metric obtained from the (finitely generated) group of labels [4].

In the paper entitled "Unlicensed Spectrum Allocation for LTE and Wi-Fi Coexistence with HAP", W. Lai et al. contribute to the determination of the optimal time ratio, δ, for the time-division multiplexing of LTE and Wi-Fi over unlicensed bands. By considering the asymmetric allocation according to QoS requirements and traffic demands, the problem is formulated as an optimization problem over the total throughput. The lower and upper bounds of δ are developed according to the QoS requirements of Wi-Fi and the admission control requirements of LTE. Simulations are conducted and demonstrate that the proposed approach improves the total throughput without compromising the fairness of Wi-Fi, as intended. Ten percent improvement in throughput compared with LTE-U can be achieved [5].

In the last paper, entitled "New Unequal Error Protection Strategy for Image Transmission Based on Bilayer-Lengthened PLDPC Code in Half-Duplex Relay System", T. Gao et al. propose new efficient UEP strategies of based on bilayer protograph-based low-density parity check (PLDPC) codes in decoding-and-forward (DF) relay systems. It jointly utilizes source coding and channel coding to design UEP strategies and then save transmission energy. Considering the different importance of DCT coefficients of image and variance statistical characteristics of image sub-blocks, bilayer-lengthened PLDPC codes are exploited to protect the transmitted image information in the half-duplex relay system. The simulation result shows that the proposed UEP schemes achieve excellent performance gains as compared to conventional equal-error protection schemes [6].

The Guest Editor hopes you will enjoy reading this Special Issue focused on cutting-edge research in channel coding and network protocols. We expect that the collected studies will motivate researchers to continue groundbreaking work in this emerging area.

Finally, the Guest Editor would like to thank the authors of all the papers submitted to this Special Issue, and the Guest Editor would like to thank the journal's editorial staff and reviewers for their efforts and help during the process.

Funding: This research was funded by the NSF of China under Grants 61871132, 62171135, 62071131, the Guangdong Basic and Applied Basic Research Foundation under Grant 2022B1515020086, and Jiangsu Specially-Appointed Professor Program in 2021.

Conflicts of Interest: The authors declare no conflict of interest.

References

1. Zhu, L.; Xiang, H.; Zhang, K. A Light and Anonymous Three-Factor Authentication Protocol for Wireless Sensor Networks. *Symmetry* **2022**, *14*, 46. [CrossRef]
2. Wang, B.; Lin, Z.; Zhang, X. A CNN-MPSK Demodulation Architecture with Ultra-Light Weight and Low-Complexity for Communications. *Symmetry* **2022**, *14*, 873. [CrossRef]
3. Kong, L.; Liu, H.; Hou, W.; Dai, B. Improving Decodability of Polar Codes by Adding Noise. *Symmetry* **2022**, *14*, 1156. [CrossRef]
4. Gomes, E.; de Carvalho, E.; Martins, C.; Brizola, E.; da Silva, E. A General Framework for Geometrically Uniform Codes and Signal Sets Matched to Groups. *Symmetry* **2022**, *14*, 1214. [CrossRef]
5. Lai, W.; Shieh, C.; Lin, Y.; Tsai, C.; Yan, Y. Unlicensed Spectrum Allocation for LTE and Wi-Fi Coexistence with HAP. *Symmetry* **2022**, *14*, 1650. [CrossRef]
6. Gao, T.; Xiao, M.; Chen, P.; Gao, D. New Unequal Error Protection Strategy for Image Transmission Based on Bilayer-Lengthened PLDPC Code in Half-Duplex Relay System. *Symmetry* **2022**, *14*, 1662. [CrossRef]

Article

A Light and Anonymous Three-Factor Authentication Protocol for Wireless Sensor Networks

Lianghong Zhu [1,†], Huaikun Xiang [1,†] and Kai Zhang [2,*]

1. School of Automotive and Transportation, Shenzhen Polytechnic, Shenzhen 518055, China; zhulianghong@szpt.edu.cn (L.Z.); xianghuaikun@szpt.edu.cn (H.X.)
2. Department of Computer Science and Engineering, National Chung Hsing University, Taichung 402, Taiwan
* Correspondence: kai.zhang@smail.nchu.edu.tw
† These authors contributed equally to this work.

Abstract: Recently, wireless sensor networks (*WSNs*) have been widely used in a variety of fields, and make people's lives more convenient and efficient. However, *WSNs* are usually deployed in a harsh and insecure environment. Furthermore, sensors with limited hardware resources have a low capacity for data processing and communication. For these reasons, research on efficient and secure real-time authentication and key agreement protocols based on the characteristics of *WSNs* has gradually attracted the attention of academics. Although many schemes have been proposed, most of them cannot achieve all known security features with satisfactory performance, among which anonymity, N-Factor security, and forward secrecy are the most vulnerable. In order to solve these shortcomings, we propose a new lightweight and anonymous three-factor authentication scheme based on symmetric cryptographic primitives for *WSNs*. By using the automated security verification tool *ProVerif*, *BAN*-logic verification, and an informal security analysis, we prove that our proposed scheme is secure and realizes all known security features in *WSNs*. Moreover, we show that our proposed scheme is practical and efficient through the comparison of security features and performance.

Keywords: authentication and key agreement; symmetric cryptographic primitives; three-factor; security analysis; wireless sensor networks

1. Introduction

A wireless sensor network (*WSN*) is a distributed and self-organizing sensor network, which is composed of a large number of sensor nodes that can perceive and understand the external world. In *WSNs*, sensor nodes cooperate to sense, collect, and process information in the network coverage area and send it to the gateway node. In recent years, *WSNs* have been widely used in various practical applications in industrial and agricultural fields [1–4], such as temperature monitoring in agriculture, power consumption monitoring in smart grids, and human health monitoring in medical care. In these application environments, many scattered users, various randomly distributed sensor nodes, and one or more relatively powerful gateway nodes form a powerful network system. For example, in the field of health care, the sensors deployed on the patient's body can monitor and obtain the patient's body data, and the medical staff can directly and remotely obtain the patient's current body temperature, blood pressure, pulse times, and other information in real-time through the wireless sensor network, so as to improve the health status of healthy patients. Figure 1 shows the network architecture of *WSNs*.

However, when sensor nodes are active in an unattended or hostile wireless network environment, attackers can easily intercept, delete, and modify transmission messages and launch various attacks [5]. Therefore, the network security and privacy of these sensors become very critical. In order to ensure that only authorized legitimate users can access sensors and protect the communication security of real-time sensing data, it is extremely

necessary for users and sensors to authenticate each other directly. Moreover, they also need to be able to establish a session key to ensure the security of future communication. Authentication and key agreement protocols are effective ways to achieve these goals. However, due to the limited resources of sensor nodes, an authentication protocol based on complex asymmetric cryptographic primitives is difficult to apply to wireless sensor networks. Therefore, the balance between security and performance is highly significant for the design of identity authentication protocols in the wireless sensor network environment.

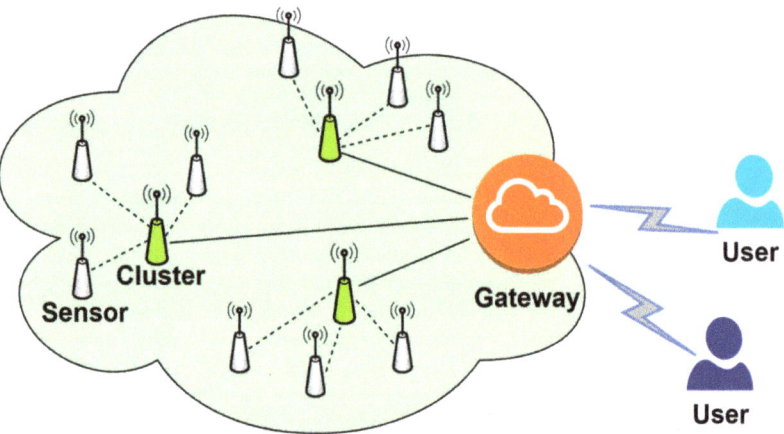

Figure 1. Network model of wireless sensor networks.

Lamport proposed the first password-based authentication and key agreement protocol in 1980 [6], and, since then, research on authentication protocols has been a hot topic. In recent years, research on authentication and key agreement protocols in *WSNs* has been conducted [7–18]. In 2006, Wong et al. [19] proposed a lightweight password-based authentication scheme for *WSNs*. However, Das et al. point out that Wong et al.'s scheme cannot resist replay attacks and stolen-verifier attacks [20]. Furthermore, Das et al. put forward an improved scheme. Unfortunately, there are also many security flaws in Das et al.'s scheme [21,22]. Based on Farash et al.'s scheme [23], Amin et al. provided an anonymity three-factor authentication scheme [24] for *WSNs* in 2016. However, Jiang et al. found that the scheme could not resist smart card stolen attacks and known session-specific temporary information attacks [25]. Although many schemes have been proposed, most of them cannot achieve all known security features with satisfactory performance.

In 2019, Shin et al. proposed a lightweight three-factor authentication and key agreement protocol for *WSNs* [26] and claimed that the protocol can achieve all known security features with satisfactory performance. This article analyzes Shin et al.'s scheme. It is found that their scheme is vulnerable to de-synchronization attacks and cannot achieve forward secrecy and three-factor security.

Our crucial contributions are as follows:

1. We review and analyze Shin et al.'s three-factor authentication scheme for *WSNs*. Further, we show that their scheme is vulnerable to de-synchronization attacks and cannot achieve forward secrecy and three-factor security.
2. We present a new, lightweight anonymous three-factor authentication with perfect forward secrecy in *WSNs*. The operation of the scheme is based on a symmetric cryptosystem, so the computational overhead of the scheme is lightweight and the scheme is suitable for *WSNs*. The new scheme can achieve all known strong security functions with satisfactory performance, including anonymity, perfect forward secrecy, n-factor security, and so on.

3. By using the automated security verification tool *ProVerif* and *BAN*-logic, we prove that our proposed scheme is secure and realizes the mutual authentication of communication participants in *WSNs*.
4. Through the comparison of security features and performance, it can be found that our proposed scheme is practical.

The rest of this paper is organized as follows. We introduce the relevant preliminaries in Section 2 and review the scheme of Shin et al. in Section 3. In Section 4, the scheme of Shin et al. is subjected to cryptanalysis and the attack method is given. The new scheme is proposed in Section 5, and the security analysis and performance analysis of the new scheme are carried out in Sections 6 and 7, respectively. Section 8 summarizes the paper.

2. Preliminaries

2.1. Fuzzy Extractor

At different times, there may be subtle differences in the biometrics extracted by the same user. The fuzzy extractor can eliminate these subtle differences. In other words, the fuzzy extractor can produce the same output even if the inputs are slightly different. Fuzzy logic is widely used in supply chains and healthcare logistics [27–29]. The fuzzy extractor consists of two parts:

1. $GEN(Bio_i) = (b_i, pair_i)$, with Bio_i as input, the probability generation mechanism GEN outputs a random string b_i and a random helper string $pair_i$.
2. $REP(Bio'_i, pair_i) = b_i$, with Bio'_i and $pair_i$ as inputs, the deterministic mechanism REP can regenerate b_i, where $dis(Bio'_i, Bio_i) \leq \Delta t$.

2.2. Adversary Model

In this paper, we adopt the most rigorous (but practical) adversary model proposed by Wang et al. [30] and Huang et al. [31]. Table 1 shows the capabilities of the adversary, A.

Table 1. The capabilities of the adversary.

Symbol	Description
C1	A can enumerate every possibility of user identity and password.
C2	A can eavesdrop, intercept, insert, delete, or block messages transmitted in the public channel.
C3	For a three-factor protocol (password, smart card, and biometric), A can capture two of the authentication factors simultaneously.
C4	Expired session keys can be captured.
C5	A can obtain the long-term private keys of users, $GWNs$, or sensors (only when evaluating forward secrecy).

2.3. Notations

The notations used thereinafter are listed in Table 2.

Table 2. Notations.

Symbol	Description
GWN	Gateway Node
U_i	User
ID_i	Identification of U_i
PW_i	Password of U_i
SC_i	Smart card of U_i
Bio_i	Biometric of U_i
b_i	Random string generated by a fuzzy extractor
$pair_i$	Random helper string generated by a fuzzy extractor
PID_i	Pseudo identification of U_i

Table 2. Cont.

Symbol	Description
S_j	Sensor Node
SID_j	Identification of S_j
SK_{ij}	Session Key of U_i and S_j
T_1, T_2, T_3, T_4	Timestamp
$\oplus$	XOR Operation
$H(*)/h(*)$	Hash Function
$\|\|$	Concatenation operation

3. Revisiting of Shin et al.'s Scheme

In 2019, Sooyeon Shin et al. proposed a lightweight anonymous three-factor authentication protocol for micro-sensors in wireless sensor networks [26]. Taking their protocol as an example, we analyze and point out the security defects of such authentication protocols.

Shin et al.'s protocol consists of four phases: the initialization phase, registration phase, authentication phase, and password update phase. The system completes the selection of parameters and encryption algorithm in the initialization phase. The registration phase realizes user registration and the distribution of smart cards. The authentication phase completes the mutual authentication and session key agreement between the user and the sensor. It should be noted that the communication channel in the authentication phase is public and insecure.

The specific process of the agreement is as follows:

3.1. Initialization Phase

Step 1: The GWN selects K_U, K_S as master secrets and stores them safely.

Step 2: For sensor S_j, the GWN chooses SID_j as the identity of S_j and calculates $X_{S_j} = h(SID_j || K_S)$.

Step 3: The sensor S_j stores X_{S_j} secretly.

3.2. User Registration Phase

Step 1: The user U_i selects his identity ID_i and password PW_i and imprints Bio_i. Then, U_i chooses a random number u_i and calculates $GEN(Bio_i) = (b_i, pair_i)$, $HPW_i = h(PW_i || b_i)$, and $TID_i = h(ID_i || u_i)$. Further, U_i sends the registration request $\{TID_i, HPW_i\}$ towards the GWN via a private secure channel.

Step 2: The GWN receives $\{TID_i, HPW_i\}$ and freely chooses PID_i^1 as a pseudonym. Then, the GWN calculates $HID_i = h(TID_i || K_U)$, $A_i = h(HPW_i || TID_i) \oplus HID_i$, $B_i = h(HPW_i || HID_i)$, and $C_i^1 = h(TID_i || HID_i) \oplus PID_i^1$. Then, the GWN writes $\{A_i, B_i, C_i^1\}$ into SC_i. and stores (PID_i^1, TID_i). Finally, the GWN transmits SC_i towards U_i via a private, secure channel.

Step 3: U_i receives SC_i and calculates $D_i = u_i \oplus h(ID_i || b_i)$. Finally, U_i write $\{D_i, pair_i\}$ into SC_i.

The process of the User registration phase is shown in Figure 2.

3.3. Authentication Phase

Step 1: U_i inserts SC_i, inputs ID_i and PW_i, and imprints Bio_i. SC_i calculates $b_i = REP(Bio_i, pair_i)$, $u_i = D_i \oplus h(ID_i || b_i)$, $TID_i = h(ID_i || u_i)$, $HPW_i^* = h(PW_i || b_i)$, $HID_i^* = A_i \oplus h(HPW_i^* || TID_i)$, and $B_i^* = h(HPW_i^* || HID_i^*)$ and verifies the equality check for B_i ? $= B_i^*$. If it does not hold true, SC_i rejects the login request. Otherwise, SC_i generates a random number r_i and the current timestamp T_1, and calculates $PID_i^1 = C_i^1 \oplus h(TID_i || HID_i^*)$, $R_i = h(TID_i || PID_i^1 || r_i)$, $M_i = r_i \oplus h(TID_i || HID_i^* || T_1)$, and $M_{UG} = h(TID_i || HID_i^* || PID_i^1 || R_i || T_1)$. Finally, SC_i transmits the login request $\{PID_i^1, M_i, M_{UG}, T_1\}$ towards the GWN.

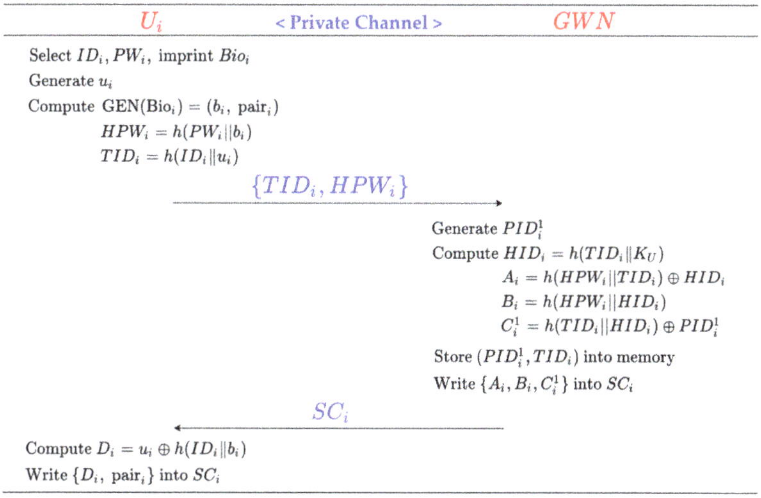

U_i	< Private Channel >	GWN
Select ID_i, PW_i, imprint Bio_i		
Generate u_i		
Compute $GEN(Bio_i) = (b_i, pair_i)$		
$\quad HPW_i = h(PW_i\|b_i)$		
$\quad TID_i = h(ID_i\|u_i)$		
	$\xrightarrow{\{TID_i, HPW_i\}}$	
		Generate PID_i^1
		Compute $HID_i = h(TID_i\|K_U)$
		$\quad A_i = h(HPW_i\|TID_i) \oplus HID_i$
		$\quad B_i = h(HPW_i\|HID_i)$
		$\quad C_i^1 = h(TID_i\|HID_i) \oplus PID_i^1$
		Store (PID_i^1, TID_i) into memory
		Write $\{A_i, B_i, C_i^1\}$ into SC_i
	$\xleftarrow{SC_i}$	
Compute $D_i = u_i \oplus h(ID_i\|b_i)$		
Write $\{D_i, pair_i\}$ into SC_i		

Figure 2. User registration phase of Shin et al.'s scheme.

Step 2: The GWN receives $\{PID_i^1, M_i, M_{UG}, T_1\}$ and checks the validity of T_1. Then, the GWN searches (PID_i^1, TID_i) in memory using PID_i^1 and calculates $HID_i^* = h(TID_i\|K_U)$, $r_i^* = M_i \oplus h(TID_i\|HID_i^*\|T_1)$, $R_i^* = h(TID_i\|PID_i^1\|r_i^*)$, and $M_{UG}^* = h(TID_i\|HID_i^*\|PID_i^1\|R_i^*\|T_1)$. Further, the GWN checks the equality of $M_{UG}^* \stackrel{?}{=} M_{UG}$. If it does not hold true, the GWN rejects the login request. Otherwise, the GWN selects SID_j, generates the current timestamp T_2, and calculates $X_{S_j} = h(SID_j\|K_S)$, $M_G = R_i^* \oplus h(X_{S_j}\|T_2)$, and $M_{GS} = h(PID_i^1\|SID_j\|X_{S_j}\|R_i^*\|T_2)$. Finally, the GWN transmits $\{PID_i^1, M_G, M_{GS}, T_2\}$ towards S_j.

Step 3: Upon the reception of $\{PID_i^1, M_G, M_{GS}, T_2\}$ from the GWN, S_j checks whether T_2 is a valid timestamp. Then, S_j calculates $R_i^* = M_G \oplus h(X_{S_j}\|T_2)$ and $M_{GS}^* = h(PID_i^1\|SID_j\|X_{S_j}\|R_i^*\|T_2)$ and verifies the equality check $M_{GS}^* \stackrel{?}{=} M_{GS}$. If the verification fails, S_j aborts the session. Otherwise, S_j generates a random number r_j and the current timestamp T_3, and calculates $R_j = h(SID_j\|r_j)$, $M_j = r_j \oplus h(X_{S_j}\|T_3)$, $SK_{ij} = h(R_i^*\|R_j)$, $M_{SG} = h(PID_i^1\|SID_j\|X_{S_j}\|R_j\|SK_{ij}\|T_3)$. Finally, S_j sends $\{M_j, M_{SG}, T_3\}$ back to the GWN.

Step 4: The GWN receives $\{M_j, M_{SG}, T_3\}$ and checks the validity of T_3. Then, the GWN calculates $r_j^* = M_j \oplus h(X_{S_j}\|T_3)$, $R_j^* = h(SID_j\|r_j^*)$, $SK_{ij}^* = h(R_i^*\|R_j^*)$, and $M_{SG}^* = h(PID_i^1\|SID_j\|X_{S_j}\|R_j^*\|SK_{ij}^*\|T_3)$ and verifies the equality check $M_{SG}^* \stackrel{?}{=} M_{SG}$. If the verification fails, the GWN aborts the session. Otherwise, the GWN generates the current timestamp T_4 and a new pseudonym PID_i^2, and calculates $C_i^2 = h(TID_i\|HID_i^*) \oplus PID_i^2$, $p_i^2 = C_i^2 \oplus h(HID_i^*\|T_4)$, $M_G' = R_j^* \oplus h(PID_i^1\|HID_i^*)$, and $M_{GU} = h(PID_i^1\|HID_i^*\|C_i^2\|R_j^*\|SK_{ij}^*\|T_4)$. Finally, the GWN sends $\{p_i^2, M_G', M_{GU}, T_4\}$ back to U_i. and replaces PID_i^1 with PID_i^2 in memory.

Step 5: U_i receives $\{p_i^2, M_G', M_{GU}, T_4\}$ and checks whether T_4 is a valid timestamp. Then, U_i calculates $R_j^* = M_G' \oplus h(PID_i^1\|HID_i^*)$, $SK_{ij}^* = h(R_i\|R_j^*)$, $C_i^2 = p_i^2 \oplus h(HID_i^*\|T_4)$, and $M_{GU}^* = h(PID_i^1\|HID_i^*\|C_i^2\|R_j^*\|SK_{ij}^*\|T_4)$ and checks the equality of $M_{GU}^* \stackrel{?}{=} M_{GU}$. If it holds true, U_i replaces C_i^1 with C_i^2 in SC_i.

The process of the authentication phase is shown in Figure 3.

U_i	< Public Channel >	GWN	< Public Channel >	S_j

U_i side:
Insert SC_i, input ID_i, PW_i, imprint Bio_i
Compute $b_i = REP(Bio_i, pair_i)$, $u_i = D_i \oplus h(ID_i \| b_i)$
$TID_i = h(ID_i \| u_i)$, $HPW_i^* = h(PW_i \| b_i)$
$HID_i^* = A_i \oplus h(HPW_i^* \| TID_i)$, $B_i^* = h(HPW_i^* \| HID_i^*)$
Check $B_i ? = B_i^*$
Generate r_i, T_1
Compute $PID_i^1 = C_i^1 \oplus h(TID_i \| HID_i^*)$, $R_i = h(TID_i \| PID_i^1 \| r_i)$
$M_i = r_i \oplus h(TID_i \| HID_i^* \| T_1)$, $M_{UG} = h(TID_i \| HID_i^* \| PID_i^1 \| R_i \| T_1)$

$\{PID_i^1, M_i, M_{UG}, T_1\} \longrightarrow$

GWN side:
Check the validity of T_1
Compute $HID_i^* = h(TID_i \| K_n)$, $r_i^* = M_i \oplus h(TID_i \| HID_i^* \| T_1)$
$R_i^* = h(TID_i \| PID_i^1 \| r_i^*)$, $M_{UG}^* = h(TID_i \| HID_i^* \| PID_i^1 \| R_i^* \| T_1)$
Check $M_{UG}^* ? = M_{UG}$
Select SID_j, generate T_2
Compute $X_{S_j} = h(SID_j \| K_S)$, $M_G = R_i^* \oplus h(X_{S_j} \| T_2)$
$M_{GS} = h(PID_i^1 \| SID_j \| X_{S_j} \| R_i^* \| T_2)$

$\{PID_i^1, M_G, M_{GS}, T_2\} \longrightarrow$

S_j side:
Check the validity of T_2
Compute $R_i^* = M_G \oplus h(X_{S_j} \| T_2)$
$M_{GS}^* = h(PID_i^1 \| SID_j \| X_{S_j} \| R_i^* \| T_2)$
Check $M_{GS}^* ? = M_{GS}$
Generate r_j, T_3
Compute $R_j = h(SID_j \| r_j)$
$M_j = r_j \oplus h(X_{S_j} \| T_3)$
$SK_{ij} = h(R_i^* \| R_j)$
$M_{SG} = h(PID_i^1 \| SID_j \| X_{S_j} \| R_j \| SK_{ij} \| T_3)$

$\longleftarrow \{M_j, M_{SG}, T_3\}$

GWN side:
Check the validity of T_3
Compute $r_j^* = M_j \oplus h(X_{S_j} \| T_3)$, $R_j^* = h(SID_j \| r_j^*)$, $SK_{ij}^* = h(R_i^* \| R_j^*)$
$M_{SG}^* = h(PID_i^1 \| SID_j \| X_{S_j} \| R_j^* \| SK_{ij}^* \| T_3)$
Check $M_{SG}^* ? = M_{SG}$
Generate T_4, PID_i^2
Compute $C_i^2 = h(TID_i \| HID_i^*) \oplus PID_i^2$, $p_i^2 = C_i^2 \oplus h(HID_i^* \| T_4)$
$M_G' = R_j^* \oplus h(PID_i^1 \| HID_i^*)$, $M_{GU} = h(PID_i^1 \| HID_i^* \| C_i^2 \| R_j^* \| SK_{ij}^* \| T_4)$
Replace PID_i^1 with PID_i^2

$\longleftarrow \{p_i^2, M_G', M_{GU}, T_4\}$

U_i side:
Check the validity of T_4
Compute $R_j^* = M_G' \oplus h(PID_i^1 \| HID_i^*)$, $SK_{ij}^* = h(R_i \| R_j^*)$
$C_i^2 = p_i^2 \oplus h(HID_i^* \| T_4)$, $M_{GU}^* = h(PID_i^1 \| HID_i^* \| C_i^2 \| R_j^* \| SK_{ij}^* \| T_4)$
Check $M_{GU}^* ? = M_{GU}$
Replace C_i^1 with C_i^2

Figure 3. Authentication phase of Shin et al.'s scheme.

3.4. Password Update Phase

Step 1: U_i inserts SC_i to the reader, inputs ID_i and PW_i, and imprints Bio_i.

Step 2: SC_i calculates $b_i = REP(Bio_i, pair_i)$, $u_i = D_i \oplus h(ID_i \| b_i)$, $TID_i = h(ID_i \| u_i)$, $HPW_i^* = h(PW_i \| b_i)$, $HID_i^* = A_i \oplus h(HPW_i^* \| TID_i)$, and $B_i^* = h(HPW_i^* \| HID_i^*)$ and verifies the equality check for $B_i ? = B_i^*$. If it does not hold true, SC_i rejects the request. Otherwise, U_i inputs a new password PW_i^{new}.

Step 3: SC_i calculates $HPW_i^{new} = h(PW_i^{new} \| b_i)$, $A_i^{new} = h(HPW_i^{new} \| TID_i) \oplus HID_i^*$, and $B_i^{new} = h(HPW_i^{new} \| HID_i^*)$. At last, SC_i replaces A_i and B_i with A_i^{new} and B_i^{new}, respectively.

4. Cryptanalysis of Shin et al.'s Scheme

We show that Shin et al.'s scheme is vulnerable to de-synchronization attacks and can not achieve forward secrecy and three-factor security in this section.

4.1. De-Synchronization Attack

Suppose that an adversary blocks $\{p_i^2, M'_G, M_{GU}, T_4\}$, which is sent from the *GWN* to U_i. On the side of the *GWN*, the pseudonym of U_i is PID_i^2 at this point. However, U_i is unable to obtain C_i^2 without $\{p_i^2, M'_G, M_{GU}, T_4\}$. Thus, the pseudonyms on the side of U_i and the *GWN* become out of synchronization. When U_i wants to access a sensor node through the *GWN* in the next session, the *GWN* will reject U_i's login request. Therefore, Shin et al.'s scheme is vulnerable to de-synchronization attacks.

4.2. Forward Secrecy

Suppose that an adversary occasionally obtains X_{S_j}, which is the long-term private key of S_j. Furthermore, the adversary intercepted $\{PID_i^1, M_G, M_{GS}, T_2\}$ and $\{M_j, M_{SG}, T_3\}$ in the previous session of U_i and S_j. The adversary could obtain the previous session key of U_i and S_j via following steps.

Step 1: The adversary calculates $R_i^* = M_G \oplus h(X_{S_j}||T_2)$, $r_j^* = M_j \oplus h(X_{S_j}||T_3)$, and $R_j^* = h(SID_j||r_j^*)$.

Step 2: The adversary obtains the previous session key of U_i and S_j, $SK_{ij} = h(R_i^*||R_j^*)$. Therefore, Shin et al.'s scheme can not achieve forward secrecy.

4.3. Three-Factor Security

For a three-factor authentication scheme, when two of the authentication factors are captured by an adversary, it is necessary to ensure that the remaining authentication factor is still secure. Suppose that an adversary captures U_i's smart card SC_i and biometric Bio_i simultaneously. The adversary is able to obtain the password of U_i via the following steps.

Step 1: The adversary extracts $\{A_i, B_i, C_i^1, D_i, pair_i\}$ from SC_i using side-channel technology and calculates $b_i = REP(Bio_i, pair_i)$.

Step 2: The adversary guesses a candidate identity ID_i^* and a candidate password PW_i^* from D_{id} and D_{pw}, where D_{id} and D_{pw} are user identity space and password space, respectively.

Step 3: The adversary calculates $u_i^* = D_i \oplus h(ID_i^*||b_i)$, $TID_i^* = h(ID_i^*||u_i^*)$, $HPW_i^* = h(PW_i^*||b_i)$, $HID_i^* = A_i \oplus h(HPW_i^*||TID_i^*)$, and $B_i^* = h(HPW_i^*||HID_i^*)$.

Step 4: The adversary checks whether $B_i \stackrel{?}{=} B_i^*$ holds. If not, the adversary repeats Steps 2–4 until he acquires the true password. Otherwise, the adversary succeeds in obtaining the true password of U_i.

The computational overhead of this attack is $(5T_h + 2T_{xor}) * |D_{id}| * |D_{pw}|$, where T_h is the running time of the one-way hash function, T_{xor} is the running time of the XOR operation, and D_{id} and D_{pw} are the spaces of user identity and password, respectively. According to the literature [20], we know that $|D_{id}| \leq |D_{pw}| \leq 10^6$. According to the experimental data from the literature [32], $T_h \approx 0.591\,\mu s$, $T_{xor} \approx 0.006\,\mu s$. The adversary can break the password of U_i in 35 days. If you use a high-performance cloud computing platform, the password will be cracked within a few hours.

5. The Proposed Scheme

The proposed protocol includes the following phases: initialization phase, user registration phase, sensor node registration phase, authentication phase, password, and biometric update phase.

The detailed description of the agreement is as follows:

5.1. Initialization Phase

The gateway node *GWN* creates two information tables in its memory (*UserInfoTable* and *SensorInfoTable*), which is used to store relevant information of users and sensors.

Then, the GWN freely chooses two master keys, K_u and K_s, and two secure hash functions, $h: \{0,1\}^* \bigoplus \{0,1\}^{128}$ and $H: \{0,1\}^* \bigoplus \{0,1\}^{256}$.

5.2. Sensor Registration Phase

The sensor registration phase is completed by the gateway node GWN. The GWN selects a unique identity SID_j for each sensor node and calculates $X_{S_j} = h(SID_j || K_s)$. Furthermore, GWN selects two random integers, n_j and c, defines and sets $N_j = NG_j = c$. Then, the GWN inserts the $\{SID_j, NG_j, X_{S_j}, n_j\}$ into *SensorInfoTable* in its memory. Before S_j is deployed, the GWN stores $\{SID_j, N_j, X_{S_j}, n_j\}$ into S_j.

5.3. User Registration Phase

Step 1: U_i chooses ID_i and PW_i freely, imprints Bio_i. Then U_i calculates $GEN(Bio_i) = (b_i, pair_i)$, $HPW_i = h(PW_i||b_i)$, and $TID_i = h(ID_i)$. Finally, U_i sends the registration request $\{TID_i, HPW_i\}$ towards the GWN via a private secure channel.

Step 2: The GWN receives $\{TID_i, HPW_i\}$ and checks if *UserInfoTable*() contains the element $(TID_i, *, *, *, *)$. If yes, the GWN rejects the registration request of U_i. Otherwise, the GWN chooses a, b randomly, and sets $NC_i = a$, $PID_i = PID_i^{new} = b$, $PID_i^{old} = Null$. Then, the GWN calculates $HID_i = h(TID_i||K_u)$, $A_i = h(HPW_i||TID_i) \bigoplus HID_i$, $B_i = h(HPW_i||HID_i) \mod n$, and $C_i = h(TID_i||HID_i) \bigoplus PID_i$, where $2^4 \le n \le 2^8$ is an integer to determine the size of (ID, PW), and inserts the element $(PID_i^{new}, PID_i^{old}, TID_i, NC_i)$ into table *UserInfoTable*. Further, the GWN writes $\{A_i, b_i, C_i, NC_i, h(\cdot), H(\cdot)\}$ into SC_i, and transmits SC_i towards U_i via a private secure channel.

Step 3: U_i receives SC_i, and defines and sets *flag* $= 0$. Finally, U_i writes $\{pair_i, flag, GEN(\cdot), REP(\cdot)\}$ into SC_i.

The process of the user registration phase is shown in Figure 4.

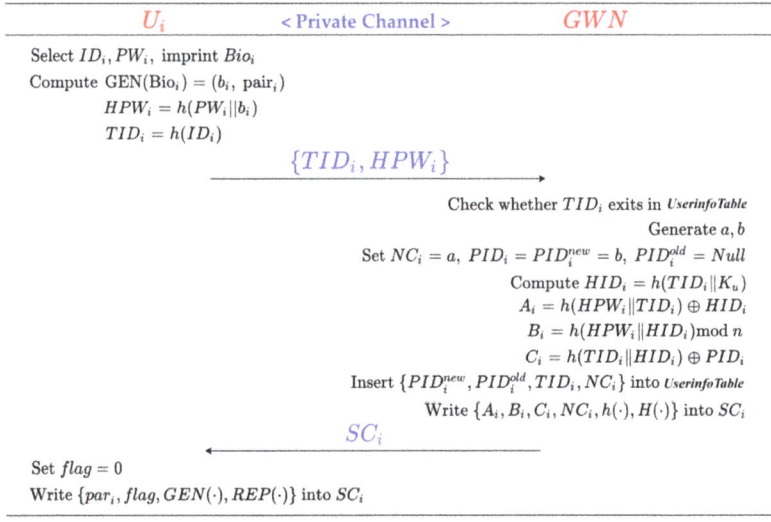

Figure 4. User registration phase of the proposed scheme.

5.4. Authentication Phase

Step 1: U_i inserts SC_i, inputs ID_i and PW_i, and imprints Bio_i. SC_i calculates $b_i = REP(Bio_i, pair_i)$, $TID_i = h(ID_i)$, $HPW_i^* = h(PW_i||b_i)$, $HID_i^* = A_i \bigoplus h(HPW_i^*||TID_i)$, and $B_i^* = h(HPW_i^*||HID_i^*) \mod n$ and verifies the equality check for $B_i^* \stackrel{?}{=} B_i$. If it does not hold true, SC_i rejects the login request. Otherwise, SC_i checks if *flag* $\stackrel{?}{=} 0$ holds.

If yes, SC_i updates $NC_i = h(NC_i)$, $flag = 1$. Then, SC_i generates the current timestamp T_1 and a random number r_i, chooses SID_j which he wants to access and calculates $PID_i = C_i \oplus h(TID_i||HID_i^*)$, $R_i = h(TID_i||PID_i||NC_i||r_i)$, $M_1 = (r_i||SID_j) \oplus H(TID_i||HID_i^*||NC_i||T_1)$, and $M_{UG} = h(TID_i||HID_i^*||PID_i||R_i||T_1)$. Finally, SC_i transmits the login request $\{PID_i, M_1, M_{UG}, T_1\}$ towards the GWN.

Step 2: The GWN receives $\{PID_i, M_1, M_{UG}, T_1\}$ and checks the validity of T_1. Then, the GWN searches $(PID_i^{new}, PID_i^{old}, TID_i, NC_i)$ in UserInfoTable using PID_i and operates as below.

Case 1: If there exists an element $(PID_i^{new}, PID_i^{old}, TID_i, NC_i)$ of UserInfoTable which satisfies $PID_i = PID_i^{new}$, then the GWN calculates $NC_i' = h(NC_i)$, $HID_i^* = h(TID_i||K_u)$, $K_i = H(TID_i||HID_i^*||NC_i'||T_1)$, $(r_i^*||SID_j) = K_i \oplus M_1$, $R_i^* = h(TID_i||PID_i^{new}||NC_i'||r_i^*)$, and $M_{UG}^* = h(TID_i||HID_i^*||PID_i^{new}||R_i^*||T_1)$. The GWN verifies the equality check $M_{UG}^* \stackrel{?}{=} M_{UG}$. If the verification fails, the GWN rejects the login request. Otherwise, the GWN chooses a new $tPID_i^{new}$ randomly, and sets $PID_i^{old} = PID_i^{new}$, $PID_i^{new} = tPID_i^{new}$, $NC_i = NC_i'$.

Case 2: If there exists an element $(PID_i^{new}, PID_i^{old}, TID_i, NC_i)$ of UserInfoTable which satisfies $PID_i = PID_i^{old}$, then the GWN calculates $HID_i^* = h(TID_i||K_u)$, $K_i = H(TID_i||HID_i^*||NC_i||T_1)$, $(r_i^*||SID_j) = K_i \oplus M_1$, $R_i^* = h(TID_i||PID_i^{old}||NC_i||r_i^*)$, and $M_{UG}^* = h(TID_i||HID_i^*||PID_i^{old}||R_i^*||T_1)$. The GWN verifies the equality check $M_{UG}^* \stackrel{?}{=} M_{UG}$. If the verification fails, the GWN rejects the login request. Otherwise, the GWN chooses a new $tPID_i^{new}$ randomly, and sets $PID_i^{new} = tPID_i^{new}$.

Case 3: If the above two cases do not exist, the GWN rejects the login request.

Further, the GWN generates the current timestamp T_2, searches $\{SID_j, NG_j, X_{S_j}, n_j\}$ in SensorInfoTable using SID_j, and updates $NG_j = NG_j + n_j$, $X_{S_j} = h(SID_j||X_{S_j})$. Then, the GWN calculates $M_2 = (R_i^*||PID_i^{old}) \oplus H(X_{S_j}||T_2)$ and $M_{GS} = h(PID_i^{old}||SID_j||X_{S_j}||R_i^*||T_2)$. Finally, the GWN transmits $\{M_2, M_{GS}, NG_j, T_2\}$ towards S_j.

Step 3: Upon the reception of $\{M_2, M_{GS}, NG_j, T_2\}$ from the GWN, S_j checks whether T_2 is a valid timestamp. Then, S_j calculates $N' = NG_j - NS_j/n_j$ and checks if $1 \leq N' \leq N$ holds, where N is the initial threshold for preserving the computing resources of sensors. If it holds true, S_j sets $X_{S_j}' = X_{S_j}$ and calculates N' times $X_{S_j}' = h(X_{S_j}'||SID_j)$. Further, S_j calculates $(R_i^*||PID_i^{old}) = M_2 \oplus H(X_{S_j}'||T_2)$ and $M_{GS}^* = h(PID_i^{old}||SID_j||X_{S_j}'||R_i^*||T_2)$ and verifies the equality check $M_{GS}^* \stackrel{?}{=} M_{GS}$. If the verification fails, S_j aborts the session. Otherwise, S_j generates the current timestamp T_3 and a random number r_j and calculates $R_j = h(SID_j||r_j)$, $M_3 = (R_j||PID_i^{old}) \oplus H(X_{S_j}'||T_3)$, $SK_{ji} = h(R_i^*||R_j)$, and $M_{SG} = h(PID_i^{old}||SID_j||X_{S_j}'||R_i^*||R_j||T_3)$. S_j updates $X_{S_j} = X_{S_j}'$, $N_j = NG_j$. Finally, S_j sends $\{SID_j, M_3, M_{SG}, T_3\}$ back to the GWN.

Step 4: The GWN receives $\{SID_j, M_3, M_{SG}, T_3\}$ and checks the validity of T_3. Then, the GWN searches $\{SID_j, NG_j, X_{S_j}, n_j\}$ in SensorInfoTable using SID_j and calculates $(R_j||PID_i^{old}) = M_3 \oplus H(X_{S_j}||T_3)$, and $M_{SG}^* = h(PID_i^{old}||SID_j||X_{S_j}||R_i^*||R_j^*||T_3)$. The GWN verifies the equality check $M_{SG}^* \stackrel{?}{=} M_{SG}$. If the verification fails, the GWN aborts the session. Otherwise, the GWN generates the current timestamp T_4 and searches $(PID_i^{new}, PID_i^{old}, TID_i, NC_i)$ in UserInfoTable using PID_i^{old}. Further, the GWN calculates $C_i^{new} = h(TID_i||HID_i^*) \oplus PID_i^{new}$, $p_i^{new} = C_i^{new} \oplus HID_i^* \oplus T_4$, $M_4 = R_j^* \oplus K_i$, and $M_{GU} = h(PID_i^{old}||HID_i^*||C_i^{new}||R_i^*||R_j^*||T_4)$. Finally, the GWN sends $\{p_i^{new}, M_4, M_{GU}, T_4\}$ to U_i.

Step 5: Upon the reception of $\{p_i^{new}, M_4, M_{GU}, T_4\}$ from the GWN, U_i checks whether T_4 is a valid timestamp. Then, U_i calculates $R_j^* = M_4 \oplus H(TID_i||HID_i^*||NC_i||T_1)$, $SK_{ij} = h(R_i||R_j^*)$, $C_i^{new} = p_i^{new} \oplus HID_i^* \oplus T_4$, and $M_{GU}^* = h(PID_i||HID_i^*||C_i^{new}||R_i||R_j^*||T_4)$. Then, U_i verifies the equality check $M_{GU}^* \stackrel{?}{=} M_{GU}$. If the verification fails, U_i aborts the session. Otherwise, U_i updates $C_i = C_i^{new}$, $flag = 0$.

The process of the authentication phase is shown in Figure 5.

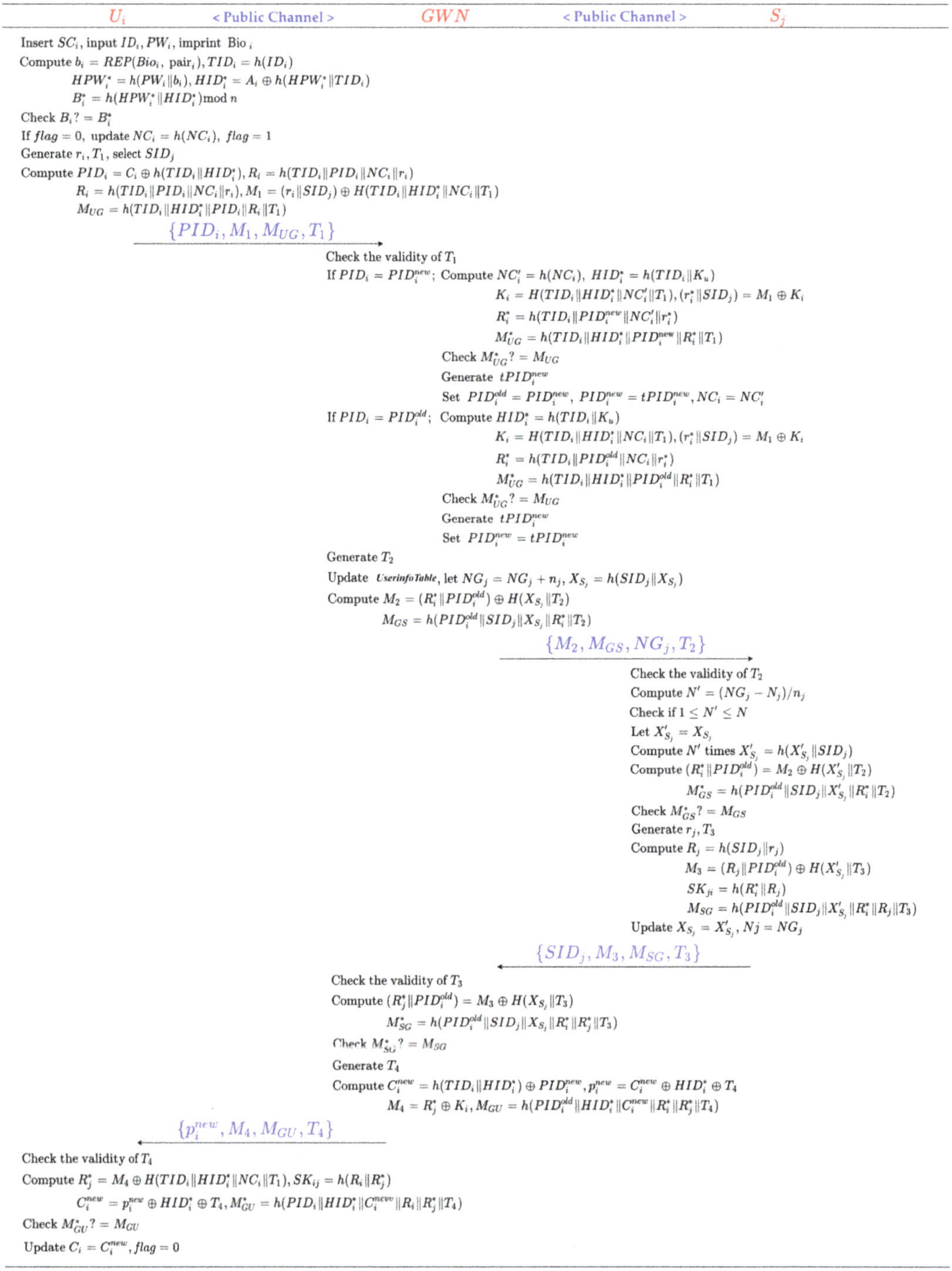

| U_i | < Public Channel > | GWN | < Public Channel > | S_j |

Insert SC_i, input ID_i, PW_i, imprint Bio_i
Compute $b_i = REP(Bio_i, pair_i)$, $TID_i = h(ID_i)$
$HPW_i^* = h(PW_i \| b_i)$, $HID_i^* = A_i \oplus h(HPW_i^* \| TID_i)$
$B_i^* = h(HPW_i^* \| HID_i^*) \bmod n$
Check $B_i ? = B_i^*$
If $flag = 0$, update $NC_i = h(NC_i)$, $flag = 1$
Generate r_i, T_1, select SID_j
Compute $PID_i = C_i \oplus h(TID_i \| HID_i^*)$, $R_i = h(TID_i \| PID_i \| NC_i \| r_i)$
$R_i = h(TID_i \| PID_i \| NC_i \| r_i)$, $M_1 = (r_i \| SID_j) \oplus H(TID_i \| HID_i^* \| NC_i \| T_1)$
$M_{UG} = h(TID_i \| HID_i^* \| PID_i \| R_i \| T_1)$

$\{PID_i, M_1, M_{UG}, T_1\} \longrightarrow$

Check the validity of T_1
If $PID_i = PID_i^{new}$; Compute $NC_i' = h(NC_i)$, $HID_i^* = h(TID_i \| K_u)$
$K_i = H(TID_i \| HID_i^* \| NC_i' \| T_1)$, $(r_i^* \| SID_j) = M_1 \oplus K_i$
$R_i^* = h(TID_i \| PID_i^{new} \| NC_i' \| r_i^*)$
$M_{UG}^* = h(TID_i \| HID_i^* \| PID_i^{new} \| R_i^* \| T_1)$
Check $M_{UG}^* ? = M_{UG}$
Generate $tPID_i^{new}$
Set $PID_i^{old} = PID_i^{new}$, $PID_i^{new} = tPID_i^{new}$, $NC_i = NC_i'$
If $PID_i = PID_i^{old}$; Compute $HID_i^* = h(TID_i \| K_u)$
$K_i = H(TID_i \| HID_i^* \| NC_i \| T_1)$, $(r_i^* \| SID_j) = M_1 \oplus K_i$
$R_i^* = h(TID_i \| PID_i^{old} \| NC_i \| r_i^*)$
$M_{UG}^* = h(TID_i \| HID_i^* \| PID_i^{old} \| R_i^* \| T_1)$
Check $M_{UG}^* ? = M_{UG}$
Generate $tPID_i^{new}$
Set $PID_i^{new} = tPID_i^{new}$
Generate T_2
Update $UserinfoTable$, let $NG_j = NG_j + n_j$, $X_{S_j} = h(SID_j \| X_{S_j})$
Compute $M_2 = (R_i^* \| PID_i^{old}) \oplus H(X_{S_j} \| T_2)$
$M_{GS} = h(PID_i^{old} \| SID_j \| X_{S_j} \| R_i^* \| T_2)$

$\{M_2, M_{GS}, NG_j, T_2\} \longrightarrow$

Check the validity of T_2
Compute $N' = (NG_j - N_j)/n_j$
Check if $1 \le N' \le N$
Let $X_{S_j}' = X_{S_j}$
Compute N' times $X_{S_j}' = h(X_{S_j}' \| SID_j)$
Compute $(R_i^* \| PID_i^{old}) = M_2 \oplus H(X_{S_j}' \| T_2)$
$M_{GS}^* = h(PID_i^{old} \| SID_j \| X_{S_j}' \| R_i^* \| T_2)$
Check $M_{GS}^* ? = M_{GS}$
Generate r_j, T_3
Compute $R_j = h(SID_j \| r_j)$
$M_3 = (R_j \| PID_i^{old}) \oplus H(X_{S_j}' \| T_3)$
$SK_{ji} = h(R_i^* \| R_j)$
$M_{SG} = h(PID_i^{old} \| SID_j \| X_{S_j}' \| R_i^* \| R_j \| T_3)$
Update $X_{S_j} = X_{S_j}'$, $Nj = NG_j$

$\longleftarrow \{SID_j, M_3, M_{SG}, T_3\}$

Check the validity of T_3
Compute $(R_j^* \| PID_i^{old}) = M_3 \oplus H(X_{S_j} \| T_3)$
$M_{SG}^* = h(PID_i^{old} \| SID_j \| X_{S_j} \| R_i^* \| R_j^* \| T_3)$
Check $M_{SG}^* ? = M_{SG}$
Generate T_4
Compute $C_i^{new} = h(TID_i \| HID_i^*) \oplus PID_i^{new}$, $p_i^{new} = C_i^{new} \oplus HID_i^* \oplus T_4$
$M_4 = R_j^* \oplus K_i$, $M_{GU} = h(PID_i^{old} \| HID_i^* \| C_i^{new} \| R_i^* \| R_j^* \| T_4)$

$\longleftarrow \{p_i^{new}, M_4, M_{GU}, T_4\}$

Check the validity of T_4
Compute $R_j^* = M_4 \oplus H(TID_i \| HID_i^* \| NC_i \| T_1)$, $SK_{ij} = h(R_i \| R_j^*)$
$C_i^{new} = p_i^{new} \oplus HID_i^* \oplus T_4$, $M_{GU} = h(PID_i \| HID_i^* \| C_i^{new} \| R_i \| R_j^* \| T_4)$
Check $M_{GU}^* ? = M_{GU}$
Update $C_i = C_i^{new}$, $flag = 0$

Figure 5. Authentication phase of the proposed scheme.

5.5. Password and Biometric Update Phase

Step 1: U_i inserts SC_i, inputs ID_i and PW_i, and imprints Bio_i. SC_i calculates $b_i = REP(Bio_i, pair_i)$, $TID_i = h(ID_i)$, $HPW_i^* = h(PW_i||b_i)$, $HID_i^* = A_i \oplus h(HPW_i^*||TID_i)$, and $B_i^* = h(HPW_i^*||HID_i^*) \bmod n$ and verifies the equality check for $B_i^*\ ? = B_i$. If it does not hold true, SC_i rejects the request. Otherwise, U_i inputs a new password PW_i^{new} and imprints a new biometric Bio_i^{new}.

Step 2: SC_i calculates $GEN(Bio_i^{new}) = (b_i^{new}, pair_i^{new})$, $HPW_i^{new} = h(PW_i^{new}||b_i^{new})$, $A_i^{new} = HID_i^* \oplus h(HPW_i^{new}||TID_i)$, and $B_i^{new} = h(HPW_i^{new}||HID_i^*) \bmod n$. At last, SC_i replaces $pair_i$, A_i and B_i, with $pair_i^{new}$, A_i^{new} and B_i^{new}, respectively.

6. Security Analysis

6.1. Security Verification Using ProVerif

ProVerif [33] is one of the widely accepted automated security verification tools for communication protocols. ProVerif supports main cryptographic primitives including hash function, encryption, digital signatures, etc. In this section, we use ProVerif to check the mutual authentication and session key secrecy of the proposed scheme.

First, we define two insecure channels, c1 for communication between users and the GWN and c2 for communication between the GWN and sensors.

```
(*–Two public channel–*)
free c1: channel. (*–The channel between users and GWN–*)
free c2: channel. (*–The channel between sensors and GWN–*)
```

Then, we define the parameters and constructors as follows:

```
(*–The basic variables–*)
free user, GWN, SN: bitstring. (*—three participants–*)
free PID: bitstring. (*—the pseudonym identity shared by user and GWN–*)
free Ku: bitstring[private]. (*—the masterkey of GWN–*)
free Ks: bitstring[private]. (*—the masterkey of GWN–*)
free XSj: bitstring[private]. (*—the shared key between GWN and sensor–*)
table Table_user_info( bitstring, bitstring, bitstring). (*—the user's info table—*)
table Table_sensor_info(bitstring, bitstring). (*—the sensor's info table—*)
(*–Encryption operation–*)
fun encrypt(bitstring, bitstring): bitstring.
fun decrypt(bitstring, bitstring): bitstring.
equation forall x: bitstring, y: bitstring; decrypt(encrypt(x, y), y) = x.
(*–Hash operation–*)
fun h1(bitstring): bitstring.
fun h2 (bitstring, bitstring): bitstring.
fun h4 (bitstring, bitstring, bitstring, bitstring):bitstring.
fun h5 (bitstring, bitstring, bitstring, bitstring, bitstring): bitstring.
fun h6 (bitstring, bitstring, bitstring, bitstring, bitstring, bitstring): bitstring.
(*–XOR operation–*)
fun XOR (bitstring, bitstring): bitstring.
equation forall x: bitstring, y: bitstring; XOR(XOR(x, y), y) = x.
(*–Concat and Divide operation–*)
fun Concat (bitstring, bitstring): bitstring.
fun Div1 (bitstring):bitstring.
fun Div2 (bitstring):bitstring.
equation forall x: bitstring, y: bitstring; Div1(Concat(x, y)) = x.
equation forall x: bitstring, y: bitstring; Div2(Concat(x, y)) = y.
(*–Check the Freshness of timestamp operation–*)
fun isFresh (bitstring, bool): bool
reduc forall T: bitstring; isFresh (T, true) = true.
```

In order to check the mutual authentication and session key secrecy, we define the following eight events and two secrets:

(*–Mutual authentication queries–*)
event beginUG(bitstring).
event endUG(bitstring).
event beginGU(bitstring).
event endGU(bitstring).
event beginGS(bitstring).
event endGS(bitstring).
event beginSG(bitstring).
event endSG(bitstring).
query x: bitstring; inj-event(endUG(x)) ==> inj-event(beginUG(x)).
query x: bitstring; inj-event(endGU(x)) ==> inj-event(beginGU(x)).
query x: bitstring; inj-event(endGS(x)) ==> inj-event(beginGS(x)).
query x: bitstring; inj-event(endSG(x)) ==> inj-event(beginSG(x)).
(*–Session key secrecy queries–*)
free secretA, secretB: bitstring [private].
query attacker(secretA);
attacker(secretB).
Three distinct processes *processUser*, *processSensor*, and *processGWN* are declared to model U_i, S_j and *GWN*, respectively.
(*————————User Ui————————*)
let processUser(IDi: bitstring, PWi: bitstring, bi: bitstring, Ai: bitstring, Bi: bitstring, Ci: bitstring, NCi: bitstring, SIDj: bitstring) =
let TIDi = h1(IDi) in
let HPWi' = h2(PWi, bi) in
let HIDi' = XOR(Ai, h2(HPWi', TIDi)) in
let Bi' = h2(HPWi',HIDi') in
if Bi'=Bi then
event beginGU(GWN);
new ri: bitstring;
new T1: bitstring;
let PIDi = XOR(Ci, h2(TIDi, HIDi')) in
let Ri = h4(TIDi, PIDi, NCi, ri) in
let M1 = XOR(Concat(ri, SIDj), h4 TIDi, HIDi', NCi, T1)) in
let MUG = h5 (TIDi, HIDi', PIDi, Ri, T1) in
out (c1, (PIDi, M1, MUG, T1));
in (c1, (M4:bitstring, MGU:bitstring, T4:bitstring));
if isFresh (T4, true) = true then
let Rj' = XOR(M4,h4(TIDi, HIDi',NCi, T1)) in
let SKij' = h2(Ri, Rj') in
let MGU' = h5(PIDi, HIDi', Ri, Rj', T4) in
if MGU' =MGU then
event endUG(user);
out(c1, encrypt(secretA, SKij')).
(*————————GWN————————*)
let processGWN() =
in(c1, (PIDi: bitstring, M1: bitstring, MUG: bitstring, T1:bitstring));
if isFresh(T1, true) = true then
get Table_user_info(=PIDi, TIDi, NCi) in
let HIDi' = h2(TIDi, Ku) in
let Ki = h4(TIDi, HIDi', NCi, T1) in
let ri' = Div1(XOR(M1,Ki)) in
let SIDj = Div2(XOR(M1,Ki)) in
let Ri' = h4(TIDi, PIDi, NCi, ri') in
event beginUG(user);

```
let MUG' = h5(TIDi, HIDi', PIDi, Ri', T1) in
if MUG' =MUG then
event beginSG(SN);
new T2: bitstring;
get Table_sensor_info(=SIDj, XSj) in
let M2 = XOR(Concat(Ri', PIDi),h2(XSj, T2)) in
let MGS = h5(PIDi, SIDj, XSj, Ri', T2) in
out(c2, (M2, MGS, T2));
in(c2,(SIDj:bitstring, M3:bitstring, MSG:bitstring, T3: bitstring));
if isFresh(T3, true) = true then
let Rj' = Div1(XOR(M3,h2(XSj, T3))) in
let PIDi = Div2(XOR(M3, h2(XSj, T3))) in
let MSG' = h6(PIDi, SIDj, XSj, Ri',Rj', T3) in
if MSG' = MSG then
new T4: bitstring;
event endGS(GWN);
let M4 = XOR(Rj',Ki) in
let MGU = h5(PIDi, HIDi', Ri', Rj', T4) in
out(c1, (M4, MGU, T4));
event endGU(GWN);
0.
(*————Sensor Sj————*)
let processSensor(SIDj:bitstring, XSj:bitstring) =
in(c2, (MG:bitstring, MGS:bitstring, T2:bitstring));
event beginGS(GWN);
let Ri' =Div1(XOR(MG, h2(XSj, T2))) in
let PIDi =Div2(XOR(MG, h2(XSj, T2))) in
let MGS' = h5(PIDi, SIDj, XSj, Ri', T2) in
if MGS'=MGS then
new T3: bitstring;
new rj: bitstring;
let Rj = h2(SIDj, rj) in
let Mj = XOR(Concat(rj, PIDi),h2(XSj, T3)) in
let SKij = h2(Ri', Rj) in
let MSG = h6(PIDi, SIDj, XSj, Ri', Rj, T3) in
out(c2, (SIDj, Mj, MSG, T3));
event endSG(SN);
out(c2, encrypt(secretB, SKij)).
```
We simulate the unbounded parallel execution of processes *processUser*, *processSensor*, and *processGWN* as follows:
```
(*–Start process–*)
process
new IDi: bitstring;
new PWi: bitstring;
new bi: bitstring;
new PIDi: bitstring;
new SIDj: bitstring;
new NCi: bitstring;
let HPWi = h2(PWi, bi) in
let TIDi = h1(IDi) in
let HIDi = h2(TIDi, Ku) in
let Ai = XOR(h2(HPWi, TIDi), HIDi) in
let Bi = h2(HPWi, HIDi) in
let Ci = XOR(h2(TIDi, HIDi),PIDi) in
```

```
let XSj = h2(SIDj, Ks) in
insert Table_user_info(PIDi, TIDi, NCi);
insert Table_sensor_info(SIDj, XSj);
(
(*– Launch an unbounded number of sessions of the user –*)
(!processUser(IDi, PWi, bi, Ai, Bi, Ci, NCi, SIDj)) |
(*– Launch an unbounded number of, sessions of the GWN–*)
(!processGWN()) |
(*– Launch an unbounded number of sessions of the sensor–*)
(!processSensor(SIDj, XSj))
)
```
The simulation results are shown as follows:
Query inj-event(endUG(x)) ==> inj-event(beginUG(x)) is true.
Query inj-event(endGU(x)) ==> inj-event(beginGU(x)) is true.
Query inj-event(endGS(x)) ==> inj-event(beginGS(x)) is true.
Query inj-event(endSG(x)) ==> inj-event(beginSG(x)) is true.
Query not attacker(secretA[]) is true.
Query not attacker(secretB[]) is true.

The results mean that the proposed scheme is able to achieve mutual authentication. Meanwhile, the session key $SKij$ generated by the user U_i and the sensor S_j is secure.

6.2. BAN-Logic

Burrows–Abadi–Needham logic (*BAN*-logic) [34] is a widely used tool for the formal analysis of authentication schemes which was proposed by Burrows et al. In this section, we use *BAN*-logic to prove the session key agreement between the user U_i and the sensor node S_j after the execution of the proposed scheme. Table 3 introduces the notations for the *BAN*-logic analysis and some basic rules for *BAN*-logic are described in Table 4.

Table 3. *BAN*-logic notations.

Symbol	Description
$P \mid \equiv X$	P believes X.
$P \triangleleft X$	P sees X.
$P \mid \sim X$	P sends X.
$P \Rightarrow X$	P has jurisdiction over X.
(X)	X is fresh.
(X, Y)	X or Y is part of (X, Y).
$(X)_K$	Use the key K to compute X.
$P \stackrel{SK}{\leftrightarrow} Q$	P and Q achieve the shared key SK for communication.

Table 4. Basic logical postulates of *BAN*-logic.

Symbol	Description
Message meaning rule	$\frac{P\mid\equiv(P\stackrel{K}{\leftrightarrow}Q),\ P\triangleleft(X)_K}{P\mid\equiv Q\mid\sim X}$
Freshness conjuncatenation rule	$\frac{P\mid\equiv(X)}{P\mid\equiv(X,Y)}$
Nonce verification rule	$\frac{P\mid\equiv(X),\ P\mid\equiv Q\mid\sim X}{P\mid\equiv Q\mid\equiv X}$
Jurisdiction rule	$\frac{P\mid\equiv Q\Rightarrow X,\ P\mid\equiv Q\mid\equiv X}{P\mid\equiv X}$
Believe rule	$\frac{P\mid\equiv Q\mid\equiv(X,Y)}{P\mid\equiv Q\mid\equiv X},\ \frac{P\mid\equiv X,P\mid\equiv Y}{P\mid\equiv(X,Y)}$

(1) The idealized form of the proposed scheme:

Message 1: $U_i \rightarrow GWN : (r_i, SID_j)_{U_i \stackrel{(HID_i, NC_i)}{\leftrightarrow} GWN}$

Message 2: $GWN \rightarrow S_j : (R_i, PID_i^{old})_{GWN \overset{X_{S_j}}{\leftrightarrow} S_j}$

Message 3: $S_j \rightarrow GWN : (R_j, PID_i^{old})_{S_j \overset{X_{S_j}}{\leftrightarrow} GWN}$

Message 4: $GWN \rightarrow U_i : (R_j)_{GWN \overset{(HID_i, NC_i)}{\leftrightarrow} U_i}$

(2) Verification goals:

Goal 1: $U_i| \equiv (U_i \overset{SK}{\leftrightarrow} S_j)$.

Goal 2: $U_i| \equiv S_j| \equiv (U_i \overset{SK}{\leftrightarrow} S_j)$.

Goal 3: $S_j| \equiv (U_i \overset{SK}{\leftrightarrow} S_j)$.

Goal 4: $S_j| \equiv U_i| \equiv (U_i \overset{SK}{\leftrightarrow} S_j)$.

(3) Assumptions about the initial state:

A1: $U_i| \equiv (r_i, r_j)$.

A2: $S_j| \equiv (r_i, r_j)$.

A3: $GWN| \equiv (r_i, r_j)$.

A4: $U_i| \equiv (U_i \overset{(PID_i, HID_i, NC_i)}{\leftrightarrow} GWN)$.

A5: $GWN| \equiv (U_i \overset{(PID_i, HID_i, NC_i)}{\leftrightarrow} GWN)$.

A6: $GWN| \equiv (GWN \overset{X_{S_j}}{\leftrightarrow} S_j)$.

A7: $S_j| \equiv (GWN \overset{X_{S_j}}{\leftrightarrow} S_j)$.

A8: $U_i| \equiv S_j \Rightarrow (U_i \overset{SK}{\leftrightarrow} S_j)$.

A9: $S_j| \equiv U_i \Rightarrow (U_i \overset{SK}{\leftrightarrow} S_j)$.

(4) Proofs:

Step 1: From Message 1, we can get: $GWN \triangleleft (r_i, SID_j)_{U_i \overset{(HID_i, NC_i)}{\leftrightarrow} GWN}$.

Step 2: According to Step 1, A5, and the message meaning rule, it can be inferred that: $GWN| \equiv U_i|\sim(r_i, SID_j)_{U_i \overset{(HID_i, NC_i)}{\leftrightarrow} GWN}$.

Step 3: According to Step 2, A3, and the nonce verification rule, we obtain: $GWN| \equiv U_i| \equiv (r_i, SID_j)_{U_i \overset{(HID_i, NC_i)}{\leftrightarrow} GWN}$.

Step 4: From Message 2, we understand that: $S_j \triangleleft (R_i, PID_i^{old})_{GWN \overset{X_{S_j}}{\leftrightarrow} S_j}$.

Step 5: According to A7 and the message meaning rule, we obtain: $S_j| \equiv GWN|\sim(R_i, PID_i^{old})_{GWN \overset{X_{S_j}}{\leftrightarrow} S_j}$.

Step 6: According to A2, $R_i = h(TID_i||PID_i||NC_i||r_i)$, and the freshness conjuncatenation rule, we can get: $S_j| \equiv (R_i)$.

Step 7: According to Step 5, Step 6, and the nonce verification rule, we get: $S_j| \equiv GWN| \equiv (R_i, PID_i^{old})_{GWN \overset{X_{S_j}}{\leftrightarrow} S_j}$.

Step 8: According to Step 3, Step 7, $SK_{ij} = h(R_i||R_j)$, and $R_i = h(TID_i||PID_i||NC_i||r_i)$, we prove: $S_j| \equiv U_i| \equiv (U_i \overset{SK}{\leftrightarrow} S_j)$ (**Goal 4**).

Step 9: According to Step 8, A9, and the jurisdiction rule, we prove: $S_j| \equiv (U_i \overset{SK}{\leftrightarrow} S_j)$ (**Goal 3**).

Step 10: According to Message 3, we get: $GWN \triangleleft (R_j, PID_i^{old})_{S_j \overset{X_{S_j}}{\leftrightarrow} GWN}$.

Step 11: According to Step10, A6, and the message meaning rule, it can be inferred that: $GWN| \equiv S_j|\sim(R_j, PID_i^{old})_{S_j \overset{X_{S_j}}{\leftrightarrow} GWN}$.

Step 12: According to Step 11, A3, $R_j = h(SID_j||r_j)$, and the nonce verification rule, we obtain: $GWN| \equiv S_j| \equiv (R_j, PID_i^{old})_{S_j \overset{X_{S_j}}{\leftrightarrow} GWN}$.

Step 13: From Message 4, we obtain: $U_i \triangleleft (R_j)_{GWN \overset{(HID_i, NC_i)}{\leftrightarrow} U_i}$.

Step 14: According to Step 13, A4, and the message meaning rule, we obtain: $U_i| \equiv GWN|\sim (R_j)_{GWN \overset{(HID_i, NC_i)}{\leftrightarrow} U_i}$.

Step 15 According to Step 14, A1, $R_j = h(SID_j||r_j)$, and the nonce verification rule, we get: $U_i| \equiv S_j| \equiv (U_i \overset{SK}{\leftrightarrow} S_j)$. (**Goal 2**).

Step 16: According to Step 15, A8, and the jurisdiction rule, we prove: $U_i| \equiv (U_i \overset{SK}{\leftrightarrow} S_j)$ (**Goal 1**).

From the proof results obtained from the above process, **Goal 1–4**, U_i, and S_j believe that they have completed the key agreement and generated the shared session key $SK_{ij} = SK_{jiji}$.

6.3. Informal Security Analysis

(1) Anonymity and un-traceability

Suppose an adversary intercepted the information transmitted to a public channel from U_i, GWN, and S_j. Obviously, the adversary cannot obtain the user's actual identity ID_i, because of the security of the one-way *hash* function. In addition, the pseudonym identity PID_i changes after each authentication, and r_i and r_j are randomly generated in each session. The adversary cannot determine whether two sessions are launched by the same user.

(2) Perfect forward secrecy

Suppose an adversary accidentally captured U_i's private key NC_i, S_j's private key (X_{S_j}, N_j), and the GWN's master key (K_u, K_s), and intercepted the information propagated in the public channel. The adversary cannot obtain the previous session key because NC_i, X_{S_j}, N_j changes after each authentication, and the adversary cannot get the NC_i, X_{S_j}, N_j in a previous session because of the security of the one-way *hash* function. Therefore, the proposed scheme can achieve perfect forward secrecy.

(3) Mutual authentication

In Section 6.1, we define eight events—event *beginUGparam*(bitstring), event *endUGparam*(bitstring), event *beginGUparam*(bitstring), event *endGUparam*(bitstring), event *beginGSparam*(bitstring), event *endGSparam*(bitstring), event *beginSGparam*(bitstring), and event *endSGparam*(bitstring)—to verify the mutual authentication of U_i, GWN, and S_j. The results show that our proposed scheme could achieve mutual authentication.

(4) Session key agreement

The user U_i and the sensor S_j reach a session key $SK_{ij} = h_2(R_i||R_j)$ for future communication after authentication. Since R_i and R_j are generated by U_i and S_j, respectively, both U_i and S_j have an influence on the outcome of the session key $SK_{ij} = h(R_i||R_j) = SK_{ji}$.

(5) Three-factor security

Suppose an adversary captured the smart card SC_i of U_i and obtained the biometrics Bio_i. The adversary can extract the values $\{A_i, b_i, C_i, NC_i, pair_i, flag\}$ in SC_i. Further, the adversary guesses (ID_i', PW_i') and calculates $b_i = REP(Bio_i, pair_i)$, $TID_i' = h(ID_i')$, $HPW_i^* = h(PW_i'||b_i)$, $HID_i^* = A_i \oplus h(HPW_i^*||TID_i')$, and $b_i^* = h(HPW_i^*||HID_i^*) \bmod n$. However, the adversary does not know the correctness of (ID_i', PW_i') because $B_i ? = h(HPW_i^*||HID_i^*) \bmod n$. is a fuzzy verification process.

(6) Resistance of other known attacks

Insider attack: An insider adversary can obtain the user's registration information $\{TID_i = h(ID_i), HPW_i = h(PW_i||b_i)\}$. Because of the security of the one-way hash function and ignorance about b_i, the adversary cannot capture PW_i. Therefore, no effective insider attack can be launched.

Stolen verifier table attack: There is no password-related or biometric-related information stored inside the GWN. Therefore, the stolen verifier table attack is infeasible in our proposed scheme.

User impersonation attack: For generating valid login request information, the adversary needs to know HID_i. While we know $b_i = REP(Bio_i, pair_i)$, $TID_i = h(ID_i)$, $HPW_i = h(PW_i || b_i)$, and $HID_i = A_i \oplus h(HPW_i || TID_i)$, where A_i and $pair_i$ are stored in SC_i. Therefore, the adversary cannot forge U_i without getting ID_i, PW_i, Bio_i and SC_i. Thus our proposed scheme could resist user impersonation attacks.

Sensor Spoofing Attack: An adversary cannot forge a sensor node S_j without getting the secrets of S_j (NS_j and X_{S_j}). Therefore, no effective sensor spoofing attack can be launched.

Known session-specific temporary information attack: In our proposed scheme, the user U_i and the micro-sensor S_j reach a session key $SK_{ij} = h(R_i || R_j) = h(h(TID_i || PID_i || NC_i || r_i) || h(SID_j || r_j))$. Even if an adversary captured the session-specific temporary information, r_i and r_j, he cannot launch a known session-specific temporary information attack without NC_i. As a result, our proposed scheme can resist known session-specific temporary information attacks.

De-synchronization attack: We analyze five possible cases of de-synchronization attacks, shown in Figure 6.

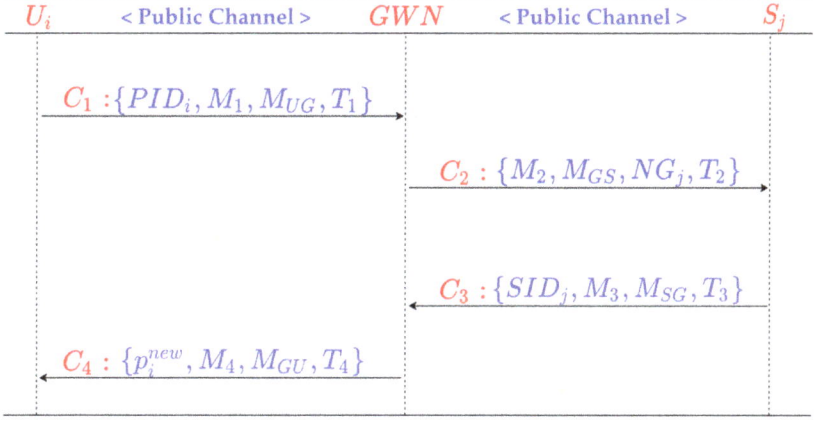

Figure 6. Possible de-synchronization attack on our proposed protocol.

Case 1: Suppose an adversary blocked $C1$: $\{PID_i, M_1, M_{UG}, T_1\}$. Since none of the participants updated the information table, the attack is infeasible.

Case 2: Suppose an adversary blocked $C2$: $\{M_2, M_{GS}, NG_j, T_2\}$, the information stored on the GWN side and sensor side would be out of synchronization. However, by calculating
, it can be known how many times the communications between S_j and the GWN are blocked. The information on two sides would be resynchronized by calculating N, times $X'_{S_j} = h(X'_{S_j} || SID_j)$ and updating $X_{S_j} = X'_{S_j}$, $N_j = NG_j$.

Case 3: If an adversary blocks $C3$: $\{SID_j, M_3, M_{SG}, T_3\}$. Both the GWN and S_j have updated the X_{S_j} and NG_j/N_j. The synchronization between U_i and the GWN is the same as Case 4.

Case 4: If an adversary blocks $C4: \{p_i^{new}, M_4, M_{GU}, T_4\}$. The communications between the GWN and S_j are in synchronization, while the communications between U_i and the GWN are out of synchronization. In this case, the GWN has completed the update of PID_i, and PID_i^{old} records the previous PID_i. Since $C4: \{p_i^{new}, M_4, M_{GU}, T_4\}$ is not received, the user U_i does not update C_i, and the PID_i calculated in the next session is not updated. However, when U_i initiates the session request again, the GWN finds that the PID_i sent by U_i is the same as the PID_i^{old} recorded in its memory. The GWN can identify the de-synchronization attack initiated by the adversary and synchronize the information according to Step 2 of the authentication phase. Therefore, the proposed new protocol can also resist the attacks of Case 3 and Case 4 of de-synchronization attacks.

In summary, our proposed scheme can resist de-synchronization attacks. On the other hand, we have shown that our proposed scheme can achieve forward secrecy in previous part of this section. Therefore, our proposed scheme can resist offline password-guessing attacks and stolen smart card attacks.

7. Performance Analysis

This section will compare and analyze the performance of the proposed new protocol with other similar protocols, including a computing cost comparison and communication cost comparison. Since the registration phase of users and sensors occurs only once, and users do not change their passwords and biometrics frequently, this section only discusses the performance comparison between authentication phases.

7.1. Comparison of Computing Costs

According to the experimental data in the literature [35], $T_h \approx 0.32$ms, the computing cost comparison between our proposed scheme and other similar schemes, is shown in Table 5. From the results, the proposed protocol has a lower computation cost than the other four similar protocols.

Table 5. Comparison of computing costs (milliseconds).

Protocol	User	GWN	Sensor	Total
Shin et al. [26]	$13T_h \approx 4.16$	$15T_h \approx 4.8$	$6T_h \approx 1.92$	$34T_h \approx 10.88$
Ostad et al. [36]	$11T_h \approx 3.52$	$17T_h \approx 5.44$	$5T_h \approx 1.6$	$33T_h \approx 10.56$
Wu et al. [13]	$10T_h \approx 3.2$	$15T_h \approx 4.8$	$5T_h \approx 1.6$	$31T_h \approx 9.92$
Amin et al. [24]	$12T_h \approx 3.84$	$15T_h \approx 3.2$	$5T_h \approx 1.6$	$32T_h \approx 10.24$
Proposed	$11T_h \approx 3.52$	$10T_h \approx 3.2$	$6T_h \approx 1.92$	$27T_h \approx 8.64$

7.2. Comparison of Communication Costs

We assume that the length of identification, random number, timestamp, and other parameters involved in the proposed protocol and other similar protocols is 128 bits, and the length of the timestamp is 32 bits. Hash functions $h: \{0,1\}^* \oplus \{0,1\}^{128}$ and $H: \{0,1\}^* \oplus \{0,1\}^{256}$ have 128-bit and 256-bit outputs, respectively. Other related protocols use hash functions (such as $MD5$) with an output length of 128 bits.

In the authentication phase of the newly proposed protocol, there are four transmission messages: $\{PID_i, M_1, M_{UG}, T_1\}$, $\{M_2, M_{GS}, NG_j, T_2\}$, $\{SID_j, M_3, M_{SG}, T_3\}$, and $\{p_i^{new}, M_4, M_{GU}, T_4\}$. The total length of the transmitted message is (128 + 256 + 128 + 32) + (256 + 128 + 128 + 32) + (128 + 256 + 128 + 32) + (128 + 128 + 128 + 32) = 2048 bits.

Table 6 shows the comparison of the communication costs between the proposed new protocol and other similar schemes. From the comparison results, our new proposed scheme is also at a good level in terms of communication costs.

Table 6. Comparison of communication costs.

Protocol	Number of Messages	Length of Interactive Information
Shin et al. [26]	4 Messages	1664 bits
Ostad et al. [36]	6 Messages	2208 bits
Wu et al. [13]	4 Messages	2176 bits
Amin et al. [24]	6 Messages	2016 bits
Proposed	4 Messages	2048 bits

8. Conclusions

Due to the insecurity of wireless sensor networks, abundant research on authentication and key agreement protocols for WSNs has been put forward. In 2019, Shin et al. proposed a lightweight three-factor authentication and key agreement protocol based on symmetric cryptographic primitives for WSNs, which looked promising. However, we found that there are some security risks in their protocol. To solve the shortcomings, we proposed a new lightweight and anonymous three-factor authentication scheme for WSNs. Furthermore, we proved that our proposed scheme is secure using the automated security verification tool *ProVerif*, BAN-logic verification, and an informal security analysis. Through a performance comparison and analysis, our new scheme shows a good level of computing and communication overhead and has high practicability. In future research, we will focus on finding a lighter mathematical model to realize the strong security of identity authentication in wireless sensor networks and apply the scheme to the actual environment.

Author Contributions: Conceptualization, L.Z.; Formal analysis, H.X.; Investigation, H.X.; Methodology, L.Z.; Supervision, H.X. and K.Z.; Validation, K.Z.; Writing—original draft, L.Z. All authors have read and agreed to the published version of the manuscript.

Funding: This research was supported by the Project of Educational Commission of Guangdong Province (No.6019210033S), Shenzhen Fundamental Research Project (No.JCYJ20180305163701198), Shenzhen Bureau of Education (No.zdzz20002).

Institutional Review Board Statement: Not applicable.

Informed Consent Statement: Not applicable.

Data Availability Statement: Not applicable.

Conflicts of Interest: The authors declare no conflict of interest.

References

1. Yick, J.; Mukherjee, B.; Ghosal, D. Wireless sensor network survey. *Comput. Netw.* **2008**, *52*, 2292–2330. [CrossRef]
2. Gnawali, O.; Jang, K.-Y.; Paek, J.; Vieira, M.; Govindan, R.; Greenstein, B.; Joki, A.; Estrin, D.; Kohler, E. The tenet architecture for tiered sensor networks. In Proceedings of the 4th International Conference on Embedded Networked Sensor Systems ACM, Boulder, CO, USA, 31 October–3 November 2006; pp. 153–166.
3. Yang, D.; Misra, S.; Fang, X.; Xue, G.; Zhang, J. Two-Tiered Constrained Relay Node Placement in Wireless Sensor Networks: Computational Complexity and Efficient Approximations. *IEEE Trans. Mob. Comput.* **2011**, *11*, 1399–1411. [CrossRef]
4. He, D.; Kumar, N.; Chilamkurti, N. A secure temporal-credential-based mutual authentication and key agreement scheme with pseudo identity for wireless sensor networks. *Inf. Sci.* **2015**, *321*, 263–277. [CrossRef]
5. He, D.; Chen, C.; Chan, S.; Bu, J.; Yang, L.T. Security Analysis and Improvement of a Secure and Distributed Reprogramming Protocol for Wireless Sensor Networks. *IEEE Trans. Ind. Electron.* **2012**, *60*, 5348–5354. [CrossRef]
6. Lamport, L. Password authentication with insecure communication. *Commun. ACM* **1981**, *24*, 770–772. [CrossRef]
7. Guo, H.; Gao, Y.; Xu, T.; Zhang, X.; Ye, J. A secure and efficient three-factor multi-gateway authentication protocol for wireless sensor networks. *Ad Hoc Networks* **2019**, *95*, 101965. [CrossRef]
8. Gope, P.; Das, A.K.; Kumar, N.; Cheng, Y. Lightweight and Physically Secure Anonymous Mutual Authentication Protocol for Real-Time Data Access in Industrial Wireless Sensor Networks. *IEEE Trans. Ind. Inform.* **2019**, *15*, 4957–4968. [CrossRef]
9. Ever, Y.K. Secure-anonymous user Authentication scheme for e-healthcare application using wireless medical sensor networks. *IEEE Syst. J.* **2018**, *13*, 456–467. [CrossRef]

10. Adavoudi-Jolfaei, A.H.; Ashouri-Talouki, M.; Aghili, S.F. Lightweight and anonymous three-factor authentication and access control scheme for real-time applications in wireless sensor networks. *Peer-to-Peer Netw. Appl.* **2019**, *12*, 43–59. [CrossRef]
11. Wang, D.; Li, W.; Wang, P. Measuring Two-Factor Authentication Schemes for Real-Time Data Access in Industrial Wireless Sensor Networks. *IEEE Trans. Ind. Inform.* **2018**, *14*, 4081–4092. [CrossRef]
12. Mishra, D.; Vijayakumar, P.; Sureshkumar, V.; Amin, R.; Islam, S.K.H; Gope, P. Efficient authentication protocol for secure multimedia communications in IoT-enabled wireless sensor networks. *Multimed. Tools Appl.* **2018**, *77*, 18295–18325. [CrossRef]
13. Wu, F.; Li, X.; Sangaiah, A.K.; Xu, L.; Kumari, S.; Wu, L.; Shen, J. A lightweight and robust two-factor authentication scheme for personalized healthcare systems using wireless medical sensor networks. *Futur. Gener. Comput. Syst.* **2018**, *82*, 727–737. [CrossRef]
14. Wu, F.; Xu, L.; Kumari, S.; Li, X. An improved and provably secure three-factor user authentication scheme for wireless sensor networks. *Peer-to-Peer Netw. Appl.* **2018**, *11*, 1–20. [CrossRef]
15. Ramachandran, S.; Shanmugam, V. A two way authentication using bilinear mapping function for wireless sensor networks. *Comput. Electr. Eng.* **2017**, *59*, 242–249. [CrossRef]
16. Gope, P.; Hwang, T. A Realistic Lightweight Anonymous Authentication Protocol for Securing Real-Time Application Data Access in Wireless Sensor Networks. *IEEE Trans. Ind. Electron.* **2016**, *63*, 7124–7132. [CrossRef]
17. Kumari, S.; Li, X.; Wu, F.; Das, A.K.; Arshad, H.; Khan, M.K. A user friendly mutual authentication and key agreement scheme for wireless sensor networks using chaotic maps. *Futur. Gener. Comput. Syst.* **2016**, *63*, 56–75. [CrossRef]
18. Xiong, L.; Peng, D.; Peng, T.; Liang, H.; Liu, Z. A Lightweight Anonymous Authentication Protocol with Perfect Forward Secrecy for Wireless Sensor Networks. *Sensors* **2017**, *17*, 2681. [CrossRef]
19. Wong, K.H.M.; Zheng, Y.; Cao, J.; Wang, S. A dynamic user authentication scheme for wireless sensor networks. In Proceedings of the IEEE International Conference on Sensor Networks, Ubiquitous, and Trustworthy Computing (SUTC '06), Taichung, Taiwan, 5–7 June 2006; Volume 1, p. 8.
20. Das, M.L. Two-factor user authentication in wireless sensor networks. *IEEE Trans. Wirel. Commun.* **2009**, *8*, 1086–1090. [CrossRef]
21. Chen, T.H.; Shih, W.K. A robust mutual authentication protocol for wireless sensor networks. *ETRI J.* **2010**, *32*, 704–712. [CrossRef]
22. He, D.; Gao, Y.; Chan, S.; Chen, C.L.P. An enhanced two-factor user authentication scheme in wireless sensor networks. *Ad Hoc Sens. Wirel. Netw.* **2010**, *10*, 361–371.
23. Farash, M.S.; Turkanović, M.; Kumari, S.; Hölbl, M. An efficient user authentication and key agreement scheme for heterogeneous wireless sensor network tailored for the Internet of Things environment. *Ad Hoc Networks* **2016**, *36*, 152–176. [CrossRef]
24. Amin, R.; Islam, S.H.; Biswas, G.; Khan, M.K.; Leng, L.; Kumar, N. Design of an anonymity-preserving three-factor authenticated key exchange protocol for wireless sensor networks. *Comput. Networks* **2016**, *101*, 42–62. [CrossRef]
25. Jiang, Q.; Zeadally, S.; Ma, J.; He, D. Lightweight three-factor authentication and key agreement protocol for internet-integrated wireless sensor networks. *IEEE Access* **2017**, *5*, 3376–3392. [CrossRef]
26. Shin, S.; Kwon, T. A Lightweight Three-Factor Authentication and Key Agreement Scheme in Wireless Sensor Networks for Smart Homes. *Sensors* **2019**, *19*, 2012. [CrossRef]
27. Fathollahi-Fard, A.M.; Dulebenets, M.A.; Hajiaghaei–Keshteli, M.; Tavakkoli-Moghaddam, R.; Safaeian, M.; Mirzahosseinian, H. Two hybrid meta-heuristic algorithms for a dual-channel closed-loop supply chain network design problem in the tire industry under uncertainty. *Adv. Eng. Inform.* **2021**, *50*, 101418. [CrossRef]
28. Fathollahi-Fard, A.M.; Ahmadi, A.; Karimi, B. Multi-Objective Optimization of Home Healthcare with Working-Time Balancing and Care Continuity. *Sustainability* **2021**, *13*, 12431. [CrossRef]
29. Fallahpour, A.; Wong, K.Y.; Rajoo, S.; Fathollahi-Fard, A.M.; Antucheviciene, J.; Nayeri, S. An integrated approach for a sustainable supplier selection based on Industry 4.0 concept. *Environ. Sci. Pollut. Res.* **2021**, 1–19. [CrossRef]
30. Wang, D.; He, D.; Wang, P.; Chu, C.-H. Anonymous Two-Factor Authentication in Distributed Systems: Certain Goals Are Beyond Attainment. *IEEE Trans. Dependable Secur. Comput.* **2015**, *12*, 428–442. [CrossRef]
31. Huang, X.; Xiang, Y.; Chonka, A.; Zhou, J.; Deng, R. A Generic Framework for Three-Factor Authentication: Preserving Security and Privacy in Distributed Systems. *IEEE Trans. Parallel Distrib. Syst.* **2011**, *22*, 1390–1397. [CrossRef]
32. Wang, D.; Gu, Q.; Cheng, H.; Wang, P. The request for better measurement: A comparative evaluation of two-factor authentication schemes. In Proceedings of the 11th ACM on Asia Conference on Computer and Communications Security ACM, Xi'an, China, 30 May–3 June 2016; pp. 475–486.
33. Blanchet, B.; Smyth, B.; Cheval, V.; Sylvestre, M. ProVerif 2.00: Automatic Cryptographic Protocol Verifier, User Manual and Tutorial. 2018. Available online: https://prosecco.gforge.inria.fr/personal/bblanche/proverif (accessed on 15 October 2021).
34. Burrows, M.; Abadi, M.; Needham, R.M. A logic of authentication. Proceedings of the Royal Society of London. *A. Math. Phys. Sci.* **1989**, *426*, 233–271.
35. He, D.; Kumar, N.; Lee, J.-H.; Sherratt, R. Enhanced three-factor security protocol for consumer USB mass storage devices. *IEEE Trans. Consum. Electron.* **2014**, *60*, 30–37. [CrossRef]
36. Ostad-Sharif, A.; Arshad, H.; Nikooghadam, M.; Abbasinezhad-Mood, D. Three party secure data transmission in IoT networks through design of a lightweight authenticated key agreement scheme. *Futur. Gener. Comput. Syst.* **2019**, *100*, 882–892. [CrossRef]

Article

A CNN-MPSK Demodulation Architecture with Ultra-Light Weight and Low-Complexity for Communications

Bingrui Wang [1], Zhijian Lin [2,*] and Xingang Zhang [1]

[1] Henan Intelligent Emergency Support Engineering Research Center, Nanyang Normal University, Nanyang 473061, China; toynbeescoot@alumni.hust.edu.cn (B.W.); xingzh6yaros@nynu.edu.cn (X.Z.)
[2] School of Advanced Manufacturing, Science Park of Fuzhou University, Jinjiang 362251, China
* Correspondence: zlin@fzu.edu.cn

Abstract: Modulation is an indispensable component in modern communication systems and multiple phase shift keying (MPSK) is widely studied to improve the spectral efficiency. It is of great significance to study the MPSK modulations of symmetric phases in practice. Based on convolutional neural networks (CNNs), we propose a generic architecture for MPSK demodulation, referred to as CNN-MPSK. The architecture utilizes a single-layer CNN and a pooling trick to crop network parameters. In comparison with conventional coherent demodulation, the CNN-MPSK eliminates three modules, i.e., carrier multiplication, bandpass filter and sampling decision. Thus, we can avoid π-inverted phenomenon from the multiplication of two carrier waves with different phases, as the carrier multiplication is not employed. In addition, we can reduce errors introduced by sampling decision. Furthermore, we conduct bit-error-rate tests for binary-PSK, 4PSK, 8PSK, and 16PSK demodulation. Experimental results reveal that the performance of CNN-MPSK is almost the same to that of conventional coherent demodulation. However, the CNN-MPSK demodulation reduces computational complexity from $O(n^2)$ to $O(n)$ as compared to the latter one. Additionally, the proposed scheme can be readily applied for demodulation of non-symmetric MPSK constellations that maybe distorted by linear and nonlinear impairments in communication systems.

Keywords: carrier multiplication; computational complexity; sampling decision; phase shift keying; coherent demodulation

Citation: Wang, B.; Lin, Z.; Zhang, X. A CNN-MPSK Demodulation Architecture with Ultra-Light Weight and Low-Complexity for Communications. *Symmetry* **2022**, *14*, 873. https://doi.org/10.3390/sym14050873

Academic Editor: Boris Malomed

Received: 28 March 2022
Accepted: 14 April 2022
Published: 25 April 2022

Publisher's Note: MDPI stays neutral with regard to jurisdictional claims in published maps and institutional affiliations.

Copyright: © 2022 by the authors. Licensee MDPI, Basel, Switzerland. This article is an open access article distributed under the terms and conditions of the Creative Commons Attribution (CC BY) license (https://creativecommons.org/licenses/by/4.0/).

1. Introduction

Modulation and demodulation techniques play an important role in data transmission. Original digital signals in communication systems may contain low-frequency components that are difficult to transmit directly through channels. Therefore, the original signals must be encoded onto high-frequency carrier signals for transmission. The encoded process is referred to as modulation [1]. The primary purpose of modulation is to match the frequency bandwidths between signals and channels [2]. Another purpose is to facilitate channel multiplexing [3]. Thus, after modulation, each signal is shifted to a different frequency band so that mutual interference will not occur during transmission. In particular, a multiple phase shift keying (MPSK) demodulation is used to convey data by changing the phase of a constant frequency reference signal. MPSK is a classic modulation that is practically displaced in the standard within orthogonal frequency-division multiplexing (OFDM) symbols for wireless communications. For instance, 4PSK is widely utilized in code division multiple access mobile communications, digital video broadcasting-satellite-second generation communications, coherent optical communications and fiber optic communications. The constellations of MPSK signals are symmetric and zero-mean that is widely used for wireless local area networks and Bluetooth communications.

Recently, a lot of research related to modulation recognition have been undertaken using deep learning technology [4–6]. In particular, deep residual networks was investigated to perform radio signal classification, taking into account the effects of carrier frequency offset, symbol rate, and multipath fading. The traditional convolutional neural networks (CNNs) achieve similar performance to residual networks, but with the increased trainable parameters [7]. A novel two-step training for CNN-based automatic modulation classification (CNN-AMC) was then proposed in order to handle complex tasks [8]. Simulation results indicate that the CNN-AMC approximates the optimal maximum likelihood (ML)-AMC. Regarding inference speed, the deep learning-based approach is more than a hundred times faster than ML-AMC by using parallel computation. The relatively simple neural network architectures were presented for space-time-block-codes multiple-input multiple-output systems (MIMO), which are sparse autoencoders-based deep neural networks (DNN) and radial basis function networks (RBFN) [9]. RBFN and DNN weights are optimized using the Broyden–Fletcher–Goldfarb–Shannon algorithm and the least square approach. For the classification of digitally modulated signals in varying channel conditions, Ali and Yang [10] proposed a fully linked two-layer feed-forward DNN with layerwise unsupervised pretraining. This system uses multiple hidden nodes and independent autoencoders for learning feature maps. The proposed DNN has good classification accuracy even when trained and tested at different signal-to-noise ratios (SNRs). To be more efficient in low SNR conditions, the deep belief network and spiking neural network were utilized to reduce execution latency associated with deep learning architectures [11]. Each feature-based AMC classifier is then studied to determine the upper and lower performance bounds within this adaptive framework.

By employing a CNN-based technique, an intelligent eye-diagram analyzer was proposed to recognize modulation formats and estimate optical SNR [12]. Aided by oscilloscope in simulation, the eye diagram images of four modulation formats can be obtained over a wide optical SNR range. It was showed that CNN achieves higher accuracy than other machine learning algorithms such as decision trees, *k*-nearest neighbors, back-propagation neural networks, and support vector machines. Using the strengths of the CNN and the long short-term memory (LSTM), the AMC is developed by dual-stream construction, which efficiently explores the feature interaction and spatial–temporal properties of raw complex temporal signals [13]. In particular, the signals first go through preprocessing to be converted to the temporal inphase/quadrature format and amplitude/phase representation. To improve modulation recognition accuracy at low SNRs, an algorithm for pre-denoising was proposed in [14] before modulation recognition. The pre-denoising algorithm consists of a fully CNN, which is similar to an auto-encoder. A residual learning is also used to speed up the learning process. Eye diagram measurements were further used to estimate coherent channel performance with deep learning [15]. The experimental results show that the proposed technique provides high accuracy in determining the modulation format, optical SNR, roll-off factor, and timing skew of a quadrature amplitude modulation. In [16], the modulation signals are transformed into two image representations of cyclic spectra and constellation diagram, respectively.

To integrate the features, a gradient descent strategy and a multi-feature fusion technique were exploited along with a two-branch CNN model. The novel framework was proposed for low-cost link adaptation for spatial modulation MIMO (SM-MIMO). Simulations demonstrate that the supervised-learning classifiers and DNN-based adaptive SM-MIMO outperform a variety of conventional optimization-driven designs [17]. The detection of modulations was presented for multi-relay cooperative MIMO systems of 5G communications in the presence of spatially correlated channels and imperfect channel state information. The simulation results show that the machine learning techniques provide gain in terms of both the modulation detection and complexity [18]. To blindly detect the modulation order of interference signals in downlink non-orthogonal multiple access systems, a machine learning algorithm based on Anderson–Darling test was investigated [19]. DNNs and machine learning were used to develop methods for monitoring optical performance, identifying modulation formats, multipath fading channels and orthogonal frequency-division multiplexing supported by compressed sensing assisted index modulation [20–23].

The previous related studies have yielded positive results. However, these studies utilize deep learning networks, which are deep and have a large output latency [24,25]. As the deep networks have a high degree of complexity, they are difficult to train and generate a large number of parameters, which is unsuitable for small embedded hardware systems. Several studies require the input data of a system to be in an image format. In such case, the received binary data have to be converted into images, and then feature extraction and other operations are carried out. Finally, the image is converted back into binary data. The exchange of binary data and images increases the delay and complexity. There are concerns regarding the system ability to process the received data in real time. Other studies perform pre-processing operations, which increases the amount of parameters and the complexity of the overall system [26,27]. Thus, it is hard to apply these studies for practical hardware implementations. Consequently, based on CNN and pooling techniques, we propose a shallow CNN-MPSK demodulation with ultra-light parameters to achieve a low complexity architecture. The goal of using CNNs with MPSK is to provide an alternative method for demodulation with the affordable computation complexity.

The sections of the study are organized as follows. In Section 2, we analyze the modulation principle of MPSK and the coherent demodulation process. In addition, the theoretical bit-error-rate (BER) formula for coherent demodulation is derived. Section 3 presents the architecture of CNN-MPSK and the computation consumed by each component. We then show the number of parameters generated by the CNN-MPSK architecture. In Section 4, we give a specific CNN-MPSK demodulation example to illustrate parameters training and perform BER tests under different SNRs. Afterwards, we discuss the multiplications and additions involved in CNN-MPSK and coherent demodulation, and conclude this paper in Section 5.

2. Conventional Modulation and Demodulation of MPSK

MPSK is one of the most widely used techniques due to its relative simplicity in modulation and demodulation. The modulation of such signals can be represented by

$$c_i(t) = \sqrt{\frac{2}{T_c}} \sin(w_c t + \theta), \qquad (1)$$
$$\theta = 2\pi i/M, i = \{0, 1, 2, \ldots, M-1\},$$

where T_c is the period of modulated signal $c_i(t)$, $T_c = \frac{2\pi}{w_c}$, w_c and θ denote frequency and phase of the carrier, respectively.

The MPSK demodulation process typically consists of two BPSK demodulation. Figure 1 illustrates the simple case of coherent demodulation for BPSK [28,29]. First, the received BPSK signal $r(t)$ is filtered to eliminate out-of-band noise using a bandpass filter. Afterwards, the filtered output $z(t)$ is multiplied by a sin wave $2\sin(w_c t)$, resulting in an output $x(t)$ that is twice the frequency of the input signal. The high frequency components in $x(t)$ are removed by the lowpass filter. The signal is then passed to the decision circuit. Based on the synchronized clock in the timing synchronizer module, we obtain the final result $o(t)$ which recovers the binary data stream. In particular, the key component in BPSK demodulation is the carrier generator. It needs to yield a local carrier with the identical frequency and phase as the input signal $r(t)$. However, the local carrier may not be properly generated, leading to a phase difference between the generated carrier and the received carrier, resulting in negative consequences for demodulation [30–32].

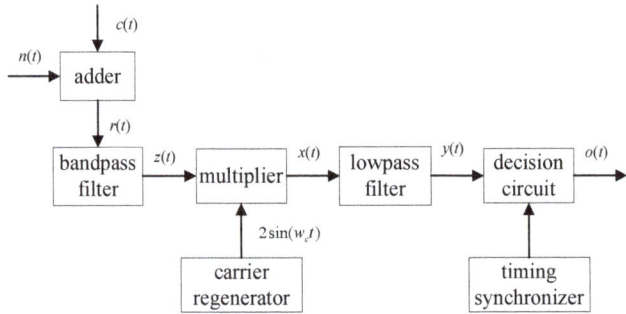

Figure 1. Block diagram of a coherent binary-PSK (BPSK) receiver.

Figure 2 depicts the two conditional probability density functions (PDF) $f_0(x)$ and $f_1(x)$ for the transmitted bits 0 and 1 with mean values of $\sqrt{2/T_c}$ and $-\sqrt{2/T_c}$, respectively.

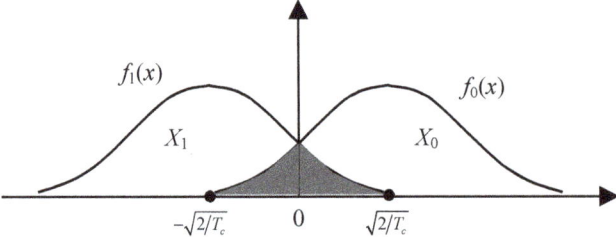

Figure 2. Conditional bit error probability density functions for BPSK demodulated signals.

In the event that the bit 1 is transmitted and the receiver determines it as 0, the conditional probability of such an error is defined by

$$P(0/1) = \int_0^{+\infty} f_1(x)dx$$
$$= \int_{\frac{\sqrt{2/T_c}}{\sqrt{2}\sigma_n}}^{\infty} \frac{1}{\sqrt{\pi}} \exp[-u^2] du \qquad (2)$$

where

$$u = \frac{(x + \sqrt{2/T_c})}{\sqrt{2}\sigma_n}. \qquad (3)$$

The lower limit of integration in Equation (2) is simplified to

$$\frac{\sqrt{2/T_c}}{\sqrt{2}\sigma_n} = \frac{\sqrt{1/T_c}}{\sqrt{N_0 B}} = \frac{\sqrt{1/T_c}}{\sqrt{N_0/T_c}} = \frac{1}{\sqrt{N_0}} = \sqrt{\frac{E_b}{N_0}} = \sqrt{snr}, \qquad (4)$$

where E_b is already normalized to one when BPSK signals are transmitted. Consequently, in terms of the complementary error function (erfc), assuming bits are equiprobable, the BER for BPSK coherent detection is given by

$$P_e = \frac{1}{2} P(0/1) + \frac{1}{2} P(1/0) = \frac{1}{2} \mathrm{erfc}(\sqrt{snr}). \qquad (5)$$

Similarly, the probability of symbol error of MPSK ($M \geq 4$) is overbounded by [33]

$$P_e = \frac{2}{\sqrt{\pi N_0}} \int_{\sqrt{E_s}\sin(\frac{\pi}{M})}^{\infty} \exp[\frac{-x^2}{N_0}]dx$$
$$= \frac{2}{\sqrt{\pi}} \int_{\sqrt{\frac{E_s}{N_0}}\sin(\frac{\pi}{M})}^{\infty} \exp[-u^2]du \qquad (6)$$
$$= erfc[\sqrt{\frac{E_s}{N_0}}\sin(\frac{\pi}{M})],$$

where $\sqrt{E_s}$ is the average energy of the transmitted symbols.

3. The Proposed CNN-MPSK Architecture

3.1. Architecture Presentation

In Figure 3, the proposed architecture takes the received signal as input and then applies one-dimensional (1D) convolution to extract features. Afterwards, the signal flows to the activation module to become unlinear. The flow continues to input a pooling component, followed by a full connection to act as a classifier on the features.

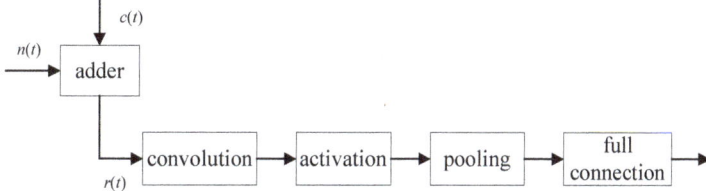

Figure 3. The architecture of a neural network for MPSK demodulation.

Next, we present the components of the CNN architecture, which consist of 1D convolution, activation, pooling, and full connection. Among these modules, convolution is the most important one. From a mathematical standpoint, convolution can be regarded as an integral operation, or an accumulation. Convolution has the property that past data have an effect on future data, and adjacent data influence current data, which makes convolution convenient to extract features from data. Given a sequence r of length d as input and a vector w of length k, the 1D convolution operation is given by

$$y(m) = \sum_k r(m+k)w(k). \qquad (7)$$

The Equation (7) involves element-by-element multiplication and summation. In particular, the elements of vector w are called weights that the network needs to learn during training. Thus, the w is often interchangeably referred to as kernel. Typically, the kernels have small size. In this study, the size of kernel w is 1×3, and the 1D output vector z is given by

$$z(j) = y + b = \sum_{i=0}^{2} r(j+i)w(i) + b, \; 0 \leq j \leq d-3, \qquad (8)$$

where $z(j)$ is the j-th element of the output, the z is also referred as extracted feature, and b is called bias which represents the baseline when all the inputs have values of zero. Note that the length of $z(j)$ is $d-2$. In order to make $z(j)$ to have the same size as the input r, we add one zero to the first and last positions of r, respectively, which produces a new input vector $r' = [\,0\;r\;0\,]$. Thus, we can rewrite Equation (8) as

$$z'(j) = \sum_{i=0}^{2} r'(j+i)w(i) + b, \; 0 \leq j \leq d-1. \qquad (9)$$

The Equation (9) can be illustrated by Figure 4, which gives a visual explanation of how 1D convolution works. In Figure 4, the convolution multiplies the kernel w by the first three elements of r', sums all the multiplications with b, and yields the first output $z'(0)$. Following this, we shift the kernel w one element to the right and perform convolution to generate another output $z'(1)$. In particular, the $r'(0)$, $r'(1)$, $r'(d)$ and $r'(d+1)$ are equal to zero, $r(0)$, $r(d-1)$ and zero, respectively. Thus, the first two items $z'(0)$ and $z'(1)$, and the last item $z'(d-1)$ are computed as

$$
\begin{aligned}
z'(0) &= r'(0)w(0) + r'(1)w(1) + r'(2)w(2) + b \\
&= r'(1)w(1) + r'(2)w(2) + b \\
&= r(0)w(1) + r(1)w(2) + b,
\end{aligned} \tag{10}
$$

$$
\begin{aligned}
z'(1) &= r'(1)w(0) + r'(2)w(1) + r'(3)w(2) + b \\
&= r(0)w(0) + r(1)w(1) + r(2)w(2) + b,
\end{aligned} \tag{11}
$$

and

$$
\begin{aligned}
z'(d-1) &= r'(d-1)w(0) + r'(d)w(1) + r'(d+1)w(2) + b \\
&= r'(d-1)w(0) + r'(d)w(1) + b \\
&= r(d-2)w(0) + r(d-1)w(1) + b.
\end{aligned} \tag{12}
$$

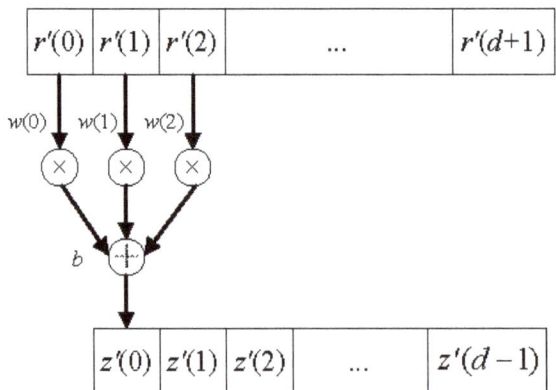

Figure 4. The operation of the 1D convolution.

It is noted that when the input data change, these three parameters, $w(0)$, $w(1)$ and $w(2)$, do not change. We need to repeat the movement $d-1$ times. This 1D convolution costs $3d$ multiplications and d additions in total.

Following by 1D convolution, there is an activation function that performs nonlinear transformation and enables the neural network to learn nonlinear features. CNNs commonly use rectifier linear units (ReLUs) as activating functions. A ReLU can lead to rapid computation with a threshold value 0. When the input is smaller than 0, the output is 0. Otherwise, the output is unchanged. Applying ReLU, the output can be represented as

$$
f(j) = \max[0, z'(j)], \ 0 \leq j \leq d-1. \tag{13}
$$

The pooling is often performed after activation for sub-sampling features. In general, the reason to subsample is that the an important feature of a sequence is seldom contained in adjacent data. The sub-sampling can produce features that are invariant to scale, translation, pose, and rotation changes. Max pooling selects the maximum value from the adjacent data, and thus we have

$$p(m) = \max\{f[ms : (m+1)s - 1]\},\ 0 \le m \le d/s - 1, \tag{14}$$

where s is the slide step size and p is the output from max pooling. To provide classification results, a full connection needs to integrate useful and hierarchical features. In a full connection, each unit is connected to all the previous input units. The connection can be expressed as a matrix multiplication, i.e.,

$$o = \sum_{m=0}^{d/s-1} p(m) w_f(m) + b_f, \tag{15}$$

where b_f is a parameter known as bias, w_f are weights, and o denotes a single unit. According to Equation (15), we can construct a structure to depict the full connection, as shown in Figure 5. In BPSK demodulation, we only need one output unit represented by bit 1 or 0. Thus, the full connection costs d/s multiplications and d/s additions for one output.

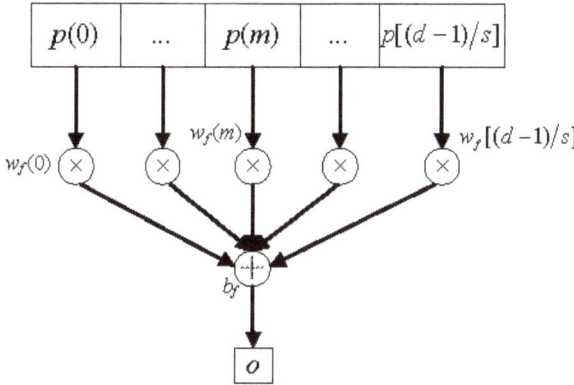

Figure 5. The operation of the full connection.

3.2. Parameter Distribution of CNN-MPSK

The CNN-MPSK network architecture is illustrated in Table 1. The network is rather straightforward. Table 1 shows the type of operation, shape of the input and output, and the number of parameters in the operation. The network takes the $1 \times n \times 1$ single-channel data sequence as input. The convolution uses one 1×3 kernel and requires three weights and a bias. The $1 \times n \times 1$ data are processed by activation. Then, the data are pooled down by a factor of 2, yielding a $1 \times n/2 \times 1$ output. Following this, the full connection module converts the $1 \times n/2 \times 1$ input to a $1 \times M$ output with a $M \times n/2$ kernel. Note that the activation as well as pooling has no parameters because there is nothing to learn. Thus, the total number of parameters is $M \times n/2 + M + 4$, which includes $M \times n/2 + 3$ weights and $1 + M$ biases. In particular, for BPSK, the value of M is equal to 1.

Table 1. The summary of CNN-MPSK structure.

Type of Operation	Input Shape	Output Shape	Size of Kernel	Parameters
convolution	$1 \times n \times 1$	$1 \times n \times 1$	1×3	4
activation	$1 \times n \times 1$	$1 \times n \times 1$	0	0
pooling	$1 \times n \times 1$	$1 \times n/2 \times 1$	0	0
full connection	$1 \times n/2 \times 1$	$1 \times M$	$M \times n/2$	$M \times n/2 + M$

4. Comparison between CNN-MPSK and Coherent Demodulation in Terms of Performance and Computational Complexity

4.1. The Accuracy and Loss Curves

The proposed MPSK modulation assumes a sine wave of one period to represent a symbol. As an example, in BPSK modulation, a sine wave of one cycle represents a 0 or a 1. Our proposed modulation can also be applied for communication systems operated at at MHz or GHz. In order to facilitate comparison, we set the carrier frequency to be 300 KHz and sampling frequency is 6 MHz for BPSK, 4PSK, 8PSK and 16PSK demodulations. Thus, the input to the CNN-MPSK network consists of 20 bits. The training process are similar for these four demodulations. We demonstrate the process by using BPSK as an example. The CNN-BPSK network only requires $n/2 + 5 = 15$ parameters in total. We generate 1 million experimental data at random, half of which is used for training and half for validating. After training the CNN-BPSK network for 15 epochs, we obtain the accuracy and loss curves versus the number of epochs, as shown in Figure 6. The epoch number is on the x-axis, while accuracy and loss are on the y-axis.

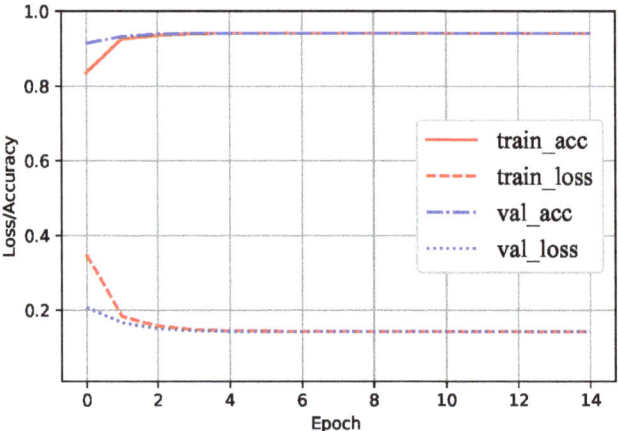

Figure 6. A plot of accuracy and loss for the CNN-BPSK network.

The accuracy in Figure 6 takes a value very near 0.95 and the loss is close to 0.15. The training and validating accuracies improve as we train, while the losses decrease. In particular, the four curves change rapidly in the first two epochs, and the top and bottom parts tend to be 0.95 and 0.15, respectively. After the four epoch, the two accuracy curves almost overlap as well as the two loss curves. The training accuracy is stable, leading to a 94.4% accuracy.

4.2. BER Comparison of CNN-MPSK and Coherent Demodulation

This part presents the demodulation performance of CNN-MPSK. In this experiment, the SNR is $snr\_db = [-5, -4, -3, -2, -1, 0, 1, 2, 3, 4, 5, 6, 7, 8, 9]$ in decibels. We need to restore the snr_db to the initial value and perform $10^{(snr\_db/10)}$ conversion. We utilize additive white Gaussian noise (AWGN) to simulate channel interference. The tested data for each SNR is 5 million bits, so the total number of noised data flows to CNN-MPSK network is 100 million. With the trained parameters, we predict the noised data and thus obtain the demodulated curve for BPSK, 4PSK, 8PSK and 16PSK, as shown in Figure 7. The blue BER curve is obtained by coherent demodulation. The horizontal axis represents the SNR in dB, while the vertical axis is the BER. The BER curves of the four demodulations from the CNN structure overlap heavily with those based on the conventional coherent demodulation.

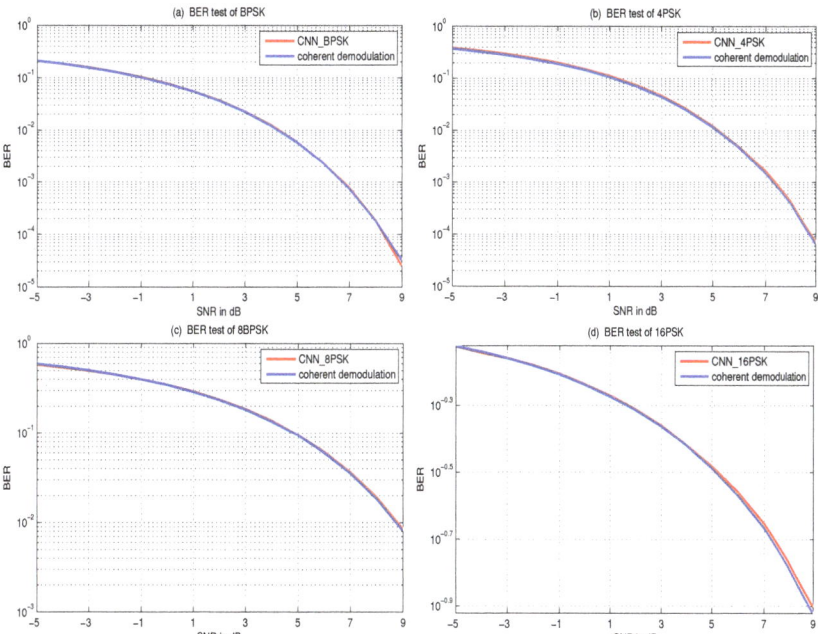

Figure 7. BER comparisons of CNN-MPSK and coherent demodulation for BPSK, 4PSK, 8PSK and 16PSK demodulations.

4.3. Comparison of Multiplications and Additions

The coherent approach for MPSK involves phase demodulation, requiring linear-phase filters and stable outputs. Therefore, finite impulse response (FIR) filters are preferred. We are concerned with linear-phase FIR filters. The output of an this filter only depends on the present and previous inputs, which can be completely described by

$$y(n) = \sum_{k=0}^{L-1} g_k x(n-k) \\ = g_0 x(n) + g_1 x(n-1) + \ldots + g_{L-1} x(n-L+1), \quad (16)$$

where $x(n)$ is the input sequence of length N, g_k denotes filter coefficients and L represents the FIR filter length. FIRs have no feedback and have stability and freedom from phase distortion. Each coefficient requires a register to hold a delayed input. With the length L of this filter and the N input samples, the length of output $y(n)$ is $N + L - 1$. This process involves $(N + L - 1)L$ multiplications and $(N + L - 1)(L - 1)$ additions [34–36]. Consequently, the corresponding computational complexity of an FIR filter is described as $O(n^2)$.

According to equation (16), when the length of the received signal is N and the bandpass filter has L_p coefficients, the operation of the bandpass filter costs $(N + L_p - 1)L_p$ multiplications and $(N + L_p - 1)(L_p - 1)$ additions. The carrier multiplier module requires N multiplications. Moreover, let L_f represent the length of the lowpass filter coefficients, the operation of this filter involves $(N + L_f - 1)L_f$ multiplications and $(N + L_f - 1)(L_f - 1)$ additions. As a result, the coherent demodulation involves the total calculations, i.e., $(N + L_p - 1)L_p + N + (N + L_f - 1)L_f = N(L_p + L_f + 1) + L_p^2 + L_f^2 - (L_p + L_f)$ multiplications, and $(N + L_p - 1)(L_p - 1) + (N + L_f - 1)(L_f - 1) = N(L_p - 1) + N(L_f - 1) + (L_p - 1)^2 + (L_f - 1)^2$ additions. Demodulating the same input signal as the coherent demodulation, we utilize the proposed CNN-BPSK architecture. In the architecture, the convolution operation requires $3N$ multiplications and N additions, and the full connection needs N/s multiplications and N/s additions, and s is the length of strides. The architecture involves $3N + N/s$ multiplications and $N + N/s$ additions in total.

In comparison with the conventional demodulation, the number of multiplications and additions of the architecture are greatly reduced, as shown in Table 2. The calculation complexity of the proposed demodulation is $O(n)$, while that of the conventional demodulation is $O(n^2)$.

Table 2. The comparison of calculation between coherent and CNN demodulation.

Type of Demodulation	Multiplications	Additions	Complexity
coherent	$N(L_p + L_f + 1) +$ $L_p^2 + L_f^2 - (L_p + L_f)$	$N(L_p - 1) + N(L_f - 1) +$ $(L_p - 1)^2 + (L_f - 1)^2$	$O(n^2)$
CNN-BPSK	$3N + N/s$	$N + N/s$	$O(n)$

Table 3 presents a comparison between the proposed deep learning technique and the existing algorithms [7,11]. We approximate the number of parameters, and the number of operations by orders of magnitude. The last three columns of Table 3 represent the demodulation accuracy for different $E_s/n0$. The proposed technique shows the similar demodulation performance as compared to the other schemes, but benefits from much reduced implementation complexity, i.e., much less operations and parameters to be trained.

Table 3. The comparison of the proposed algorithms and others.

Type of Algorithms	Parameters	Multiplications	Additions	−5 dB	0 dB	10 dB
our CNN BPSK	10	10	10	78.6%	92%	99.9%
our CNN 4PSK	10	10	10	50.9%	70.8%	99.8%
our CNN 8PSK	10	10	10	24%	40.9%	99%
our CNN 16PSK	10	10	10	12%	21.8%	61.6%
ResNet BPSK [7]	10^5	10^7	10^7	50%	97%	99%
ResNet 4PSK [7]	10^5	10^7	10^7	7%	70%	99%
ResNet 8PSK [7]	10^5	10^7	10^7	7%	25%	99%
ResNet 16PSK [7]	10^5	10^7	10^7	6%	40%	85%
DBN BPSK [11]	10^2	10^3	10^3	75%	97%	99%
DBN 4PSK [11]	10^2	10^3	10^3	60%	80%	99%
CNN based BPSK [11]	10^5	10^6	10^6	61%	90%	99%
CNN based 4PSK [11]	10^5	10^6	10^6	50%	75%	99%

5. Conclusions

This paper proposes a simplified and light-weight CNN-MPSK demodulation architecture based on deep learning technology. The proposed CNN-MPSK can be implemented without requiring the carrier synchronization and timing synchronization that make the system complex. Thus, the design complexity can be greatly reduced and the inverse π phenomenon is avoided. The simulation tests are conducted on BER performance of the proposed CNN structure for 4PSK, 8PSK and 16PSK, respectively. We see that the proposed CNN-MPSK shows the similar performance to the coherent demodulation and the existing deep learning demodulations. More importantly, the CNN-MPSK structure has the advantage of greatly reduced computational complexity. As compared with the coherent demodulation, the computation complexity of the proposed architecture is reduced from $O(n^2)$ to $O(n)$. Thus, the proposed architecture can be seen as an alternative scheme for low-complexity signal demodulation in communications.

Author Contributions: Conceptualization, B.W. and Z.L.; methodology, B.W.; software, X.Z.; validation, B.W., Z.L. and X.Z.; formal analysis, Z.L.; investigation, Z.L.; resources, X.Z.; data curation, X.Z.; writing—original draft preparation, B.W.; writing—review and editing, Z.L.; visualization, X.Z.; supervision, X.Z.; project administration, B.W.; funding acquisition, Z.L. All authors have read and agreed to the published version of the manuscript.

Funding: This research was funded by Science and Technology Research Program of Henan Province (No. 202102310530), Nsf of fujian province (No. 2020J01301), and the key scientific research projects of colleges and universities in Henan Province (No. 21A520032, 21A520033).

Institutional Review Board Statement: Not applicable.

Informed Consent Statement: Not applicable.

Data Availability Statement: Not applicable.

Acknowledgments: The authors would like to thank the reviewers for their thoughtful remarks and recommendations, which considerably enhanced the paper's presentation.

Conflicts of Interest: The authors declare no conflict of interest.

References

1. Koh, K.; Mortazavi, S.Y.; Afroz, S. Time Interleaved RF Carrier Modulations and Demodulations. *IEEE Trans. Circuits Syst. I Regul. Pap.* **2014**, *61*, 573–586. [CrossRef]
2. Harper, A.D.; Reed, J.T.; Odom, J.L.; Lanterman, A.D.; Ma, X. Performance of a Linear-Detector Joint Radar-Communication System in Doubly Selective Channels. *IEEE Trans. Aerosp. Electron. Syst.* **2017**, *53*, 703–715. [CrossRef]
3. Abd El-Rahman, A.I.; Cartledge, J.C. Evaluating the Impact of QAM Constellation Subset Selection on the Achievable Information Rates of Multidimensional Formats in Fully Loaded Systems. *J. Lightw. Technol.* **2018**, *36*, 712–720. [CrossRef]
4. Wang, Y.; Liu, M.; Yang, J.; Gui, G. Data-driven deep learning for automatic modulation recognition in cognitive radios. *IEEE Trans. Veh. Technol.* **2019**, *68*, 4074–4077. [CrossRef]
5. Njoku, J.N.; Morocho-Cayamcela, M.E.; Lim, W. CGDNet: Efficient hybrid deep learning model for robust automatic modulation recognition. *IEEE Netw. Lett.* **2021**, *3*, 47–51. [CrossRef]
6. Wang, T.; Hou, Y.; Zhang, H.; Guo, Z. Deep learning based modulation recognition with multi-cue fusion. *IEEE Wirel. Commun. Lett.* **2021**, *10*, 1757–1760. [CrossRef]
7. O'Shea, T.J.; Roy, T.; Clancy, T.C. Over-the-air deep learning based radio signal classification. *IEEE J. Sel. Top. Signal Process.* **2018**, *12*, 168–179. [CrossRef]
8. Meng, F.; Chen, P.; Wu, L.; Wang, X. Automatic modulation classification: A deep learning enabled approach. *IEEE Trans. Veh. Technol.* **2018**, *67*, 10760–10772. [CrossRef]
9. Shah, M.H.; Dang, X. Low-complexity deep learning and RBFN architectures for modulation classification of space-time blockcode (STBC)-MIMO systems. *Digit. Signal Process.* **2020**, *99*, 102656. [CrossRef]
10. Ali, A.; Fan, Y. Unsupervised feature learning and automatic modulation classification using deep learning model. *Phys. Commun.* **2017**, *25*, 75–84. [CrossRef]
11. Ghasemzadeh, P.; Banerjee, S.; Hempel, M.; Sharif, H. A novel deep learning and polar transformation framework for an adaptive automatic modulation classification. *IEEE Trans. Veh. Technol.* **2020**, *69*, 13243–13258. [CrossRef]
12. Wang, D.; Zhang, M.; Li, Z.; Li, J.; Fu, M.; Cui, Y.; Chen, X. Modulation format recognition and OSNR estimation using CNN-based deep learning. *IEEE Photonics Technol. Lett.* **2017**, *29*, 1667–1670. [CrossRef]
13. Zhang, Z.; Luo, H.; Wang, C.; Gan, C.; Xiang, Y. Automatic modulation classification using CNN-LSTM based dual-stream structure. *IEEE Trans. Veh. Technol.* **2020**, *69*, 13521–13531. [CrossRef]
14. Liu, Y.; Liu, Y. Modulation recognition with pre-denoising convolutional neural network. *Electron. Lett.* **2020**, *56*, 255–257. [CrossRef]
15. Zhang, Y.; Ren, Y.; Wang, Z.; Liu, B.; Zhang, H.; Li, S.A.; Fang, Y.; Huang, H.; Bao, C.; Pan, Z.; et al. Eye diagram measurementbased joint modulation format, OSNR, ROF, and skew monitoring of coherent channel using deep learning. *J. Light. Technol.* **2019**, *37*, 5907–5913. [CrossRef]
16. Wu, H.; Li, Y.; Zhou, L.; Meng, J. Convolutional neural network and multi-feature fusion for automatic modulation classification. *Electron. Lett.* **2019**, *55*, 895–897. [CrossRef]
17. Yang, P.; Xiao, Y.; Xiao, M.; Guan, Y.L.; Li, S.; Xiang, W. Adaptive spatial modulation MIMO based on machine learning. *IEEE J. Sel. Areas Commun.* **2019**, *37*, 2117–2131. [CrossRef]
18. Chikha, H.B.; Almadhor, A.; Khalid, W. Machine Learning for 5G MIMO Modulation Detection. *Sensors* **2021**, *21*, 1556. [CrossRef]
19. Zhang, N.; Cheng, K.; Kang, G. A machine-learning-based blind detection on interference modulation order in NOMA systems. *IEEE Commun. Lett.* **2018**, *22*, 2463–2466. [CrossRef]
20. Khan, F.N.; Zhong, K.; Al-Arashi, W.H.; Yu, C.; Lu, C.; Lau, A.P.T. Modulation format identification in coherent receivers using deep machine learning. *IEEE Photonics Technol. Lett.* **2016**, *28*, 1886–1889. [CrossRef]

21. Chen, L.; Chen, P.; Lin, Z. Artificial intelligence in education: A review. *IEEE Access* **2020**, *8*, 5264–5278. [CrossRef]
22. Khan, F.N.; Lu, C.; Lau, A.P.T. Joint modulation format/bit-rate classification and signal-to-noise ratio estimation in multipath fading channels using deep machine learning. *Electron. Lett.* **2016**, *52*, 1272–1274. [CrossRef]
23. Liu, H.; Lu, S.; El-Hajjar, M.; Yang, L.L. Machine learning assisted adaptive index modulation for mmWave communications. *IEEE Open J. Commun. Soc.* **2020**, *1*, 1425–1441. [CrossRef]
24. Ye, N.; Li, X.; Yu, H.; Wang, A.; Liu, W.; Hou, X. Deep Learning Aided Grant-Free NOMA Toward Reliable Low-Latency Access in Tactile Internet of Things. *IEEE Trans. Ind. Inform.* **2019**, *15*, 2995–3005. [CrossRef]
25. Mohammed, S.A.; Shirmohammadi, S.; Altamimi, S. A Multimodal Deep Learning-Based Distributed Network Latency Measurement System. *IEEE Trans. Instrum. Meas.* **2020**, *69*, 2487–2494. [CrossRef]
26. Fang, Y.; Bu, Y.; Chen, P.; Lau, F.C.; Al Otaibi, S. Irregular-Mapped Protograph LDPC-Coded Modulation: A Bandwidth-Efficient Solution for 6G-Enabled Mobile Networks. *IEEE Trans. Intell. Transp. Syst.* **2022**, in press. [CrossRef]
27. Won, Y.S.; Hou, X.; Jap, D.; Breier, J.; Bhasin, S. Back to the basics: Seamless integration of side-channel pre-processing in deep neural networks. *IEEE Trans. Inf. Forensics Secur.* **2021**, *16*, 3215–3227. [CrossRef]
28. Mesiya, M.F. Digital Information Transmission Using Carrier Modulation. In *Contemporary Communication Systems*; Lange, M., Ed.; McGraw-Hill: New York, NY, USA, 2013; pp. 600–610.
29. Fang, Y.; Chen, P.; Cai, G.; Lau, F.C.; Liew, S.C.; Han, G. Outage-Limit-Approaching Channel Coding for Future Wireless Communications: Root-Protograph Low-Density Parity-Check Codes. *IEEE Veh. Technol. Mag.* **2019**, *14*, 85–93. [CrossRef]
30. Safak, M. Optimum Receiver in AWGN Channel. In *Digital Communications*; Wiley, John Wiley and Sons: West Sussex, UK, 2017; pp. 298–319.
31. Chen, P.; Xie, Z.; Fang, Y.; Chen, Z.; Mumtaz, S.; Rodrigues, J.J.P.C. Physical-Layer Network Coding: An Efficient Technique for Wireless Communications. *IEEE Netw.* **2020**, *34*, 270–276. [CrossRef]
32. Haykin, S. Signaling over AWGN Channels. In *Digital Communication Systems*; Knecht, J., Ed.; John Wiley and Sons: Hoboken, NJ, USA, 2014; pp. 323–410.
33. Haykin, S.; Moher, M. Digital band-pass transmission techniques. In *Communication Systems*; Hong, S., Melhom, A., Eds.; John Wiley and Sons: Hoboken, NJ, USA, 2009; pp. 313–350.
34. Tan, L.; Jiang, J. Finite impulse response filter design. In *Digital Signal Processing: Fundamentals and Applications*; Merken, S., Ed.; Academic Press: Stanford, CA, USA, 2018; pp. 229–236, 550–558.
35. Chen, P.; Wang, L.; Lau, F.C.M. One Analog STBC-DCSK Transmission Scheme not Requiring Channel State Information. *IEEE Trans. Circuits Syst. I Regul. Pap.* **2013**, *360*, 1027–1037. [CrossRef]
36. Rao, K.D.; Swamy, M.N.S. FIR Digital Filter Design. In *Digital Signal Processing: Theory and Practice*; Springer: Singapore, 2018; pp. 325–338.

Article

Improving Decodability of Polar Codes by Adding Noise

Lingjun Kong [1], Haiyang Liu [2,*], Wentao Hou [3] and Bin Dai [4]

[1] Faculty of Network and Telecommunication Engineering, Jinling Institute of Technology, Nanjing 211169, China; kong@jit.edu.cn
[2] Institute of Microelectronics of Chinese Academy of Sciences, Beijing 100029, China
[3] College of Telecommunications and Information Engineering, Nanjing University of Posts and Telecommunications, Nanjing 210003, China; 1220013235@njupt.edu.cn
[4] School of Internet of Things, Nanjing University of Posts and Telecommunications, Nanjing 210003, China; daibin@njupt.edu.cn
* Correspondence: liuhaiyang@ime.ac.cn

Abstract: This paper presents an online perturbed and directed neural-evolutionary (Online-PDNE) decoding algorithm for polar codes, in which the perturbation noise and online directed neuro-evolutionary noise sequences are sequentially added to the received sequence for re-decoding if the standard polar decoding fails. The new decoding algorithm converts uncorrectable received sequences into error-correcting regions of their decoding space for correct decoding by adding specific noises. To reduce the decoding complexity and delay, the PDNE decoding algorithm and sole neural-evolutionary (SNE) decoding algorithm for polar codes are further proposed, which provide a considerable tradeoff between the decoding performance and complexity by acquiring the neural-evolutionary noise in an offline manner. Numerical results suggest that our proposed decoding algorithms outperform the other conventional decoding algorithms. At high signal-to-noise ratio (SNR) region, the Online-PDNE decoding algorithm improves bit error rate (BER) performance by more than four orders of magnitude compared with the conventional simplified successive cancellation (SSC) decoding algorithm. Furthermore, in the mid-high SNR region, the average normalized complexity of the proposed algorithm is almost the same as that of the SSC decoding algorithm, while preserving the decoding performance gain.

Keywords: fifth generation; channel coding; polar code; perturbation noise; neuro-evolution

1. Introduction

The development of fifth generation (5G) communication technology is driven not only by the requirements of faster and higher-capacity extreme mobile broadband (eMBB) applications, but also by the rapidly evolving area of Internet of Things (IoT) that needs a massive connectivity of devices with ultra-reliable and ultra-low-latency connectivity over Internet Protocol [1–4]. Channel coding is an integral part of any communication system, which plays an important role in meeting the system reliability requirements [5–7]. A prominent feature of 5G new radio (NR) is the adoption of a new class of error correction codes, i.e., polar codes, for control channels [8,9]. Future wireless communication technologies are proliferating in the connection between people and things, and their scenarios will place new requirements on the channel coding performances [10].

Polar codes were proposed by Arıkan [11] in 2009, who also originally indicated the symmetry of polar codes for binary-input discrete memoryless channels (B-DMCs). With the symmetry, the output vector can be divided into equivalence classes in terms of their transition probabilities. Based on the channel polarization theory that entails channel combining and channel splitting, this new coding scheme is capacity achieving as opposed to just capacity approaching in symmetric B-DMCs with efficient construction and low complexity [12,13]. Several decoding algorithms have recently been developed for polar codes in the literature [14–21]. The successive cancellation (SC) algorithm proposed by Arıkan [11] is an effective method for decoding polar codes. To reduce the decoding latency and algorithmic complexity of the SC decoder, a simplified successive cancellation (SSC) decoder was proposed in [14]. In [15], Tal and Vardy proposed the successive cancellation list (SCL) decoder to tackle the problem that only one decoding path was reserved for SC decoding, which may lead to the loss of the correct path. CRC (cyclic redundancy check)-aided decoding schemes were proposed to improve the performance of polar codes in [16]. In addition, the recent development of deep learning methods provides a new insight into the decoding of linear codes [22–27]. However, deep-learning-based channel decoding is doomed by the curse of dimensionality, in which the learning process is limited by the complexity as the number of information bits increases.

In the signal processing area, it can be shown that the performance of a suboptimal detector may be improved by adding noise to the received data under certain conditions [28,29]. Inspired by this method, some researchers have investigated how to improve the decoding performance of a (suboptimal) decoder by adding noise. In [30], a belief propagation list (BPL) decoding algorithm was proposed, in which adding a small amount of noise enables the decoder to handle non-convergent errors. A dynamic perturbation decoding method for Polar-CRC concatenation codes through dynamically controlling the interference noise was proposed in [31]. In [32], a generalized framework for multi-round BP decoding with input perturbation for short low-density parity-check (LDPC) codes was proposed, where the perturbation is done iteratively on a few symbols to widen the search space.

In [33], a CRC-assisted perturbation decoding algorithm for polar codes was proposed, which is called the PB-SSC decoding algorithm in this paper. When the CRC check of the SSC decoder fails, the PB-SSC decoding algorithm can provide multiple possible candidate vectors for re-decoding by adding disturbance noises. However, the performance gain achieved by the PB-SSC decoding algorithm is limited. A decoding algorithm for polar codes based on the perturbation with a convolution neural network (CNN) was proposed in [34]. In [35], a post-processing technique was proposed to improve the performance of the SSC polar decoder in the 2D intersymbol interference (ISI) data storage system, namely the post-processing SSC (PP-SSC) decoding algorithm, in which the perturbation algorithm and the genetic algorithm (GA) successively generate perturbation vectors that accelerate the convergence of the decoder. Unfortunately, the secondary generation of perturbation noise by the GA is performed online, which greatly increases the delay and complexity of the decoder.

In order to address these issues, this paper proposes several decoding algorithms for polar codes by applying the idea of adding noise, which generalizes the methods in our previous work [36]. However, more effective operations in the GA training process are used in this work. We first propose an online perturbed and directed neural-evolutionary (Online-PDNE) decoding algorithm. Then, a simplified version of Online-PDNE decoding algorithm, called the PDNE decoding algorithm, is proposed by using the genetic process in an offline manner. Finally, to further reduce the decoding complexity, we further propose a sole neural-evolutionary (SNE) decoding algorithm, which only invokes the pre-trained offline directed neuro-evolutionary noise and provides a considerable balance between the decoding performance and complexity. Simulation results suggest that our proposed decoding algorithms outperform the other conventional algorithms for decoding polar codes. In addition, the algorithms in this paper have more generality compared with the algorithm in [36].

The main contributions of this paper are summarized as follows:

1. An online perturbed and directed neural-evolutionary (Online-PDNE) decoding algorithm is proposed, which makes polar codes have enhanced error correction ability.
2. To avoid the online training process, the PDNE decoding algorithm is proposed, in which perturbation noise and pre-trained offline directed neuro-evolutionary noise sequences are sequentially employed for re-decoding.
3. In order to further reduce the decoding complexity, the SNE decoding algorithm is further proposed, where only the pre-trained offline directed neuro-evolutionary noise by the GA algorithms is employed to improve the decoding performance.
4. The decoding algorithms proposed in this paper are more suitable for the scenarios where the channel quality gradually degrades, such as the storage channel. A good balance can be achieved in terms of the performance and complexity.

The rest of the paper is organized as follows. Section 2 reviews the related work on polar decoding algorithms. In Section 3, the proposed decoding algorithms of polar codes are presented. Simulation results are provided in Section 4. Finally, Section 5 concludes the paper.

2. Related Works

In this paper, the error correction performance of polar codes is improved by adding specific noises. In this section, we briefly review the related works.

2.1. Conventional Perturbation Based Decoding Algorithms

The concept of stochastic perturbation opens a new perspective where systems can benefit from adding artificial noise. In 1981, Benzi [37] found that the addition of suitable noise under certain conditions leads to an increase in a measure of the quality of signal transmission performance, which could be explained by the phenomenon of stochastic resonance [38,39]. It can be shown that the performance of certain suboptimal detector may be improved by adding some white Gaussian noise [28], where the loss of detectability caused by lowering the signal-to-noise ratio (SNR) is offset by the increased sensitivity of the new noise.

Based on the similar concept, a perturbed decoding algorithm (PA) was proposed for a concatenated CRC and convolutional code system [40]. The original signal is first decoded by the conventional Viterbi algorithm. If the CRC check fails, a perturbed received signal is created and then decoded by the inner Viterbi decoder. The perturbation by artificial noise injection is expected to increase the possibility that the transmitted codeword is obtained.

In [30], a theoretical analysis was presented to gain further insight into stochastic resonance phenomenon, where the performance of a stochastic resonance enhanced detector was derived in terms of the probability of detection and the probability of false alarm. The theory behind PA was elaborated in [41]. The distribution of the numbers of perturbed decoding was derived for independent Gaussian perturbations. The dominant terms of the distribution indicate that the complexity of PA is highly dependent on the geometric structure of the error control code. If an ML decoder is employed as the inner decoder, the distribution for the numbers of perturbed decoding can be well approximated by a function of SNR, signal-to-perturbation-noise ratio (SPNR), and the two-centroid code spectrum, which provides theoretical support for related works.

A BPL decoder that relied on artificial noise as a frame error rate (FER) or bit error rate (BER) performance booster in a subject of coding theory was presented in [30]. Artificially generated noises with different intensities are added to the received signal to avoid false convergence in a BP-based decoder. A dynamic perturbation decoding method for polar-CRC cascaded codes was proposed in [31]. Dynamic perturbation decoding can adjust the variance of the added perturbation noise according to the currently decoded codeword, so that the sequences obtained after each perturbation are as different as possible. Based on the analysis of FER and BER, a noise-assisted decoding algorithm for polar codes was proposed to improve the decoding performance [42]. The algorithm is realized by adding the human-made noise, which is a post-compensation processing method for the existing algorithms. The disadvantage of the algorithm is that the noise power needs to be set artificially, and a large number of decoding attempts are performed without any direction, which greatly increases the decoding complexity.

2.2. GA Based Decoding Algortithms

Since the overall search strategy in the optimization process of the GA does not depend on gradient information or other auxiliary knowledge [43], it provides a general framework for solving complex system problems in various areas, such as combinatorial optimization, machine learning, signal processing, and adaptive control.

The GA has been used in LDPC decoding [43,44]. However, its application in polar decoding is still in the early stages. The authors in [33,35] employed the GA to generate perturbation noise, so as to perturb the received signal that failed to decode. Inspired by the GA of AI technology, the authors in [45] used the mean of the log-likelihood ratio (LLR) distribution as the fitness function of each individual to update the successive cancellation flip (SCF) decoding algorithm of the population. Simulation results verified that the improved SCF decoding algorithm based on new constructed candidate flipping positions sets can achieve competitive decoding performance compared with some state-of-the-art SCF decoding algorithms.

In addition, the GA has also achieved good results in polar code constructions [46–49]. In [46], the authors proposed a GA-based framework to construct polar codes using the BER as the fitness function of the GA, thereby reducing the size of the SCL list and the number of iterations. In [47], the authors proposed a scheme for constructing polar codes based on a hash table update population, which reduced the computational complexity of repeated candidates. Aiming at the joint detector and decoder over the resistive random-access memory (ReRAM) channel model, effective polar codes were constructed using the GA in [48].

3. Conventional Schemes

In this section, we first provide the perturbation decoding principle. Then, we briefly summarize the recent related works, including the PB-SSC decoding algorithm [33] and the PP-SSC decoding algorithm [35].

3.1. Perturbation Decoding Principle

The perturbation of the received signal can make each received signal have multiple decoding outputs, which can improve the reliability of the transmission process and avoid retransmission of erroneously decoded information [34]. The perturbation of the received signal can be interpreted as adding independent random noise to improve the performance of suboptimal decoders.

As shown in Figure 1, for each valid codeword $c(c \in \{c_1, c_2, \ldots, c_S\})$, an error correction region $a(a \in \{a_1, a_2, \ldots, a_S\})$ in the decoding space is specified, where S is the total number of valid codewords. When the received signal y^N falls into the error correction region, the decoder succeeds in decoding, where N is the code length. However, if the received signal y^N falls outside the error correction region, the decoder fails in decoding. At this point, adding a random noise n to the received signal may convert the perturbed signal $y^N + n$ into the error correction region, resulting in a successful decoding.

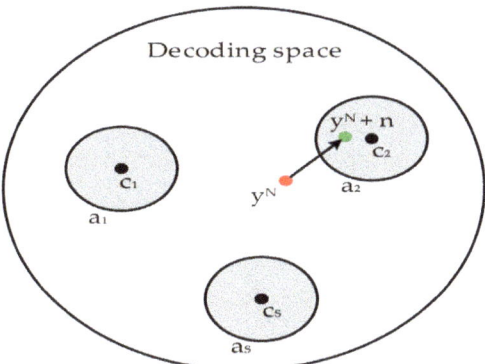

Figure 1. Schematic diagram of perturbation decoding principle.

3.2. PB-SSC Decoding Algorithm

According to the perturbation decoding principle in Section 3.1, the PB-SSC decoding algorithm has been proposed to improve the performance of the SSC decoder in [33].

When the SSC decoding fails, the PB-SSC decoding algorithm is activated. The perturbed noise is added to the received signal y^N to help the received signal to approach the error correction domain. The perturbed received signal y_1^N can be expressed by

$$y_1^N = y^N + Q_p \cdot \text{randn}(1, N), \tag{1}$$

where Q_p is the variance of the perturbed noise, and randn generates random numbers from the standard normal distribution. The decoding is an iterative process that continues until a valid codeword is obtained or the prescribed maximum number of iterations, T_1, is reached. We refer the readers to [33] for further details on the PB-SSC decoding algorithm.

3.3. PP-SSC Decoding Algorithm

The PP-SSC decoding algorithm [35] has been proposed to improve the performance of polar codes in data storage systems, where the GA procedure is employed to enhance the iteration process by producing perturbation vectors that are inherently better than the directed perturbed ones.

The fitness function of an individual is evaluated as

$$F_c = 1 / \sqrt{\sum_{k \in A} [d(k) - d_p(k)]^2 / |A|}, \tag{2}$$

where d and d_p are the decoded sequences of the received signal and the perturbed signal, respectively, and A is the information set of the polar code.

Selection operations in the GA are used to select the parents of the next offspring at each evolution stage, where fitter individuals are forwarded as parents for the upcoming offspring. Then, the surviving individuals will then encounter evolutionary transformations, namely, mutations and crossovers, to generate offspring which would represent the new population. The perturbed vector generated by the GA process in the PP-SSC decoding algorithm will be added to the received signal y^N again for decoding, until a valid codeword is obtained or the prescribed maximum number of generations T_2 is reached. We refer the readers to [31] for further details on the PP-SSC decoding algorithm.

4. Proposed Decoding Algorithms

In this section, three decoding algorithms for polar codes are proposed by adding noise based on the perturbation decoding principle. The computational complexities are then analyzed.

4.1. Online-PDNE Decoding Algorithm

For the GA, the choice of the fitness function plays an important role in the quality of the final solution and the speed of convergence. The evolutionary search process of the GA is only based on the fitness of each individual in the population. Therefore, the selection of the fitness function directly affects the convergence speed of the GA and whether the optimal solution can be found.

In Equation (2), d is the failed decoding sequence output by the decoder, and d_p is the corresponding perturbed decoded sequence. There is no guarantee that their difference can converge effectively unless d is the correct decoding result. However, in the PP-SSC decoder, the GA-based decoding is performed only if the previous perturbed decoding fails. Therefore, we need better fitness function to carry out the genetic process to find the optimal solution.

Similar to the PP-SSC decoder, we propose an online perturbed and directed neural-evolutionary (Online-PDNE) decoding algorithm for polar codes, which adopts the same decoding structure, but with a new fitness function:

$$F_c = 1/(1 + \sum CRC\_Calc(d_p)), \quad (3)$$

where CRC_Calc(·) is the CRC check operation [50].

Fitness function is used to measure whether an individual is the optimal solution in the GA process, which requires the individual's fitness value to be as high as possible. Depending on the fitness function and the selection algorithm, the population can continuously evolve towards the local optimal solution. In this paper, we take the sum of the CRC check remainders as the fitness function. When using Equation (3), it is ensured that the more number of zeros in the CRC remainder, the larger the value of F_c, which meets the requirements of the fitness function. To ensure the evolution direction of the GA population, the roulette wheel selection strategy is used to select the offspring, which is selected according to the cumulative probability. The fitness score of an individual is calculated by

$$F_s = F_c(j) / \sum_{j=1}^{T_1} F_c(j). \quad (4)$$

As shown in Figure 2, when the maximum number of decoding attempts T_1 in the second round is exceeded, the directed neural-evolutionary noise (NE) $n_{ne}^{(k)}$ will be generated online by the NE noise generator and added to the received signal y^N as

$$y_2^N = y^N + n_{ne}^{(k)}. \quad (5)$$

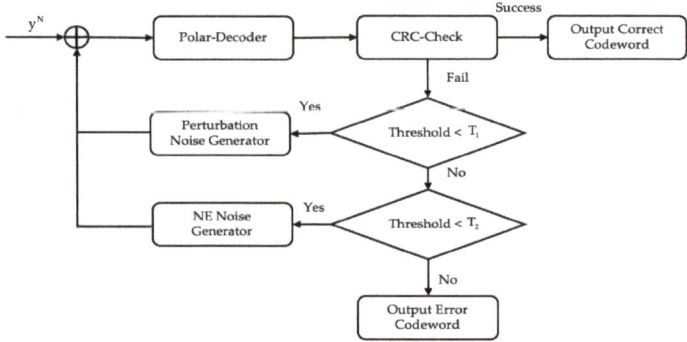

Figure 2. Block diagram of the Online-PDNE decoding algorithm.

In this paper, the GA is employed to realize neuro-evolution to obtain the required directed neural-evolutionary noise. The genetic process NE(·) is as follows:

1. Initialization: Unlike the initialization method in [31], which adopts the perturbation noise when the second round of decoding fails as the initial value. In this paper, the initial population $S_n^{(0)} = \{n_{ne}^{(i)} | i = 1, 2, \ldots, T\}$ is randomly generated, where T is the number of individuals in the population.
2. Selection: According to Equations (3) and (4), the individuals which have high fitness scores with roulette wheel selection from the initial population are forwarded as parents for the upcoming offspring.
3. Population reproduction: This step includes the crossover and mutation. The evolution of GA towards the (sub)optimal solution is mainly due to the crossover operation. The mutation operation guarantees more diversity and reduces the occurrence of a famous phenomenon called premature convergence.
4. Termination criterion: The new directed neural-evolutionary noise generated in the above steps is added to the input of the decoder, and if the CRC checking is successful, the decoding result is output. Otherwise, the GA is continued until the decoding is successful or the maximum number of generations T_2 is reached. The details of the Online-PDNE decoding algorithm are given in Algorithm 1.

Algorithm 1: Online-PDNE Decoding algorithm

Input: y^N // Received signal
       Q_p // Variance of the perturbed noise
       T_1 // Maximum number of the perturbed attempts
       T_2 // Maximum number of generations
       T   // Number of individuals in the population
Output: $\hat{u}_1^N$ // Estimated codeword
1: Initialization: $\hat{u}_1^N \leftarrow 0$, $i \leftarrow 1$, $k \leftarrow 1$.
2: $\hat{u}_1^N \leftarrow$ Polar_decoder(y^N)
3: if CRC($\hat{u}_1^N$) == success
4:     break
5: else
6:     while $i \leq T_1$ do
7:         $y_1^N = y^N + Q_p \cdot \text{randn}(1, N)$
8:         $\hat{u}_1^N \leftarrow$ Polar_decoder(y_1^N)
9:         $i \leftarrow i + 1$
10:        if CRC($\hat{u}_1^N$) == success
11:           break
12:        end if
13:     end while
14:     Initial population $S_n^{(0)} = \{n_{ne}^{(i)} | i = 1, 2, \ldots, T\}$
15:     for $j = 1, \ldots, T_2$ do
16:         $S_n^{(j)} = \text{NE}(S_n^{(j-1)})$
17:         while $k \leq T$ do
18:            Choose $n_{ne}^{(k)} \in S_n^{(j)}$
19:            $y_2^N = y^N + n_{ne}^{(k)}$
20:            $\hat{u}_1^N \leftarrow$ Polar_decoder(y_2^N)
21:            $k \leftarrow k + 1$
22:            if CRC($\hat{u}_1^N$) == success
23:               break
24:            end if
25:         end while
26:     end for
27: end if
28: Return $\hat{u}_1^N$

4.2. PDNE Decoding Algorithm

On account of the iterative genetic evolution, the proposed online-PDNE decoding algorithm needs to seek the optimal solution in an online manner. Although the error correction performance of the polar code is greatly improved, it is achieved at the expense of increasing the complexity and delay of the decoder. To this end, a perturbed and directed neural-evolutionary (PDNE) decoding algorithm for polar codes is proposed, in which the perturbation noise and pre-trained offline directed neuro-evolutionary noise sequences are sequentially added to the received sequence for re-decoding, as given in Equations (1) and (5).

In the PDNE decoding algorithm, n_{ne} is chosen from a set S_n^* of noise patterns that is generated offline according to the method described in the following. This perturbed decoding process is performed until the cardinality T_s of the set S_n^* is reached.

In the offline training, population $S_n^{(t)}$ at generation t (t = 0, 1, ..., $T_2 - 1$) are constructed in an iterative process, where the initial population $S_n^{(0)}$ is the first generation randomly created. The new population noise produced by each generation is sequentially and independently added to the decoding failed channel output sequence. The fitness function is defined as the same as Equation (5) in the proposed online-PDNE decoding algorithm. As shown in Figure 3, if the decoding is successful, the current neural-evolutionary noise n_{ne} will be stored in a set S_n^*. Otherwise, the genetic process is continued on the population noise until the correct directed individual is obtained or the maximum number of generations T_2 is reached to reinitialize the population for the next round of evolution. The details of the PDNE decoding algorithm are given in Algorithm 2.

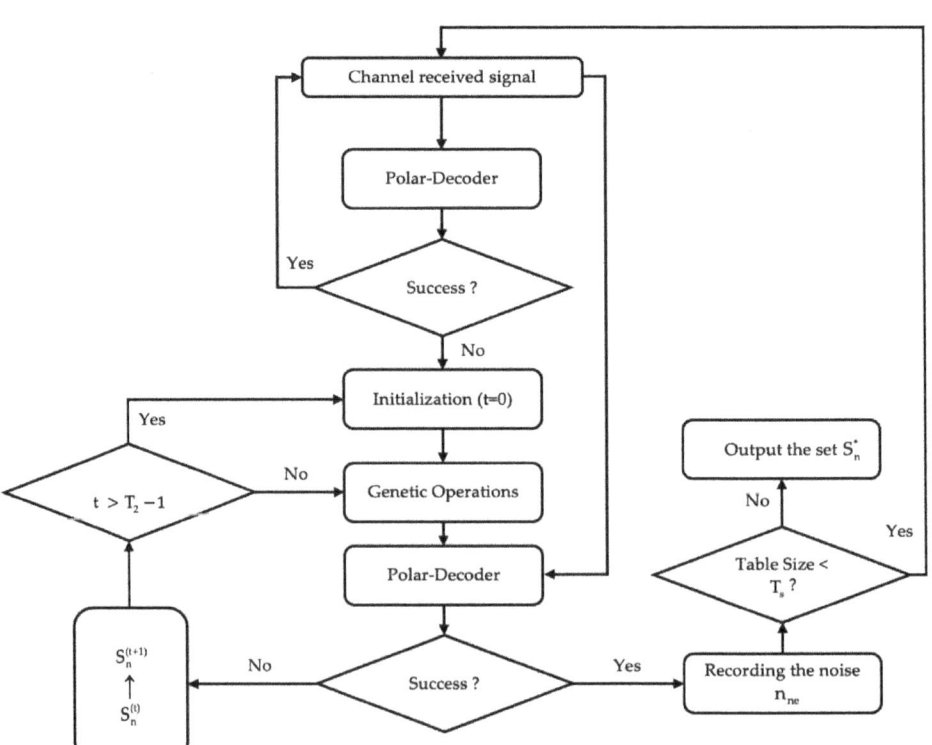

Figure 3. Block diagram of training a directed neural evolutionary noise in an offline manner.

Compared with the algorithm in [36], the proposed PDNE decoding algorithm in this paper has the following advantages:

1. The proposed PDNE decoding algorithm adopts the fitness function shown in Equation (3) instead of the bit error rate (BER)-based one in [36].
2. The mutation operations in this paper judge whether the individual needs to be mutated bit by bit, thereby increasing the variation diversity, while the operations in [36] only mutate one of the first $\lfloor N \cdot p_m \rfloor$ positions of each individual, where p_m is the mutation probability.
3. Different from the optimization of the set S_n^* for each SNR value in [36], the proposed PDNE decoding algorithm in this paper only needs to optimize one set S_n^*, which greatly shortens the optimization process and reduces the spaces for storing the noises from the perspective of implementation. This indicates the algorithm in the paper has better generality.

Algorithm 2: PDNE Decoding algorithm

Input: y^N // Received signal
       Q_p // Variance of the perturbed noise
       T_1 // Maximum number of the perturbed attempts
       T_s // Cardinality of the set S_n^*
       S_n^* // Set of the noise patterns
Output: $\hat{u}_1^N$ // Estimated codeword

1: Initialization: $\hat{u}_1^N \leftarrow 0$, $i \leftarrow 1$, $j \leftarrow 1$.
2: $\hat{u}_1^N \leftarrow \text{Polar\_decoder}(y^N)$
3: if $\text{CRC}(\hat{u}_1^N) ==$ success
4:     break
5: else
6:     while $i \leq T_1$ do
7:        $y_1^N = y^N + Q_p \cdot \text{randn}(1, N)$
8:        $\hat{u}_1^N \leftarrow \text{Polar\_decoder}(y_1^N)$
9:        $i \leftarrow i + 1$
10:        if $\text{CRC}(\hat{u}_1^N) ==$ success
11:           break
12:        end if
13:     end while
14:     while $j \leq T_s$ do
15:        Choose $n_{ne}^{(j)} \in S_n^*$
16:        $y_2^N = y^N + n_{ne}^{(j)}$
17:        $\hat{u}_1^N \leftarrow \text{Polar\_decoder}(y_2^N)$
18:        $j \leftarrow j + 1$
19:        if $\text{CRC}(\hat{u}_1^N) ==$ success
20:           break
21:        end if
22:     end while
23: end if
24: Return $\hat{u}_1^N$

4.3. SNE Decoding Algorithm

In order to further simplify the PDNE decoder structure and reduce the processing delay of the decoder, a sole neural-evolutionary (SNE) decoding algorithm of polar codes is proposed, in which only pre-trained offline directed neuro-evolutionary noise sequences are added to the received sequence for re-decoding. When the SSC decoding fails, the pre-trained neural-evolutionary noise is directly called, which greatly reduces the decoding delay. The details of the SNE decoding algorithm are given in Algorithm 3.

Algorithm 3: SNE Decoding algorithm

Input: y^N //Received signal
  T_s // Cardinality of the set S_n^*
  S_n^* // Set of the noise patterns
Output: $\hat{u}_1^N$ // Estimated codeword
1: Initialization: $\hat{u}_1^N \leftarrow 0$, $j \leftarrow 1$.
2: $\hat{u}_1^N \leftarrow$ Polar_decoder(y_1^N)
3: if CRC($\hat{u}_1^N$) == success
4:   break
5: else
6:   while $j \leq T_s$ do
7:     Choose $n_{ne}^{(j)} \in S_n^*$
8:     $y_2^N = y^N + n_{ne}^{(j)}$
9:     $\hat{u}_1^N \leftarrow$ Polar_decoder(y_2^N)
10:    $j \leftarrow j+1$
11:    if CRC($\hat{u}_1^N$) == success
12:      break
13:    end if
14: end while
15: end if
16: Return $\hat{u}_1^N$

4.4. Complexity Analysis

The additional complexities required by the proposed three decoding algorithms for polar codes are discussed in this sub-section. Note that the complexity required for CRC check is ignored in the following analysis. Table 1 compares the computational complexity of the proposed algorithms and other decoding schemes, where C_p and C_g are the unit calculations required in the perturbation operation and genetic operation, as shown in Table 2.

Table 1. Computational complexity of different decoding algorithms.

Decoding Algorithms	Computational Complexity
SSC [14]	$O(N\log N)$
PB-SSC [33]	$O(C_p N\log N)$
PP-SSC [35]	$O(C_p N\log N) + O(C_g N\log N)$
Proposed Online-PDNE	$O(C_p N\log N) + O(C_g N\log N)$
Proposed PDNE	$O(C_p N\log N)$
Proposed SNE	$O(C_p^+ N\log N)$

Table 2. Unit calculations in GA process.

Perturbation Operation Calculations (C_p)	Genetic Operation Calculations (C_g)
Multiplication $C_p^\times$ (generation of perturbation noise) Addition C_p^+ (perturbing the received signal)	Division, square root (fitness value evaluation) Summation, division (fitness score evaluation) Comparison (selection) Comparison, addition (crossover) Comparison, addition (mutation) Addition (perturbing the received signal)

When the standard polar decoding fails, the Online-PDNE or PDNE decoding algorithm is activated, in which multiple perturbation noises are generated for the first T_1

attempts. Given the code length N, the number of computations required to generate multiple candidate codewords by perturbing the output signal in the worst case is $C_p T_1 N$. The number of computations required for the worst-case genetic operation process can be estimated as $C_g T_2 N$. Therefore, the overall additional complexity brought by the proposed Online-PDNE decoder is $C_p T_1 N + C_g T_2 N$, which is the same as the PP-SSC decoder.

In the PDNE decoding algorithm, the genetic process runs in an offline manner, so the extra complexity required is only $C_p T_1 N$, which is due to perturbation operations.

As for the SNE decoding algorithm, the pre-trained noise set S_n^* is directly called for secondary decoding when the SSC decoding fails. Compared with the PDNE decoding algorithm, the SNE decoding algorithm only needs to perform the addition operation C_p^+ in the perturbation operation.

5. Simulation Results

In this section, the performance of the proposed decoding algorithms is evaluated on a BPSK-modulated additive white Gaussian noise (AWGN) channel, in which the SSC decoder is employed for the standard polar decoding. However, it can easily be extended for other decoding algorithms. In the simulations, we use the same polar codes from [10] with code rates 1/2 and 3/4, and both codes have length N = 1024. The parameters and related values used in the training process are shown in Table 3.

Table 3. Parameters of the training process.

Parameters	Value
Maximum number of the perturbed attempts T_1	10
Maximum number of generations T_2	100
Number of individuals in the population T	10
Crossover probability p_c	0.8
Mutation probability p_m	0.1
Cardinality T_s of the set S_n^*	10
Variance of the perturbed noise Q_p	0.25

Figures 4 and 5 illustrate the BER and the FER performances of the rate-1/2 polar code with the proposed decoding algorithms, the SSC algorithm [14], the PB-SSC algorithm [33], as well as the PP-SSC algorithm [35], respectively. As shown in Figure 4, the performance of the proposed three decoding algorithms is better than that of the other algorithms. The performance of the proposed Online-PDNE decoding algorithm is about 1.0 dB, 0.6 dB and 0.5 dB superior to that of the conventional SSC algorithm, the PB-SSC algorithm, and the PP-SSC algorithm at the BER of 10^{-5}, respectively. When SNR = 3.5 dB, we can see from the figure that our proposed Online-PDNE decoding algorithm can improve BER performance by nearly four orders of magnitude compared with the SSC algorithm, nearly three orders of magnitude compared with the PB-SSC algorithm, and more than two orders of magnitude compared with the PP-SSC algorithm.

In addition, among the three proposed decoding algorithms, the Online-PDNE decoding algorithm has the best performance, followed by the PDNE decoding algorithm. The reason why the Online-PDNE decoding algorithm has the best performance is that the directed neural-evolutionary noise is generated online by the GA process for the uncorrectable sequence, which converts the received signal into the error correction region of its decoding space more accurately.

Since the PDNE decoding algorithm and the SNE decoding algorithm use the offline GA process to generate the directed neural-evolutionary noise, the decoding complexity and delay are greatly reduced compared with the Online-PDNE decoding algorithm. However, due to the limitation of the size of the directed noise set and uncorrectable error codewords not encountered during offline training, their performances suffer slightly. Compared with the PDNE decoding algorithm, the performance of the SNE decoding algorithm decreases slightly, about 0.2 dB, but its decoding complexity and delay are the lowest, and it only depends on the directed neural-evolutionary noise of offline training to decode correctly.

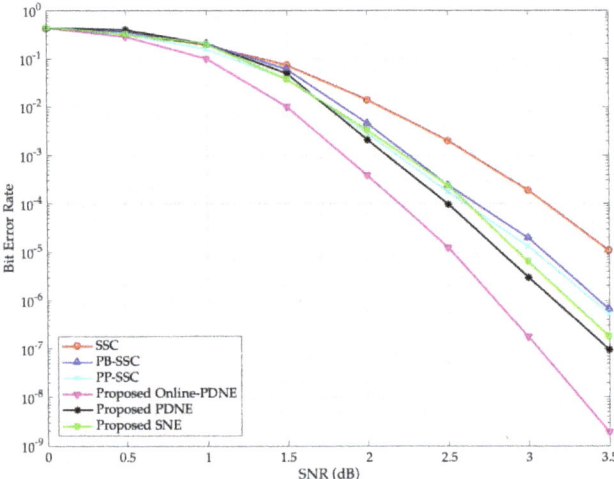

Figure 4. BER performance of the (1024, 512) polar code with different decoding algorithms. The SSC algorithm is in [14], the PB-SSC algorithm is in [33], and the PP-SSC algorithm is in [35].

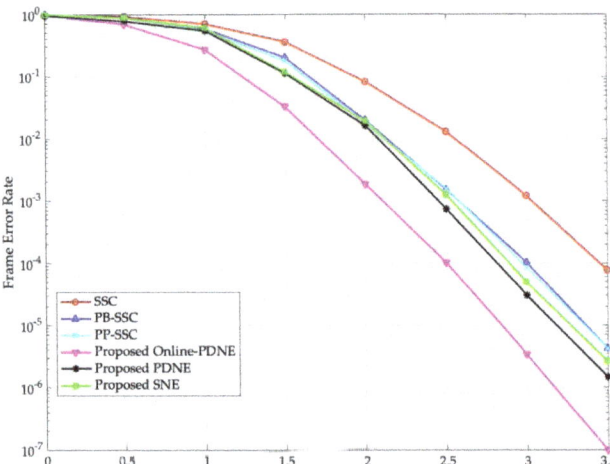

Figure 5. FER performance of the (1024, 512) polar code with different decoding algorithms. The SSC algorithm is in [14], the PB-SSC algorithm is in [33], and the PP-SSC algorithm is in [35].

From Figure 5, it can be seen that our proposed three decoding algorithms achieve better performance than the others. This conclusion agrees with the results in Figure 4. When SNR = 3.5 dB, we can see from the figure that our proposed Online-PDNE decoding algorithm can improve FER performance by three orders of magnitude compared with the SSC algorithm, more than one order of magnitude compared with the PB-SSC algorithm and the PP-SSC algorithm.

To further evaluate the error correction performance of the proposed decoding algorithms as described in Section 3, we also simulate the rate-3/4 polar code. In Figures 6 and 7, we compare the BER and FER performances of the designed decoding algorithms with other decoding algorithms for the rate-3/4 polar code, respectively. We also see that the proposed decoding algorithms have better error correction performance than other decoding algorithms when the code rate increases.

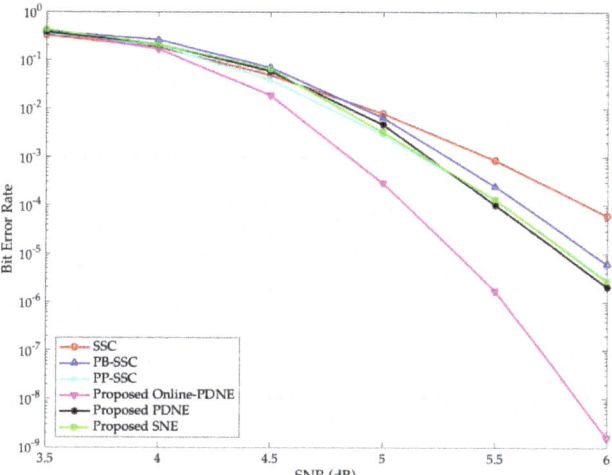

Figure 6. BER performance of the (1024, 768) polar code with different decoding algorithms. The SSC algorithm is in [14], the PB-SSC algorithm is in [33], and the PP-SSC algorithm is in [35].

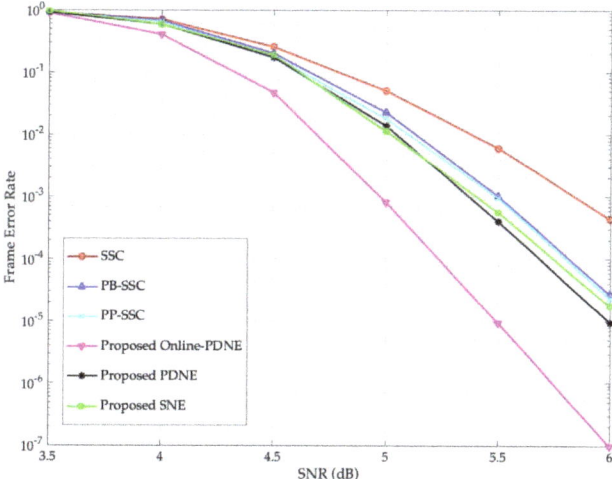

Figure 7. FER performance of the (1024, 768) polar code with different decoding algorithms. The SSC algorithm is in [14], the PB-SSC algorithm is in [33], and the PP-SSC algorithm is in [35].

In Figure 6, when SNR = 6.0 dB, we can see from the figure that our proposed Online-PDNE decoding algorithm can improve the BER performance by more than four orders of magnitude compared with the SSC algorithm, more than three orders of magnitude compared with the PB-SSC algorithm and the PP-SSC algorithm.

As can be seen from Figure 7 that when SNR = 6.0 dB, the proposed Online-PDNE decoding algorithm improves the FER performance by more than three orders of magnitude compared with the SSC algorithm and more than two orders of magnitude compared with the PB-SSC algorithm and PP-SSC algorithm. Note that compared to the proposed PDNE decoding algorithm, the SNE decoding algorithm significantly reduces the decoding complexity with negligible performance degradation, which coincide with the results in Figures 4 and 5.

In Figures 8 and 9, we compare the average normalized complexities of the proposed Online-PDNE decoding algorithm, the proposed PDNE decoding algorithm, the SNE decoding algorithm and other decoding algorithms for polar codes with two rates, respectively. The average normalized complexity of these algorithms is normalized by the SSC decoding algorithm.

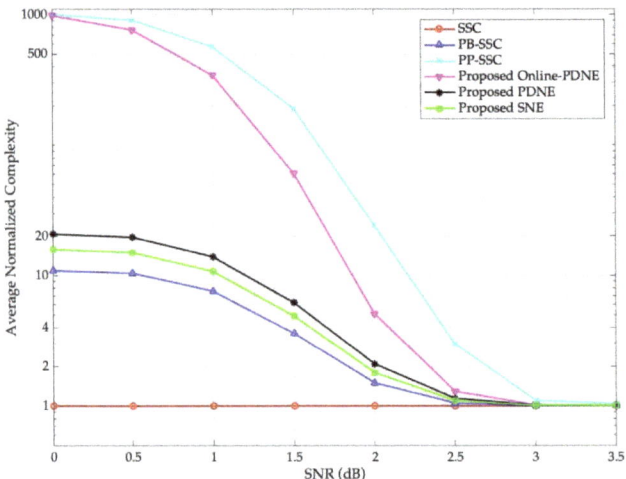

Figure 8. The average normalized complexities for the (1024, 512) polar code. The SSC algorithm is in [14], the PB-SSC algorithm is in [33], and the PP-SSC algorithm is in [35].

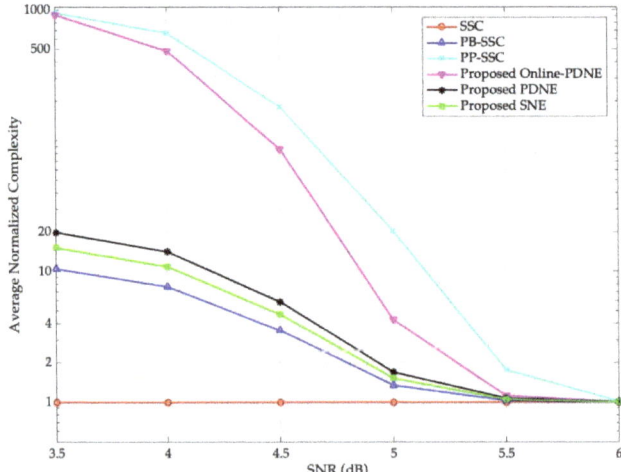

Figure 9. The average normalized complexities for the (1024, 768) polar code. The SSC algorithm is in [14], the PB-SSC algorithm is in [33], and the PP-SSC algorithm is in [35].

It can be observed that the average normalized complexity of the proposed PDNE decoding algorithm and SNE decoding algorithm is much lower than that of the PP-SSC decoding algorithm, which is due to the offline training. Among the proposed decoding algorithms, the online-PDNE decoding algorithm has the best error correction performance and the highest complexity, but it is still much less complicated than the PP-SSC decoding algorithm. As the SNR increases, the complexity of the proposed decoding algorithms reduces to the same level as the SSC decoding algorithm. The proposed decoding algorithms can benefit from more reliable channel conditions and require smaller perturbation attempts to successfully decode, thereby reducing the normalized decoding delay.

It can also be seen from Figures 4 and 8 that the proposed PDNE and SNE decoding algorithms have slightly higher average normalized complexity compared with the PB-SSC algorithm at low SNR region. When SNR $\geq$ 2.5 dB, their complexities are almost the same, but the performance of the proposed PDNE and SNE algorithms is much better than that of the PB-SSC algorithm. In Figures 6 and 8, when SNR $\geq$ 5.5 dB, similar conclusions can be drawn, which coincides with the results in Figures 4 and 8.

Tables 4 and 5 provide the average normalized complexities corresponding to some fixed SNR values of polar codes with two rates under different decoding algorithms, respectively. Taking Table 4 as an example, when the SNR increases from 0.5 dB to 2.5 dB, the average normalized complexity of the proposed Online-PDNE decoding algorithm drops sharply from 767.300 to 1.293, which is the same order of magnitude as the SSC decoding algorithm.

Table 4. The average normalized complexities for the (1024, 512) polar code for certain SNR values.

Decoding Algorithms	SNR 0.5 dB	1.5 dB	2.5 dB	3.5 dB
SSC [14]	1	1	1	1
PB-SSC [33]	10.440	3.602	1.004	1.002
PP-SSC [35]	910.800	189.900	2.982	1.042
Proposed Online-PDNE	767.300	60.500	1.293	1.001
Proposed PDNE	19.640	6.195	1.142	1.007
Proposed SNE	15.040	4.902	1.124	1.005

Table 5. The average normalized complexities for the (1024, 768) polar code for certain SNR values.

Decoding Algorithms	SNR 3.5 dB	4.5 dB	5.5 dB	6.0 dB
SSC [14]	1	1	1	1
PB-SSC [33]	10.475	3.544	1.031	1.002
PP-SSC [35]	951.757	181.610	1.767	1.016
Proposed Online-PDNE	917.032	86.376	1.119	1.007
Proposed PDNE	19.842	5.865	1.075	1.005
Proposed SNE	15.168	4.704	1.052	1.003

6. Conclusions

In this paper, three decoding algorithms were proposed for polar codes by exploiting the perturbed and directed neural-evolutionary noise, in which uncorrectable received sequences can be transformed into error-corrected regions of their decoding space. In addition to the SSC decoding algorithm, the proposed algorithms are also applicable to other standard polar code decoding algorithms. Simulation results verified that our proposed Online-PDNE decoding algorithm can achieve better performance than other algorithms and obtain up to four orders of magnitude compared with the SSC algorithm, and no error floor is observed down to a BER of 10^{-9}. The performance of the proposed Online-PDNE decoding algorithm is about 1.0 dB, 0.6 dB and 0.5 dB superior to that of the conventional SSC algorithm, the PB-SSC algorithm, and the PP-SSC algorithm at the BER of 10^{-5}, respectively. This is due to the directed neural-evolutionary noise is generated online by the GA process for the uncorrectable sequences, which converts the received signal into the error correction region of its decoding space more accurately. To further reduce the decoding complexity and simplify the decoding structure, the PDNE and SNE decoding algorithms were proposed. While ensuring the error correction performance, the complexity is reduced by employing the offline neuro-evolution. In addition, it is worth mentioning that the proposed decoding algorithms can be extended to other channel codes in a straightforward manner. As a future work, we plan to apply the proposed decoding algorithms to the polar codes in the 5G standard.

Author Contributions: Conceptualization, L.K. and H.L.; methodology, L.K. and H.L.; software, W.H. and L.K.; validation, W.H. and L.K.; formal analysis, W.H.; investigation, W.H. and B.D.; resources, W.H.; data curation, W.H.; writing—original draft preparation, L.K.; writing—review and editing, H.L.; visualization, W.H. and B.D.; supervision, B.D.; project administration, L.K. and H.L.; funding acquisition, L.K. and H.L. All authors have read and agreed to the published version of the manuscript.

Funding: This research was funded by the JITSF (grant No. jit-b-202110) and the NSFC (grant No. 61871376).

Data Availability Statement: Not applicable.

Conflicts of Interest: The authors declare no conflict of interest.

References

1. Vaezi, M.; Azari, A.; Khosravirad, S.R.; Shirvanimoghaddam, M.; Azari, M.M.; Chasaki, D.; Popovski, P. Cellular, wide-area, and non-terrestrial IoT: A survey on 5G advances and the road towards 6G. *IEEE Commun. Surv. Tutor.* **2022**, *24*, 1117–1174. [CrossRef]
2. Fang, Y.; Bu, Y.; Chen, P.; Lau, F.C.; Al Otaibi, S. Irregular-mapped protograph LDPC-coded modulation: A bandwidth-efficient solution for 6G-enabled mobile networks. *IEEE Trans. Intell. Transp. Syst.* **2022**, 1–14. [CrossRef]
3. Miah, M.S.; Schukat, M.; Barrett, E. Sensing and throughput analysis of a MU-MIMO based cognitive radio scheme for the internet of things. *Comput. Commun.* **2020**, *154*, 442–454. [CrossRef]
4. Chen, L.; Chen, P.; Lin, Z. Artificial intelligence in education: A review. *IEEE Access* **2020**, *8*, 75264–75278. [CrossRef]
5. Hui, D.; Sandberg, S.; Blankenship, Y.; Andersson, M.; Grosjean, L. Channel coding in 5G new radio: A tutorial overview and performance comparison with 4G LTE. *IEEE Veh. Technol. Mag.* **2018**, *13*, 60–69. [CrossRef]
6. Chen, P.; Xie, Z.; Fang, Y.; Chen, Z.; Mumtaz, S.; Rodrigues, J.J. Physical-layer network coding: An efficient technique for wireless communications. *IEEE Netw.* **2020**, *34*, 270–276. [CrossRef]
7. Dai, L.; Fang, Y.; Yang, Z.; Chen, P.; Li, Y. Protograph LDPC-coded BICM-ID with irregular CSK mapping in visible light communication systems. *IEEE Trans. Veh. Technol.* **2021**, *70*, 11033–11038. [CrossRef]
8. Bioglio, V.; Condo, C.; Land, I. Design of polar codes in 5G new radio. *IEEE Commun. Surv. Tutor.* **2021**, *23*, 29–40. [CrossRef]
9. Zhang, H.; Li, R.; Wang, J.; Dai, S.; Zhang, G.; Chen, Y.; Luo, H.; Wang, J. Parity-check polar coding for 5G and beyond. In Proceedings of the IEEE International Conference on Communications (ICC), Kansas City, MO, USA, 20–24 May 2018; pp. 1–7.
10. Tataria, H.; Shafi, M.; Molisch, A.F.; Dohler, M.; Sjöland, H.; Tufvesson, F. 6G wireless systems: Vision, requirements, challenges, insights, and opportunities. *Proc. IEEE* **2021**, *109*, 1166–1199. [CrossRef]
11. Arikan, E. Channel polarization: A method for constructing capacity-achieving codes for symmetric binary-input memoryless channels. *IEEE Trans. Inf. Theory* **2009**, *55*, 3051–3073. [CrossRef]
12. Tal, I.; Vardy, A. How to construct polar codes. *IEEE Trans. Inf. Theory* **2012**, *59*, 6562–6582. [CrossRef]
13. Trifonov, P. Efficient design and decoding of polar codes. *IEEE Trans. Commun.* **2012**, *60*, 3221–3227. [CrossRef]
14. Alamdar-Yazdi, A.; Kschischang, F.R. A simplified successive-cancellation decoder for polar codes. *IEEE Commun. Lett.* **2011**, *15*, 1378–1380. [CrossRef]
15. Tal, I.; Vardy, A. List decoding of polar codes. *IEEE Trans. Inf. Theory* **2015**, *61*, 2213–2226. [CrossRef]
16. Niu, K.; Chen, K. CRC-aided decoding of polar codes. *IEEE Commun. Lett.* **2012**, *16*, 1668–1671. [CrossRef]
17. Chen, K.; Niu, K.; Lin, J. Improved successive cancellation decoding of polar codes. *IEEE Trans. Commun.* **2013**, *61*, 3100–3107. [CrossRef]
18. Yuan, B.; Parhi, K.K. Early stopping criteria for energy-efficient low-latency belief-propagation polar code decoders. *IEEE Trans. Signal Process.* **2014**, *62*, 6496–6506. [CrossRef]
19. Leroux, C.; Raymond, A.J.; Sarkis, G.; Gross, W.J. A semi-parallel successive-cancellation decoder for polar codes. *IEEE Trans. Signal Process.* **2013**, *61*, 289–299. [CrossRef]
20. Li, B.; Shen, H.; Tse, D. An adaptive successive cancellation list decoder for polar codes with cyclic redundancy check. *IEEE Commun. Lett.* **2012**, *16*, 2044–2047. [CrossRef]
21. Balatsoukas-Stimming, A.; Parizi, M.B.; Burg, A. LLR-based successive cancellation list decoding of polar codes. *IEEE Trans. Signal Process.* **2015**, *63*, 5165–5179. [CrossRef]
22. Niu, K.; Dai, J.; Tan, K.; Gao, J. Deep learning methods for channel decoding: A brief tutorial. In Proceedings of the IEEE/CIC International Conference on Communications in China (ICCC), Xiamen, China, 28–30 July 2021; pp. 144–149.

23. Cammerer, S.; Gruber, T.; Hoydis, J.; Brink, S.T. Scaling deep learning-based decoding of polar codes via partitioning. In Proceedings of the IEEE Global Communications Conference, Singapore, 4–8 December 2017; pp. 1–6.
24. Doan, N.; Ali Hashemi, S.; Gross, W.J. Neural successive cancellation decoding of polar codes. In Proceedings of the IEEE International Workshop on Signal Processing Advances in Wireless Communications (SPAWC), London, UK, 31 August–3 September 2018; pp. 1–6.
25. Wang, X.; Zhang, H.; Li, R.; Huang, L.; Dai, S.; Huangfu, Y.; Wang, J. Learning to flip successive cancellation decoding of polar codes with LSTM networks. In Proceedings of the IEEE International Symposium on Personal, Indoor and Mobile Radio Communications (PIMRC), Istanbul, Turkey, 8–11 September 2019; pp. 1–5.
26. Xu, W.; Tan, X.; Be'ery, Y.; Ueng, Y.L.; Huang, Y.; You, X.; Zhang, C. Deep learning-aided belief propagation decoder for polar codes. *IEEE J. Emerg. Sel. Top. Circuits Syst.* **2020**, *10*, 189–203. [CrossRef]
27. Liu, X.; Wu, S.; Wang, Y.; Zhang, N.; Jiao, J.; Zhang, Q. Exploiting error-correction-CRC for polar SCL decoding: A deep learning-based approach. *IEEE Trans. Cogn. Commun. Netw.* **2020**, *6*, 817–828. [CrossRef]
28. Kay, S. Can detectability be improved by adding noise? *IEEE Signal Process. Lett.* **2000**, *7*, 8–10. [CrossRef]
29. Sutera, A. Stochastic perturbation of a pure connective motion. *J. Atmos. Sci.* **2010**, *37*, 245–249. [CrossRef]
30. Arli, A.; Gazi, O. Noise-aided belief propagation list decoding of polar codes. *IEEE Commun. Lett.* **2019**, *23*, 1285–1288. [CrossRef]
31. Xiao, D.; Gu, Z. Dynamic perturbation decoding of polar-CRC cascaded code. In Proceedings of the IEEE International Wireless Communications, and Mobile Computing, Limassol, Cyprus, 5–19 June 2020; pp. 42–45.
32. Lee, H.; Kil, Y.S.; Jang, M.; Kim, S.H.; Park, O.S.; Park, G. Multi-round belief propagation decoding with impulsive perturbation for short LDPC codes. *IEEE Wirel. Commun. Lett.* **2020**, *9*, 1491–1494. [CrossRef]
33. Gerrar, N.K.; Zhao, S.; Kong, L. A CRC-aided perturbed decoding of polar codes. In Proceedings of the 14th International Conference on Wireless Communications, Networking and Mobile Computing (WiCOM 2018), Chongqing, China, 18–20 September 2018. [CrossRef]
34. Zhao, S.; Xu, P.; Zhang, N.; Kong, L. A decoding algorithm of polar codes based on perturbation with CNN. *J. Electron. Inf. Technol.* **2021**, *43*, 1900–1906.
35. Gerrar, N.K.; Zhao, S.; Kong, L. Error correction in data storage systems using polar codes. *IET Commun.* **2021**, *15*, 1859–1868. [CrossRef]
36. Kong, L.; Liu, H.; Hou, W.; Meng, C. A perturbed and directed neural-evolutionary decoding algorithm for polar codes. *Electron. Lett.* **2022**, Submitted.
37. Benzi, R.; Sutera, A.; Vulpiani, A. The mechanism of stochastic resonance. *J. Phys. A Math. Gen.* **1981**, *14*, L453–L457. [CrossRef]
38. McDonnell, M.D.; Abbott, D. What is stochastic resonance? definitions, misconceptions, debates, and its relevance to biology. *PLoS Comput. Biol.* **2009**, *5*, e1000348. [CrossRef] [PubMed]
39. Chen, H.; Varshney, P.K.; Michels, J.H.; Kay, S. Approaching near optimal detection performance via stochastic resonance. In Proceedings of the IEEE International Conference on Acoustics Speech and Signal Processing Proceedings (ICASSP), Toulouse, France, 14–19 May 2006; p. III. [CrossRef]
40. Shih, K.; Shiu, D. Perturbed decoding algorithm for concatenated error correcting and detecting codes system. In Proceedings of the IEEE International Symposium on Personal, Indoor and Mobile Radio Communications (PIMRC), Helsinki, Finland, 11–14 September 2006; pp. 1–5.
41. Wang, W.; Shiu, D. The theory behind perturbed decoding algorithm. In Proceedings of the IEEE International Symposium on Personal, Indoor and Mobile Radio Communications (PIMRC), Athens, Greece, 3–7 September 2007; pp. 1–5.
42. He, Z.; Li, X.; Wang, S.; Qi, Y. A noise-assisted polar code attempt decoding algorithm. In Proceedings of the IEEE International Conference on Computer Research and Development (ICCRD), Beijing, China, 5–7 January 2021; pp. 73–77.
43. Nishikawa, M.; Nakamura, Y.; Kanai, Y.; Osawa, H.; Okamoto, Y. A study on iterative decoding with LLR modulator by neural network using adjacent track information in SMR system. *IEEE Trans. Magn.* **2019**, *55*, 1–5. [CrossRef]
44. Petrović, V.L.; Marković, M.M.; El Mezeni, D.M.; Saranovac, L.V.; Radošević, A. Flexible high throughput QC-LDPC decoder with perfect pipeline conflicts resolution and efficient hardware utilization. *IEEE Trans. Circuits Syst. I Regul. Pap.* **2020**, *67*, 5454–5467. [CrossRef]
45. Wang, X.; Ma, Q.; Li, J.; Zhang, H.; Xu, W. An improved SC flip decoding algorithm of polar codes based on genetic algorithm. *IEEE Access* **2020**, *8*, 222572–222583. [CrossRef]
46. Elkelesh, A.; Ebada, M.; Cammerer, S.; Brink, S.T. Decoder-tailored polar code design using the genetic algorithm. *IEEE Trans. Commun.* **2019**, *67*, 4521–4534. [CrossRef]
47. Zhou, H.; Gross, W.J.; Zhang, Z.; You, X.; Zhang, C. Low-complexity construction of polar codes based on genetic algorithm. *IEEE Commun. Lett.* **2021**, *10*, 3175–3179. [CrossRef]
48. Sun, C.; Cai, K.; Song, G.; Quek, T.Q.; Fei, Z. Belief propagation based joint detection and decoding for resistive random access memories. *IEEE Trans. Commun.* **2022**, *70*, 2227–2239. [CrossRef]
49. Huang, L.; Zhang, H.; Li, R.; Ge, Y.; Wang, J. AI coding: Learning to construct error correction codes. *IEEE Trans. Commun.* **2020**, *68*, 26–39. [CrossRef]
50. Moreloszaragoza, R.H. *The Art of Error Correcting Coding*, 2nd ed.; John Wiley & Sons: Chichester, UK, 2006; pp. 39–41.

Article

A General Framework for Geometrically Uniform Codes and Signal Sets Matched to Groups

Eduardo Michel Vieira Gomes [1,†], Edson Donizete De Carvalho [2,†], Carlos Alexandre Ribeiro Martins [3,†], Evandro Mazetto Brizola [4,†] and Eduardo Brandani Da Silva [4,*,†,‡]

1. Department of Mathematics, UTFPR—Universidade Técnica Federal do Paraná, Francisco Beltrão 85601-970, PR, Brazil; eduardogomes@utfpr.edu.br
2. Department of Mathematics, UNESP—Universidade Estadual Paulista, Ilha Solteira 15385-000, SP, Brazil; edson.donizete@unesp.br
3. Department of Mathematics, UTFPR—Universidade Técnica Federal do Paraná, Pato Branco 85503-390, PR, Brazil; carlos@utfpr.edu.br
4. Department of Mathematics, UEM—Universidade Estadual de Maringá, Av. Colombo 5790, Maringá 87020-900, PR, Brazil; pg54135@uem.br
* Correspondence: ebsilva@uem.br
† These authors contributed equally to this work.
‡ Brizola, E. M. was supported by Capes, process 88882.449187/2019-01.

Abstract: Geometrically uniform codes are fundamental in communication systems, mainly for modulation. Typically, geometrically uniform codes are dependent on a given alphabet. The current work establishes the necessary and sufficient conditions for obtaining a matched labeling between a group G and a signal set S. It introduces the concept of the G-isometric signal set, allowing for the establishment of equivalences between different types of signal sets. In particular, we obtain isometries between groups and geometrically uniform codes with a minimal generator. We also draw attention to the influence of the environment metric space, the group metric, and the matched mapping on the labeling of a signal set. The results are valid for all environment metric spaces. The alphabet emerges naturally from the relationship between the signal set S and the label group derived from its symmetry group, $\Gamma(S)$.

Keywords: geometrically uniform codes; matched labeling; signal sets; left invariant metric; groups; signal constellations

1. Introduction

Forney [1] introduced the concept of geometrically uniform (GU) codes, which included Lattice Codes and Slepian Group Codes [2]. The elements of the generator group were regarded as arbitrary isometries of the Euclidean space $\mathbb{R}^n$ in that approach. Then, it was possible to put together these two kinds of codes, which had little in common and were treated separately until that time, as part of the same code class.

Besides encompassing these two categories of codes, Forney extended the process of signal set partitioning created by Ungerboeck. This is a technique that brings significant gains in signal coding and it was the starting point of coded modulation. Furthermore, GU codes have good symmetry properties: all Voronoi's regions are congruent, the signals have the same error probability, and the distance profile is the same for each signal, among others things.

Another important concept developed at the same time was "matched labeling", proposed by Loeliger [3]. This concept created a fairly adequate way to associate a signal set with an appropriate algebraic structure. The main motivation was the search for certain linearity to the code. Originally, code linearity was achieved by associating it with a vector space structure or module. In more complex contexts, linearity occurs through an association via an application with the simplest possible algebraic structure. In this work, the application is called matched labeling, and the algebraic structure used is the group structure. In his main result, Loeliger proved that signal sets matched to groups are equivalent to Slepian signals. He also demonstrated that if the group is commutative, any set of signals is equivalent to phase modulation encoded with linear codes over $\mathbb{Z}_M$. Both concepts were discussed in the context of Euclidean spaces, and they have a strong relationship with each other. Loeliger proved that, under certain conditions, such concepts are equivalent.

Because of the good characteristics of GU codes, several studies have been developed to provide the theoretical basis necessary to extend them to larger classes of signal sets.

In this sense, for instance, signal labeling from a QAM constellation of cardinality M by elements of a finite group coming from a finite field appeared in the works [4,5], and only by elements of an additive group G of cardinality M that need not necessarily come from a finite field, as shown in [6]. The alphabets in these papers are coset representatives derived from the quotient of integer rings by proper ideals. Labeling groups are matched via a discrete Mannheim metric. These signal sets are subsets of signal spaces identified by the integer rings $\mathbb{Z}[i]$ and $\mathbb{Z}[\omega]$, where i and ω are the fourth and third roots of unity, respectively.

The signals of these constellations in $\mathbb{Z}[i]$ and $\mathbb{Z}[\omega]$ can be described geometrically as a finite set of points coming from a set of barycenters of squares taken from a regular tessellation by squares and by a set of barycenters of regular hexagons taken from a hexagonal tessellation, respectively.

In addition, working in environments outside of the Euclidean space has proven to be a very promising approach since certain properties of these spaces can be effectively exploited in the design of new codes.

For instance, Albuquerque et al. [7] demonstrated that using two-dimensional surfaces with genus $g \geq 2$, it is possible to obtain a more efficient quantum error-correcting codes in terms of error probability, and it is known that the inherent geometry of such surfaces is hyperbolic geometry. In [8], Silva et al. introduced signal constellations in the hyperbolic plane as an alternative to the traditional signal constellations in the Euclidean plane, and such constellations were used to achieve better performance for the transmission of digital signals, for example, in line power transmission. The regular tessellation $\{p, q\}$ exists in the hyperbolic plane, where q regular hyperbolic polygons with p sides meet at each vertex if and only if $(p - 2)(q - 2) > 4$. Thus, there are an infinite number of tessellations with regular polygons in hyperbolic space, whereas in Euclidean space there are only three classes, given by squares, hexagons, and equilateral triangles. These are some of the main features that make the hyperbolic space extremely conducive to the construction of GU codes.

The authors of [9] proposed a generalization of the concept of geometrically uniform codes from Euclidean to hyperbolic space, as well as a characterization of the equivalence proved by Loeliger in [3] in both Euclidean and hyperbolic spaces, using the concept of G-linearity. We recall that G-linearity is a generalization of the $\mathbb{Z}_4$-linearity, and it was used in order to ensure the geometrical uniformity of nonlinear codes. An essential aspect of this concept is the search for labeling between environment spaces instead of labeling between codes [9,10]. A code S is G-linear if it is the image of a group code on G by an isometry between the environment spaces (the formal definition of G-linearity will be given in Section 2). In that approach, it is necessary to have a group G, a right invariant metric (or bi-invariant metric in some cases) for G, and an alphabet.

Because the hyperbolic plane, unlike the Euclidean plane, lacks a vector space structure, determining the group of labels for a signal constellation becomes more difficult when they are characterized as a finite set of points derived from a set of barycenters of polygons taken from a hyperbolic tessellation, because we must consider these signals as representing lateral classes of a quotient group $G'' = G'/H$. If we consider G' as the symmetry group associated with signal points in the hyperbolic plane, then H must be a normal subgroup in G'.

Gomes et al. [11] presented a systematic way of labeling geometrically uniform codes in hyperbolic environments arising from surfaces. In this case, the authors worked with triangular tilings on the double torus and, despite explicitly providing the labels for the codes, the metric used was the hyperbolic metric coming from the ambient space. There were no alternatives to labels with discrete metrics, which is a desirable feature in many cases.

In this paper, we propose a general treatment of the metric, providing a necessary and sufficient condition for an isometry between a group G and a signal set S to be considered a matched labeling. We present the definition of G-isometric signal set, which allows us to connect the various concepts discussed in this work. Despite emphasizing through examples the hyperbolic case because of its rich properties and Euclidean cases for historical reasons and applications, the results are valid for any metric space. Another key aspect of the current proposal is the emphasis on the role of environment metric space, the G group metric, and the matched map $m : G \rightarrow S$ in the signal set labeling process. This new approach, unlike G-linearity, does not require an a priori alphabet. For the labeling process, the alphabet is obtained naturally from the relationship between the set S and the group of labels derived from its symmetry group $\Gamma(S)$. The fact that it does not require prior knowledge of an alphabet is a very useful feature, since in the applications we have only the set S and the environment space in which S is considered, which makes such a need an artificial hypothesis.

In summary, in our context, the search for "linearity" is performed by extracting a subgroup of the symmetries group from the metric space and then by searching for a matched labeling between the signal set and the elements of this group, according to Definition 8. The metric used is of fundamental importance in this process, a fact that will become evident throughout the present work.

Section 2 presents basic concepts, notations and results concerning GU codes and matched labeling. In Section 3, we introduce the G-isometric signal sets, as well as the main results. Section 4 presents several examples of constructions of G-isometric signal sets and matched labelings to a group G. We have signal sets in the Euclidean and hyperbolic spaces. Finally, Section 5 concludes the article.

2. Definitions and Basic Results

In this section, we give the basic definitions and results that are fundamental to the work.

If M is a non-empty set and d is a metric on M, then M is a metric space denoted by (M, d). The group of all isometries of M is denoted by $ISO(M)$, where the composition operation is the group operation.

A code is any non-empty subset S of M, and if in addition, S is discrete, then it will be called a signal set.

Definition 1. *A signal set S is geometrically uniform (GU) if, given any two points s and s' of S, there exists an isometry $u_{ss'} : M \rightarrow M$ such that $u_{ss'}(s) = s'$ and $u_{ss'}(S) = S$.*

Thus, if $\Gamma(S)$ denotes the symmetry group of S, then it is geometrically uniform if the action of $\Gamma(S)$ on S is transitive, that is, if the orbit of any point s_0 in S on the action of $\Gamma(S)$ is S.

A geometrically uniform set S is called a uniform constellation if it is finite, and a regular array if it is infinity.

Example 1 ([1]). *Let $S = \{(-1, -1), (-1, 1), (1, -1), (1, 1)\}$ be the signal set given by the four vertices of a square in the metric space $M = \mathbb{R}^2$. The symmetric group $\Gamma(S)$ is given by eight symmetries of the square, i.e., $\Gamma(S) = D_4$ (dihedral group).*

(a) If we take $U(S) = \Gamma(S)$, we obtain that S is invariant under the action of $\Gamma(S)$, which means that the signal set S is geometrically uniform.

(b) Consider the rotation subgroup R_4 of $\Gamma(S)$, that is, the set of rotations multiples of $2\pi/4 = \pi/2$. We also obtain that S is invariant under the action of

$$U(S) = R_4 = \langle R_{\frac{\pi}{2}} \rangle = \{id, R_{\pi/2}, R_\pi, R_{3\pi/2}\},$$

where R_c represents the rotational angle c. Therefore, S is geometrically uniform.

(c) Let us consider the subgroup V^2 of $\Gamma(S)$ generated by the compositions of the reflections about axis x and axis y. We also find that S is invariant when $U(S) = V^2$ is applied. Therefore, S is geometrically uniform.

We saw in Example 1 that non-trivial subgroups of the symmetry group $\Gamma(S)$ associated with a signal set S can be used to show that S is geometrically uniform. As we will see below, these are the $\Gamma(S)$ subgroups of interest that are sought in practice. In this sense, we consider Definition 2.

Definition 2. *Given a signal set S, a subgroup $U(S)$ of $\Gamma(S)$ is a generator group of S, if $S = \{u(s_0), u \in U(S)\}$ for an arbitrarily fixed s_0, and $U(S)$ is minimal, if the map $m : U(S) \to S$ defined by $m(u) = u(s_0)$ is bijective.*

It is clear that the map m induces on S the group structure of $U(S)$. Thus, m may be considered an isomorphism between groups.

Example 2. *Let S be the signal set in $\mathbb{R}^2$ given by $S = \{z = \omega^j s_0 \in \mathbb{C} : 0 \leq j \leq M-1\}$, where $\omega = e^{i2\pi/M}$ (the M-th root of unity) and $0 \neq s_0 \in \mathbb{C}$. In communication theory, S is called an M-PSK signal set. We have that $U(S) = R_M$ is a natural generating group for S, where R_M is the group of rotation multiples of $2\pi/M$, which is isomorphic to $\mathbb{Z}_M$ (the additive group of integers modulo M).*

Let $\Gamma(S) = VR_M$ be the composition of the elements of R_M with the elements of the group V, where V is the group formed by the identity and the reflection between the line determined by the origin and the midpoint of two adjacent signals of S. Then, VR_M is the group of symmetries of S. The M-ary dihedral group D_M (semidirect product of R_M by V) is isomorphic to $\Gamma(S)$. If M is an even number, we have a particular generator set, $U(S) = V.R_{M/2}$.

Remark 1. *The signal set $S = \{(-1,-1),(-1,1),(1,-1),(1,1)\}$ of Example 1, is obtained through a $\pi/4$ rotation of the 4-PSK signal set described in the form $S' = \{z = \omega^j s_0 \in \mathbb{C} : 0 \leq j \leq 3\}$, where $\omega = e^{i2\pi/4}$ (the 4-th root of the unit) and $s_0 = \sqrt{2}$. Or rather, $S = R_{\pi/4}S'$, where $R_{\pi/4}$ is an isometry of $\mathbb{R}^2$ given by a $\pi/4$ rotation matrix.*

Remark 2. *It is not true that all geometrically uniform code has a minimal generator, see [1]. Moreover, if there is a minimal generator group, it is not necessarily unique, i.e., there are geometrically uniform codes which allow more than one minimal generator group, such that they are not isomorphic to each other, as we saw in Example 1, where the groups R_4 and V^2 are groups with distinct minimal generators and are not isomorphic to each other.*

The following theorem establishes a sufficient condition for signal sets to be *GU*.

Theorem 1. *Let S be a signal set and $\Gamma(S)$ be its group of symmetries. If a subgroup H of $\Gamma(S)$ acts transitively on S, then it is geometrically uniform.*

Proof. Let H be a subgroup of $\Gamma(S)$ that acts transitively on S. Then, for a fixed $s_0 \in S$ we have that $S = \{u(s_0); u \in H\}$. We claim that S is *GU*. Indeed, for given $s, s' \in S$, there exist u_s and $u_{s'}$ in H, such that $u_s(s_0) = s$ and $u_{s'}(s_0) = s'$. Taking $u_{s,s'} = u_{s'}u_s^{-1} \in H$, we have

$$u_{s,s'}(s) = (u_{s'}u_s^{-1})(s) = u_{s'}(u_s^{-1}(s)) = u_{s'}(s_0) = s'.$$

Now, since $u_s^{-1}, u_{s'} \in H \leq \Gamma(S)$, it follows that $u_s^{-1}(S) = S$ and $u_{s'}(S) = S$. Thus,

$$u_{s,s'}(S) = (u_{s'}u_s^{-1})(S) = u_{s'}(u_s^{-1}(S)) = u_{s'}(S) = S.$$

Therefore, S is GU. □

Loeliger [3] introduced the notion of signal sets matched to groups, which is closely related to geometrically uniform codes.

Definition 3. *A signal set S is matched to a group G if exists a map m from G onto S such that, for all g and h in G,*

$$d(m(g), m(h)) = d(m(g^{-1}h), m(e)),$$

where e denotes the neutral element of G. A map m satisfying this condition is called a matched map. If we also have that m is injective, then m^{-1} is called a matched labeling.

Theorem 2. *If Λ is a transitive group of isometries of a signal set S in a metric space (M, d), then S is matched to Λ and, for all $s \in S$, the mapping $m_s : \Lambda \to S$ given by $m_s(f) = f(s), f \in \Lambda$, is a matched map. Reciprocally, if the signal set S is matched to a group G, then there exists a homomorphism from G onto a transitive subgroup of $\Gamma(S)$.*

Proof. Since Λ is a transitive group, then m_s is onto. For all f, g in Λ one has

$$d(m_s(f), m_s(g)) = d(f(s), g(s)) = d(f^{-1}f(s), f^{-1}g(s))$$
$$= d(s, f^{-1}g(s)) = d(m_s(e), m_s(f^{-1}g)).$$

Reciprocally, let m be a matched mapping from the group G onto the signal set S. For all $h \in G$, let us consider the map $f_h : S \to S$ such that, given $s \in S$. let $g \in G$ with $s = m(g)$. Then, $f_h : s = m(g) \mapsto m(hg)$, which is well defined. If $s = m(g)$ and $s' = m(g')$ for some g and g' in G, then

$$d(f_h(s), f_h(s')) = d(f_h(m(g)), f_h(m(g'))) = d(m(hg), m(hg'))$$
$$= d(m(g), m(g')) = d(s, s'),$$

which shows that f_h is an isometry of S, defined for each $h \in G$. Thus, we have a map $f : G \to \Gamma(S)$. Let $\Lambda = \{f_h : h \in G\} \subset \Gamma(S)$. Then,

$$f(hh') = f_{hh'}(s) = f_h(f_{h'}(s)) = f_h \circ f_{h'}(s) = f(h) \circ f(h')(s),$$

and it follows that f is a homomorphism from G onto Λ. Thus, Λ is a group. Furthermore, Λ is transitive. Indeed, for $e \in G$ let $s = m(e)$. Let s' be any element of S and let $h \in G$ satisfying $m(h) = s'$. Thus, $f_h(s) = s'$, implying that $\Lambda(s) = S$. □

As a result, a signal set S is matched to a group G via a matched map $m : G \to S$ if and only if G is homomorphic to a transitive subgroup of $\Gamma(S)$, the symmetry group of S. This result is due to Loeliger for the Euclidean case, but the result is valid regardless of the metric used. Therefore, it is also valid in hyperbolic spaces. As a consequence of this theorem, one has the following result, which is fundamental in this work:

Corollary 1. *If there exists a matched labeling between the signal set S and the group G, then G is isomorphic to a transitive subgroup of $\Gamma(S)$.*

Proof. This follows in a similar way to the reciprocal of Theorem 2, but in this case we have that m is a bijection, then we obtain that f is an injection. Thus, G is isomorphic to $Im(f) \leq \Gamma(S)$, which acts transitively on S. Therefore, the result follows. □

Remark 3. *The reciprocal of Corollary 1 is not true. Consider the signal set $S = \{(-1,-1),(-1,1),(1,-1),(1,1)\}$ of the Example 1. We have seen that $\Gamma(S) = D_4$ acts transitively on S. There are eight symmetries of the square and these symmetries are the elements of the dihedral group D_4. Taking $G = D_4 = \Gamma(S)$, as $|G| = 8$ and $|S| = 4$ (the number of elements in $\Gamma(S)$ is greater than the number of elements in S), it follows that there is no bijection between G and S, so there will be no matched labeling between them. However, there will be matched map from group $\Gamma(S) = D_4$ onto signals set S.*

The next result follows immediately using the Corollary 1 and the Theorem 1. It is interesting because S does not need to have a minimal generator $U(S)$. It seems to be new in the literature.

Corollary 2. *If there exists a matched labeling between the signal set S and the group G, then S is geometrically uniform.*

Definition 4. *Let G be a group. A function $d_G : G \times G \to \mathbb{R}$ is compatible with the group operation if*
$$d_G(g,h) = d_G(gh^{-1},e).$$
Moreover, if d_G is a metric on G, then d_G is a group metric.

Example 3. *Let $G = \mathbb{Z}_M = \{0,\ldots,M-1\}$ be the additive group of integers modulo M. Taking in $\mathbb{Z}_M$ the map given by $d_{\mathbb{Z}_M}(g,h) = \min\{(g-h) \bmod M, (h-g) \bmod M\}$, it is easily proved that $d_{\mathbb{Z}_M}$ defines a metric in $\mathbb{Z}_M \times \mathbb{Z}_M$. On the other hand, we have that $h^{-1} = -h$ and $e = 0$ in $\mathbb{Z}_M$, it follows that*
$$d_{\mathbb{Z}_M}(g-h,0) = \min\{((g-h)-0) \bmod M, (0-(g-h)) \bmod M\}$$
$$= \min\{(g-h) \bmod M, (h-g) \bmod M\} = d_{\mathbb{Z}_M}(g,h),$$
for all $h,g \in \mathbb{Z}_M$. So, by the Definition 4, $d_{\mathbb{Z}_M}$ is a group metric.

Remark 4. *If d_G is a group metric on a group G, then $d_G^n : G^n \times G^n \to \mathbb{R}$, given by*
$$d_G^n((f_1,\ldots,f_n),(h_1,\ldots,h_n)) = \sum_{i=1}^n d_G(f_i,h_i),$$
is a group metric on G^n.

Definition 5. *Let G be a group, d_G a group metric in G and $C \subseteq A^n$ a code of length n on the alphabet A, with a metric d' on A^n. We say that C is G-linear if C, or an equivalent code C', is an image of a group code H on the group G, that is, $C = \Phi(H)$, where $\Phi : G^n \to A^n$ is an isometry between G^n and A^n.*

We now have a result that demonstrates the importance of having a minimal generator set $U(S)$ for geometrically uniform codes S.

Theorem 3. *Let S be a signal set in a metric space (M,d). Then they are equivalent:*
(a) *S is a geometrically uniform code with a minimal generator $U(S)$;*
(b) *a matched labeling exists between $U(S)$ and S.*
(c) *S is a $U(S)$-linear code with $m : U(S) \to S$.*

Proof. $(a) \Rightarrow (b)$ Since S is GU with minimal generator $U(S)$, $S = \{u(s_0) : u \in U(S)\}$ for an $s_0 \in S$ fixed. Thus, $m : U(S) \to S$, given by $m(u) = u(s_0)$ is a bijection. Now, for every $u, v \in U(S)$ we have that

$$d(m(u), m(v)) = d(u(s_0), v(s_0)) = d(u^{-1}u(s_0), u^{-1}v(s_0))$$
$$= d(s_0, u^{-1}v(s_0)) = d(m(e), m(u^{-1}v)).$$

Thus, m^{-1} is a matched labeling.

$(b) \Rightarrow (a)$ It follows from Theorem 1, since we assuming we have $U(S)$.

$(c) \Rightarrow (a)$ Again, since we are assuming we have $U(S)$, it follows that S is geometrically uniform with minimal generator $U(S)$.

$(a) \Rightarrow (c)$ Since S is GU with minimal generator $U(S)$, $S = \{u(s_0) : u \in U(S)\}$ for a fixed $s_0 \in S$, and $m : U(S) \to S$, given by $m(u) = u(s_0)$ is a bijection. Considering in $U(S)$ the induced metric of S by m^{-1}, it follows that m will be an isometry. Therefore, we have that S is $U(S)$-linear. □

Remark 5. We have two minimal groups $U(S)$ given by R_4 and V^2 that act transitively on S, implying that S is geometrically uniform, for the signal set S from Example 1. On the other hand, we know that the group of rotations $R_4 = \langle R_\pi/2 \rangle = \{id, R_{\pi/2}, R_\pi, R_{3\pi/2}\} \simeq \mathbb{Z}_4$ and the group $V^2 = \langle r_x, r_y \rangle = \{id, r_x, r_y, r_xr_y\}$, where id denotes the identity, r_x and r_y denote the reflection about x axis and y axis, respectively. We also have that $r_x^2 = r_y^2 = id$ and $V^2 \simeq \mathbb{Z}_2 \times \mathbb{Z}_2$. As a result of Theorem 3, from the signal set S and the two distinct non-isomorphic subgroups of the symmetry group $\Gamma(S)$, we obtain two different codes S that have the properties of being G-linear, one with a label group given by $G = \mathbb{Z}_4$ and another with a label group given by $G = \mathbb{Z}_2 \times \mathbb{Z}_2$.

Definition 6. Let U be a subset of a group G and let $U^{-1} = \{u^{-1} : u \in U\}$. Then G is generated by U if, for all $g \in G$ there exists $n \in \mathbb{N}$ such that $g = u_1u_2 \ldots u_n$, where $u_i \in U \cup U^{-1}$ for all $1 \leq i \leq n$. If U is finite, then G is called finitely generated.

Every finitely generated group admits, quite naturally, a metric. In fact, given a generator set U of G, every element g in G can be written as a finite combination of elements of $U \cup U^{-1}$. Consider that the number of elements of $U \cup U^{-1}$ required to write g is a length associated with g. We may now define the norm of g as follows: $\| g \|$ is the least of all possible lengths for g. This norm induces a metric on G as follows: for every $f, g \in G$ let $d(f, g) = \| f^{-1}g \|$. This metric is known as the word metric.

It must be observed that for all $h \in G$ one has

$$d(hf, hg) = \| (hf)^{-1}hg \| = \| f^{-1}h^{-1}hg \| = \| f^{-1}g \| = d(f, g).$$

3. Isometries and G-Isometric Signal Sets

In this section, we introduce some more concepts as well as the main results. We will seek to clarify the reasons for the current proposal and its relation to previous works.

Two signal sets S and S' in a metric space (M, d) are equivalent if there is an isometry $f : M \to M$ such that $f(S') = S$.

Let M' be the space formed by all signal sets in the metric space M. It is verified that the equivalence between signal sets in M' defines an equivalence relation; that is, signal sets that are equivalent are in the same equivalence class in M'.

Example 4. Consider the 4-PSK signal set described in Remark 1, which is given by $S' = \{z = \sqrt{2}\omega^j s_0 \in \mathbb{C} : 0 \leq j \leq 3\}$, where $\omega = e^{i.2\pi/4}$. Let S^θ be the signal set given by $R_\theta S'$, where R_θ denotes rotation matrices of $\mathbb{R}^2$ with rotation angle θ. So, the set $M' = \{S^\theta, 0 \leq \theta < 2\pi\}$ denotes the set of all signal sets that are in the same equivalence class in M' and whose class representative is the signal set S'.

Definition 7. *Given a group G and a metric d on G, then d is left invariant if $d(fg, fh) = d(g, h)$ for all $f, g, h \in G$. Similarly, d is right invariant if $d(gf, hf) = d(g, h)$ for all $f, g, h \in G$. If d is both left and right invariant, then d is bi-invariant.*

Example 5. *Let $G = \mathbb{Z}_M = \{0, \ldots, M-1\}$ be the additive group of integers modulo M. When we consider the group metric $d_{\mathbb{Z}_M}$ defined in Example 3, we obtain*

$$d_{\mathbb{Z}_M}(f+g, f+h) = \min\{((f+g)-(f+h)) \bmod M, ((f+h)-(g+h)) \bmod M\}$$
$$= \min\{(g-h) \bmod M, (h-g) \bmod M\} = d_{\mathbb{Z}_M}(g, h),$$

for all $f, g, h \in \mathbb{Z}_M$. Thus, we can conclude that the group metric $d_{\mathbb{Z}_M}$ is left invariant. Similarly, it is proved that $d_{\mathbb{Z}_M}$ is right invariant. Therefore, $d_{\mathbb{Z}_M}$ is bi-invariant.

For more details about invariant metrics, see [12]. Now, we introduce a main definition to the work, which was inspired by the concept of G-linear codes, see [13].

Definition 8. *Let G be a group and S a signal set of a metric space M. S is G-isometric if there is an isometry $m : (G, d_G) \to (S, d_S)$, where d_G is a metric on G, d_S is the metric in $S \subset M$, and d_G is left invariant.*

Example 6. *Let S be the M-PSK signal set in $\mathbb{R}^2$ given by the vertices of a polygon with M sides inscribed in the unit circle, that is, $S = \{z \in \mathbb{C} : z = e^{i \cdot 2k\pi/M} \text{ with } k \in \{0, 1, \ldots, M-1\}\}$.*

The elements of S can be seen as images of the map $m : \mathbb{Z}_M \to S$ given by $m(k) = e^{i 2k\pi/M}$, that is, each element $m(k) \in S$ is a label of an element $k \in \mathbb{Z}_M$. For convenience we also denote $m(k) = e^{i 2k\pi/M}$ by k.

The Lee metric (see [14]) on S is defined as follows

$$d_S = d_{Lee}(a, b) = \min\{|a-b|, M - |a-b|\},$$

where a, b are vertices of a polygon of M sides that assumes labels in ascending order of elements $\mathbb{Z}_M = \{0, \ldots, M-1\}$. We prove that the map m defines an isometry $m : (\mathbb{Z}_M, d_{\mathbb{Z}_M}) \to (S, d_S)$, where $d_S = d_{Lee}$. Let $k, k' \in \mathbb{Z}_M$. We have that

$$d_{\mathbb{Z}_M}(k, k') = \min\{(k-k') \bmod M, (k'-k) \bmod M\}. \tag{1}$$

On the other hand,

$$d_S = d_{Lee}(m(k), m(k')) = d_{Lee}(k, k') = \min\{|k-k'|, M - |k-k'|\}, \tag{2}$$

In (1) one has $d_{\mathbb{Z}_M}(k, k') = (k-k') \bmod M = |k-k'| = d_{Lee}(k, k')$, if $k \geq k'$, and $d_{\mathbb{Z}_M}(k, k') = (k'-k) \bmod M = M - (k-k') = M - |k-k'| = d_{Lee}(k, k')$, if $k < k'$.

Thus, $d_{\mathbb{Z}_M}(k, k') = d_S(m(k), m(k'))$, for all $k, k' \in \mathbb{Z}_M$. Therefore, the map m is an isometry between $(\mathbb{Z}_M, d_{\mathbb{Z}_M})$ and (S, d_{Lee}).

Example 7. *Let $G = \mathbb{Z}_8$ and S be the 8-PSK signal set given by $S = \{z \in \mathbb{C} : z = e^{i \cdot 2k\pi/8} \text{ with } k \in \{0, 1, \ldots, 7\}\}$. Then, we have:*

(1) Taking $k = 5$ and $k' = 2$, we have that $d_{\mathbb{Z}_8}(5, 3) = d_{\mathbb{Z}_8}(5-3, 3-3) = d_{\mathbb{Z}_8}(2, 0) = 2$. When we take the vertices in the regular octagon labeled by 5 and 3, we have $d_{Lee}(5, 3) = \min\{|5-3|, 8-|5-3|\} = \min\{2, 6\} = 2$, as can be seen in Figure 1.

(2) Taking $k = 2$ and $k' = 7$, we have that $d_{\mathbb{Z}_8}(2, 7) = d_{\mathbb{Z}_8}(2-7, 7-7) = d_{\mathbb{Z}_8}(-5, 0) = -5 \equiv 3 \bmod 8$. Taking the vertices in the regular octagon labeled 2 and 7, we obtain $d_{Lee}(2, 7) = \min\{|2-7|, 8-|2-7|\} = \min\{3, 3\} = 3$, as can be seen in Figure 1.

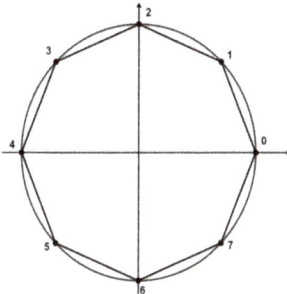

Figure 1. The 8-PSK signal set.

Remark 6. *Note that when $M = 2$, the Lee metric in a signal set in $\mathbb{R}^2$ coincides with the Hamming metric.*

Remark 7. *By environment metric space, we are referring to the space where the signal sets are being constructed. As a consequence of Definition 8, we conclude that the concept of G-isometric is an algebraic invariant that is preserved for all signal sets that are part of the same equivalence class in the space M'. That is, if S and S' are two equivalent signal sets, then, S is G-isometric if and only if, S' also is G-isometric.*

Remark 8. *Definition 8 requires an isometry between the code S and the group G, instead of an isometry between the code S and a group code on G, as we have in the G-linearity (see Definition 5). Moreover, we do not require an isometry between the environment spaces. The isometry is just between G and S. The metric for the group G must be left invariant, and we do not need right invariance, as required for G-linearity. Another important point is that it is not necessary to have an alphabet for S. Once the isometry with the group G is determined, the alphabet is presented.*

The next theorem shows that the left invariance of the group metric is the main condition for an isometry between a group and a signal set to be a matched labeling. That is, an isometry labels a signal set by a group only if the group metric is left invariant.

Theorem 4. *Let $m : (G, d_G) \to (S, d)$ be an isometry. If d_G is left invariant, then the map m^{-1} is a matched labeling.*

Proof. For all $f, g \in G$ one has

$$d_S(m(f), m(g)) = d_G(f, g) = d_G(f^{-1}f, f^{-1}g)$$
$$= d_G(f^{-1}g, e) = d_S(m(f^{-1}g), m(e)),$$

where e is the neutral element of G. Since m is bijective we obtain that m^{-1} is a matched labeling. □

It follows from Theorem 3 that if S is GU with minimal generator, we always have a matched labeling between $U(S)$ and S but, from Theorem 4, for an isometry $m : U(S) \to S$ be a matched labeling, we need compatibility between the metric of the space $ISO(M)$ and the group structure of $U(S)$, that is, the natural metric of $U(S)$ (that one inherited from $ISO(M)$ is useful in the process of labeling by isometries, if the metric gives left invariance to the labeling group $U(S)$.

However, even when we do not have such compatibility, it is possible, in some cases, to endow $U(S)$ with a different metric than the one of $ISO(M)$, so that we may ensure the left invariance property for the group of labels. The following corollary provides an alternative in this direction.

Corollary 3. *Let S be a signal set. If there is a finitely generated group G and a bijection $m : G \to S$, then m^{-1} is a matched labeling.*

Proof. Let G be a finitely generated group. Then, we endowed G with the word metric, which is left invariant. Since $m : G \to S$ is a bijection from G to S, then it is enough to consider on S the metric induced by G through m, instead of consider the metric given by M. Thus, m is an isometry, and by Theorem 4, m^{-1} is a matched labeling. □

In other words, under the above conditions, any bijection between a finitely generated group and a signal set can be considered a matched label. To accomplish this, simply apply the map m to S and induce the metric of G. In this case, all the code properties, both algebraic and metric, are inherited from the group G regardless of the environment metric space of S.

Example 8. *Let $G = \mathbb{Z}_8$, which is a finitely generated group.*
(1) Let $S = \{z \in \mathbb{C} : z = e^{i \cdot 2k\pi/8} \text{ with } k \in \{0, 1, \ldots, 7\}\}$ a signal set in $\mathbb{R}^2$. Considering the bijection given by $m : \mathbb{Z}_8 \to S$ given by $m(k) = e^{i2k\pi/8}$, by Corollary 3 we conclude that m^{-1} is a matched labeling.
(2) Let $S' = \{z \in \mathbb{C} : z = z_0 e^{i \cdot 2k\pi/8} \text{ with } k \in \{0, 1, \ldots, 7\} \text{ and } |z_0| < 1\}$ be a signal set in $\mathbb{D}$ (hyperbolic plane). Moreover, considering the bijection given by $m : \mathbb{Z}_8 \to S$ given by $m(k) = z_0 e^{i2k\pi/8}$, by Corollary 3 we conclude that m^{-1} is a matched labeling.

Theorem 5. *Let G be a group and d_G be any metric on G. If m^{-1} is a matched labeling, where $m : G \to S$ is an isometry, then d_G is left invariant.*

Proof. Given $f, g \in G$ one has

$$d_G(f, g) = d_S(m(f), m(g)) = d_S(m(f^{-1}g), m(e)) = d_G(f^{-1}g, e).$$

Thus, d_G is left invariant. □

The previous result requires that G has a metric d_G, and also that there is an isometry for that metric. The next result shows that it is enough to have a matched labeling between G and S, such that we can induce a metric in G and obtain an isometry.

Theorem 6. *Let m^{-1} be a matched labeling where $m : G \to S$. If we consider on G the metric induced by S through m^{-1}, then d_G is left invariant.*

Proof. Considering on G the metric of S induced by m^{-1}, the construction implies that m is also an isometry, and by Theorem 5, it follows that d_G is left invariant. □

This theorem says that a matched labeling may also be considered an isometry. It is enough to consider in the group G the metric induced from the signal set S by m^{-1}. This is independent of the metric of M and always gives a left invariant metric to the group of labels.

The next result is the main result of the current work, where we obtain that, if a signal set is G-isometric, then this is equivalent to the existing matched labeling between G and S.

Theorem 7. *Let S be a signal set and G be a group. Then, S is G-isometric if, and only if, m^{-1} is a matched labeling, where $m : G \to S$.*

Proof. Let S be a G-isometric signal set. It follows from Theorem 4 that m^{-1} is a matched labeling. Conversely, suppose that there is a matched labeling between G and S, that is, $m : G \to S$ is a bijection, and it satisfies

$$d(m(g), m(h)) = d(m(g^{-1}h), m(e)),$$

for every g and h in G. According to Theorem 6, d_G is left invariant, where d_G is the metric induced by S through $m - 1$. Thus, we have that m is an isometry, and therefore, it follows that S is G-isometric. So, it follows the result. □

Example 9. *Let $G = \mathbb{Z}_8$ and $S = \{z \in \mathbb{C}; z = e^{i \cdot 2k\pi/8} \text{ with } k \in \{0, 1, \ldots, 7\}\}$ be signal sets in $\mathbb{R}^2$ and $S' = \{z \in \mathbb{C}; z = e^{i \cdot 2k\pi/8} \text{ with } k \in \{0, 1, \ldots, 7\}\}$ be a signal set in $\mathbb{D}$. As a consequence of Example 8 and the Theorem 7, we conclude that the signal set S in $\mathbb{R}^2$ is $\mathbb{Z}_8$-isometric and the signal set S' in $\mathbb{D}$ is also $\mathbb{Z}_8$-isometric.*

Remark 9. *We conclude from Example 9 that the 8-PSK signal set S^θ given in the form $S^\theta = R_\theta S$, that is in the same equivalence class of the signal set S, is $\mathbb{Z}_8$-isometric, where R_θ denotes an isometry of $\mathbb{R}^2$ given by rotation matrix with angle θ.*

We have seen in this section that if a signal set S in a metric space is G-isometric, then the signal sets in M that have S as equivalence class representant are also G-isometric, as illustrated in item (a) of Example 9. As shown in item (b) of Example 9, there are signal sets S and S' that are G-isometric at the same time, but they are not in the same equivalence class and even in different metric spaces.

In the next section, we will discuss situations of this nature in greater depth, where we will see in particular that they are associated with the metric structure of the minimal groups $U(S)$ that we will take as subgroups of the isometry group $ISOM(M)$ in the metric space in question.

Corollary 4. *Let S be a signal set in a metric space (M, d). Then, the following statements are equivalent:*

(a) *the code S is geometrically uniform with minimal generator $U(S)$;*
(b) *there exists a matched labeling between $U(S)$ and S;*
(c) *the code S is $U(S)$-isometric.*

Proof. The equivalence between (a) and (b) follows from Theorem 3, and the equivalence between (c) and b) follows from Theorem 7. □

The last two results give a characterization of the equivalence established by Loeliger. Since the result does not depend on the metric space under consideration, it is valid for hyperbolic and Euclidean cases. The aim is to search for isometries between signal sets and groups with a left invariant metric. Note that the advantage of this result in relation to Theorem 3 is that we do not need a group code or an alphabet.

Remark 10. *Consider the signal set 4-PSK, S^θ of Example 8. As the signal sets S^θ are in the same equivalence class, using the alphabet given by the group of labels $G = \mathbb{Z}_4$, we conclude that each signal set/codes S^θ is $\mathbb{Z}_4$-isometric. Similarly, using of the alphabet given by the label group $G = \mathbb{Z}_2 \times \mathbb{Z}_2$, we conclude that each one of the signal sets / codes S^θ and S' are $\mathbb{Z}_2 \times \mathbb{Z}_2$-isometric.*

However, it is worth noting that, depending on the application we are considering, there are representatives S^θ in the equivalence class that are more convenient because of the geometric arrangement of the signals, as is the case when looking for a signal set of maximum diversity, that is, when all the components of the signal points of the signal set are distinct, which is useful in transmission models in Rayleigh channels.

4. Construction of G-iSometric Signal Sets and Matched Labelings to the Group G

In any matched labeling, the algebraic structure is always given by the group of labels, but in relation to the metric proprieties, there are three distinct ways to proceed: (1) consider in the group of labels for the metric given by $ISO(M)$; (2) define in the group of labels other metric than the one of $ISO(M)$, in order that the algebraic and metric structures of $U(S)$ are compatible; and (3) consider the metric structure of S inherited of space M.

In the first case, it is necessary to have a previous compatibility between the metric of $ISO(M)$ and the group structure of $U(S)$; in the second case, such compatibility is obtained by imposition. However, in both cases, the idea is to obtain a matched labeling from an isometry. On the other hand, in the last case, we have the opposite idea. We want a matched labeling that is an isometry. It is possible to endow the group of labels with the geometric properties of the space M using this method. This is not the case in cases (1) and (2). Thus, it is under this approach that the search of metric spaces to obtain new signal sets matched to groups becomes more interesting because, in this way, the geometrical properties of M may be used in the labeling process. Euclidean space is a particular case of this approach.

Case 1: In the first example, we consider the space metric M given by the Euclidean plane $\mathbb{R}^2$, the metric of $ISO(M)$ is the same, [15]. In this case, we do not have any change if we use either the metric of M or the metric of the $ISO(M)$.

Example 10. Consider the signal set $S = \mathbb{Z}^2 + (\frac{1}{2}, \frac{1}{2}) \subset \mathbb{R}^2$, see Figure 2. A minimal generator group for S is

$$U(S) = T(\mathbb{Z}^2) = \{T_{(m,n)} \in \Gamma(S) : T_{(m,n)}(x,y) = (x,y) + (m,n) \, \forall \, (x,y) \in \mathbb{R}^2\},$$

the group of translations by integers in each coordinate. On the other hand, we know that the symmetry group of S is $\Gamma(S) = D_4 \ltimes T(\mathbb{Z}^2)$, where D_4 denotes the Dihedral Group of order 8 and $\ltimes$ denotes the semi-direct product of the groups. Thus, one has two possibilities for the generator group of S, $U(S) = R_4 \ltimes T(2\mathbb{Z}^2)$ (these symmetries are characterized by the composition of a rotation with a translation) and $U(S) = V^2 \ltimes T(2\mathbb{Z}^2)$ (these symmetries are characterized by the composition of a reflection and a translation), where R_4 is the set of rotations by multiples of $\pi/2$, and V^2 is the group of reflections on any axis. For more details, see [1].

Therefore, by Corollary 4, there is a matched labeling m^{-1} where $m : U(S) \to S$ for each one of the three groups. Hence, in each case, imposing to S the group metric of the labels, induced by m, it follows that m is an isometry. On the other hand, as we have a matched labeling, we can induce the metric of S for the label group, and it follows from Theorem 6 that m is also an isometry.

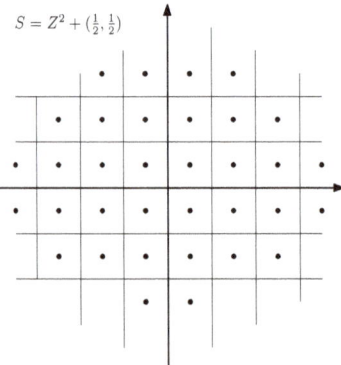

Figure 2. Signal set in the plane for Example 10.

The following example shows three possibilities for the minimal generator group $U(S)$ of a signal set S, where the three groups are not isomorphic to each other.

Example 11. *Let S be the signal constellation in $\mathbb{R}^3$ given by the vertices of a unit cube, in which we consider its center of mass at the origin $(0,0,0)$ and its edges parallel to the coordinate axes. There are three non-isomorphic groups acting on S. These groups are: a) $U(S) = D_4$ the group generated by θ_4, a rotation of order four around the axis Oz, and θ_2, a rotation of order two around the axis Oy; b) $U(S) = \mathbb{Z}_2 \times \mathbb{Z}_4$, the group generated by θ_4, a rotation around the axis Oy, and r_{xy}, a reflection in the plane xy, and c) $U(S) = \mathbb{Z}_2^3$ the group generated by r_{xy}, r_{xz} and r_{yz}, the reflections on the planes xy, xz and yz, respectively. See Figure 3.*

According to Corollary 4, there is a matched labeling m^{-1} in each case, where $m: U(S) \to S$. We can take on $U(S)$ the metric of $\mathbb{R}^3$ through the map m^{-1} for each of these groups of labels, and from Theorem 6, $d_{U(S)}$ is left invariant, so it is compatible with the group structure of $U(S)$ and m is an isometry.

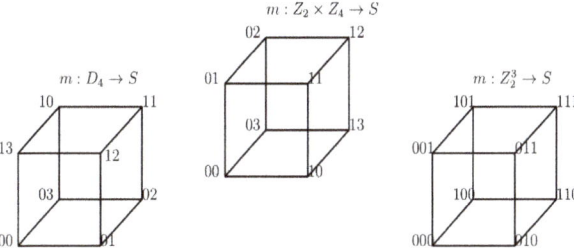

Figure 3. Signals set for Example 11.

Example 12. *Let S be a M-PSK signal set in $\mathbb{R}^2$ as described in Example 2. Taking $M = 8$ and $U(S) = R_8$ as the group of Euclidean rotations by angle $2\pi/8$ around the origin, it follows that m^{-1} is a mached labeling where $m: U(S) \to S$.*

Case 2: Here we show an example in the hyperbolic plane, which is a non-Euclidean space.

Example 13. *In the model of Poincaré disc $\mathbb{D}$ for the hyperbolic plane, let us consider the Fuchsian group*

$$G = \langle a_1, a_2, b_1, b_2 : [a_1, b_1][a_2, b_2] = e \rangle,$$

where $[a_1, b_1][a_2, b_2] = a_1 b_1 a_1^{-1} b_1^{-1} a_2 b_2 a_2^{-1} b_2^{-1}$. The group G has as a fundamental region a regular hyperbolic octagon P_0, and G generates the regular hyperbolic tiling $\{8,8\}$, that is, a tiling of $\mathbb{D}$ such that, in each vertex, there are eight copies of P_0 (see Figure 4). The group G is a group associated with a compact surface with genus 2 (a bitorus) and P_0 is a flat model of such a surface. From this information, one has

$$(i)\ \mathbb{D} = \bigcup_{\gamma \in G} \gamma(P_0),$$

$(ii)\ \gamma(P_0) \cap \beta(P_0) = \varnothing$ *for all $\gamma, \beta \in G, \gamma \neq \beta$,*

$(iii)\ \gamma(P_0)^0 \neq \varnothing$ *for all $\gamma \in G$,*

where $\gamma(P_0)^0$ denotes the interior of $\gamma(P_0)$.

Now, c_i represents the center of the i-th octagon P_i of the tiling $\{8,8\}$, and g_i represents an isometry of G that applies P_0 to P_i, $i \in \mathbb{N}$. Thus, if $S = \{c_i : i \in \mathbb{N}\}$, the map $m: G \to S$ given by

$m(g_i) = c_i$ ($m(g_0) = m(e) = c_0$ is a map such that a point of S is associated with each isometry of the group G. From this construction, (i), (ii), and (iii), we have that m is well defined and it is bijective.

Because G is a transitive group on S, Theorem 2 states that m is a matched map, but because m is a bijection, m^{-1} is a matched labeling. Note that the metric of M in this case is the hyperbolic metric of $\mathbb{D}$, and the metric of ISO(M) is the Euclidean metric of $\mathbb{R}^4$. Whatever metric we adopt, it gives distinct geometric properties.

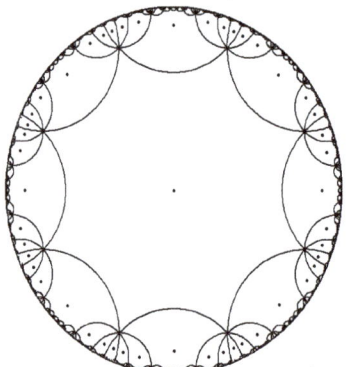

Figure 4. Signal set for Example 13.

Example 14. *Let us consider the triangular arithmetic Fuchsian group* (5, 5, 5), *which has a normal subgroup N of index 5 associated to the bitorus* [16,17]. *Therefore,* $\frac{(5,5,5)}{N} \simeq \mathbb{Z}_5 = G$, *and it follows that P_G subdivides P_N into 5 congruent regions, where P_G and P_N denote the fundamental regions of G and N, respectively. The fundamental region P_N is the regular polygon of the tessellation* {10, 5} *and the fundamental region P_G is the polygon with 4 equal sides and alternating internal angles $\frac{\pi}{5}$ and $\frac{2\pi}{5}$. Thus, we have a tessellation of the flat double torus such that, considering as a signal set S given by the centers of these 5 regions (see Figure 5) we obtain that $\mathbb{Z}_5$ is a group of labels for S.*

Taking U(S) as the group of hyperbolic rotations by an angle of $\frac{2\pi}{5}$ around the origin of $\mathbb{D}$, it follows that m^{-1} is a matched labeling where $m : U(S) \to S$.

Case 3: In the next example, we have a geometrically uniform code, which may be seen as a signal constellation on a flat torus. For more details, see [18]. As we will see, in this example, it is possible to label using three non-isomorphic groups of labels, each one containing 16 elements.

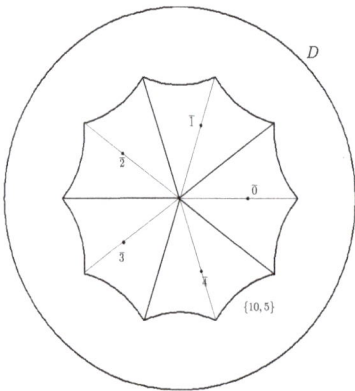

Figure 5. The double torus.

Example 15. Let S be the same set of Example 1. The three possible choices for $U(S)$ preserve S and have the subgroup $G_1 = \langle T_{e_1}, T_{e_2} \rangle$, $G_2 = \langle R_{\pi/2}, T_{2e_1}, T_{2e_2} \rangle$, $G_3 = \langle R_v, R_h, T_{2e_1}, T_{2e_2} \rangle$, where T_c is the translation by c, $R_{\pi/2}$ is the rotation of $\pi/2$ around the origin, R_v is the reflection on the axis y and R_h is the reflection on the x axis. These three symmetry groups preserve S and have in common the subgroup $G' = \langle T_{4e_1}, T_{4e_2} \rangle$. Consider the signal set $\overline{S} = \frac{S}{G'}$ in the torus $T_\alpha = \frac{\mathbb{R}^2}{G'}$, $\alpha = \{4e_1, 4e_2\}$, which can be seen as the set of vertices of a regular graph in T_α (see Figure 6). Each one of the three choices for $U(S)$ induces a different label for the 16 points of $\overline{S}$, that is, for the tessellation in the torus. We have $\frac{U(S)}{G} \simeq \mathbb{Z}_4^2$, $\frac{U(S)}{G} \simeq \mathbb{Z}_2^4$ and $\frac{U(S)}{G} \simeq \mathbb{Z}_4 \times \mathbb{Z}_2^2$. In a similar way to Example 4, endowing the group of labels with the metric of the flat torus, the matched labeling m^{-1} is an isometry.

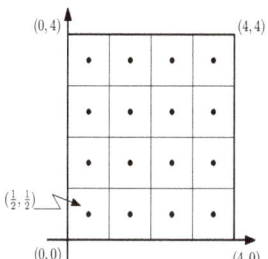

Figure 6. The signal set in the flat torus.

Remark 11. It is worth noting that in item (c) of Example 11, we saw that $U(S) = \mathbb{Z}_2^3$ is one of the possibilities. Notice that the alphabet is obtained naturally from the relationship between the set S and the group of labels $\mathbb{Z}_2^3$ coming from its symmetry group $\Gamma(S)$ during the labeling process, and in this case, the natural distance matched to S is the Hamming metric.

In Example 15, we saw that there are three possibilities for the group of labels $\frac{\overline{U(S)}}{G}$ for the signal set $\overline{S}$ in the double torus, among these we have $\frac{\overline{U(S)}}{G} \simeq \mathbb{Z}_4^2$ and $\frac{\overline{U(S)}}{G} \simeq \mathbb{Z}_2^4$. For the case where $\frac{\overline{U(S)}}{G} \simeq \mathbb{Z}_2^4$, we have that the alphabet is obtained naturally from the relationship between the set $\overline{S}$ and the group of labels $\mathbb{Z}_2^4$ coming from its symmetry group $\Gamma(S)$ during the labeling process and in this case the natural distance matched to $\overline{S}$ is the Hamming metric.

In the case where $\frac{\overline{U(S)}}{G} \simeq \mathbb{Z}_4^2$, the alphabet is obtained naturally from the relationship between the set $\overline{S}$ and the group of labels $\mathbb{Z}_4^2$ derived from its symmetry group $\Gamma(S)$ during the labeling process, and the natural distance matched to $\overline{S}$ is the Lee metric. The fact that it does not require prior knowledge of an alphabet is a very useful feature, since in the applications we have only the set S and the environment space in which S is considered, which makes such a need an artificial hypothesis.

5. Conclusions and Discussions

The procedure proposed in this article allowed to reproduce groups of labels (alphabet) matched to a signal set/code S via already known discrete metrics and naturally from the relationship between the set $\overline{S}$ and the group of labels coming from its symmetry group $\Gamma(S)$ during the labeling process. Additionally, the article opens up new possibilities for applying discrete metrics that come from the group metric obtained from the (finitely generated) group of labels.

Another important point is to expand the possibilities for new theoretical and practical constructions based on these labels, since, in this approach, we do not necessarily need to use the metric of the ambient space.

As a possible future application of the results presented in this work, we note that advanced machine learning approaches are available to search for optimum solutions of complex and unknown functions under uncertainties. The recent paper [19] can give connections in this direction.

Author Contributions: Conceptualization, E.M.V.G. and E.B.d.S.; methodology, E.M.V.G. and C.A.R.M.; software, E.M.V.G. and E.M.B.; validation, E.M.V.G., E.D.d.C. and E.B.d.S.; formal analysis, E.M.V.G. and E.M.B.; investigation, E.M.V.G.; resources, E.M.V.G.; data curation, E.M.B.; writing, E.M.V.G.; original draft preparation, E.B.d.S.; writing—review and editing, E.M.V.G. and E.B.d.S.; visualization, C.A.R.M.; supervision, E.B.d.S.; project administration, E.M.V.G.; funding acquisition, C.A.R.M. All authors have read and agreed to the published version of the manuscript.

Funding: PROAP/CAPES—processo n° 88881.595307/2020-01-CPF 024.712.759-07.

Data Availability Statement: Not applicable.

Conflicts of Interest: The authors declare no conflict of interest.

References

1. Forney, G.D., Jr. Geometrically uniform codes. *IEEE Trans. Inform. Theory* **1991**, *37*, 1241–1260. [CrossRef]
2. Slepian, D. Group codes for the gaussian channel. *Bell Syst. Tech. J.* **1968**, *37*, 575–602. [CrossRef]
3. Loeliger, H.A. Signal sets matched to groups. *IEEE Trans. Inform. Theory* **1991**, *37*, 1675–1682. [CrossRef]
4. Huber, K. Codes over gaussian integers. *IEEE Trans. Inf. Theory* **1994**, *40*, 207–216. [CrossRef]
5. Nobrega, T.P.; Interlando, J.C.; Favareto, O.M.; Elia, M.; Palazzo, R., Jr. Lattice constellations and codes from quadratic number fields. *IEEE Trans. Inf. Theory* **2001**, *47*, 1514–1527.
6. Carvalho, E.D.; Firer, M.; Palazzo, R., Jr. On the construction and labelling of geometrically uniform signal sets in $\mathbb{R}^2$ matched to additive quotient groups. *J. Appl. Math. Comput.* **2008**, *27*, 1–6. [CrossRef]
7. Albuquerque, C.D.; Palazzo, R., Jr.; Silva, E.B. Topological quantum codes on compact surfaces with genus $g \geq 2$. *J. Math. Phys.* **2009**, *50*, 023513. [CrossRef]
8. Silva, E.B.; Firer, M.; Costa, S.R.; Palazzo, R., Jr. Signal constellations in the hyperbolic plane: A proposal for new communication systems. *J. Franklin Inst.* **2006**, *343*, 69–82. [CrossRef]
9. Lazari, H.; Palazzo, R., Jr. Geometrically uniform hyperbolic codes. *Comp. Appl. Math.* **2005**, *37*, 173–192. [CrossRef]
10. Cavalcante, R.G.; Lazari, H.; Lima, J.D.; Palazzo, R., Jr. A new approach to the design of digital communication systems. *AMS-DIMACS Ser.* **2005**, *68*, 145–177.
11. Gomes, E.M.V.; Carvalho, E.D.; Martins, C.A.R.; Soares, W.S., Jr.; Silva, E.B. Hyperbolic geometrically uniform codes and Ungerboeck partitioning on the double torus. *Symmetry* **2022**, *14*, 449. [CrossRef]
12. Klee, V.L. Invariant Metrics in groups (solution of a problem of Banach). *Proc. Amer. Math. Soc.* **1952**, *3*, 484–487. [CrossRef]
13. Alves, M.M.S.; Gerônimo, J.R.; Palazzo, R., Jr.; Costa, S.I.R.; Interlando, J.C.; Araujo, M.C. Relating propelinear and binary G-linear codes. *Discret. Math.* **2002**, *243*, 187–194. [CrossRef]
14. Berlekamp, E.R. *Algebraic Coding Theory*; McGraw-Hill: New York, NY, USA, 1968.
15. Beardon, A. *The Geometry of Discrete Groups*; Springer: Berlin/Heidelberg, Germany, 1983.
16. Kuribayashi, I. On an algebraization of the Riemann Hurwitz relation. *Kodai Math. J.* **1984**, *7*, 222–237. [CrossRef]
17. Takeuchi, K. Arithmetic triangle groups. *J. Math. Soc. Jpn.* **1977**, *29*, 91–106. [CrossRef]
18. Costa, S.I.R.; Muniz, M.; Agustini, E.; Palazzo, R., Jr. Graphs, tessellations and perfect codes on flat tori. *IEEE Trans. Inform. Theory* **2004**, *50*, 2363–2377. [CrossRef]
19. Tutsoy, O.; Barkana, D.E.; Balikci, K. A Novel Exploration-Exploitation-Based Adaptive Law for Intelligent Model-Free Control Approaches. *IEEE Trans. Cybern.* **2021**, 1–9. [CrossRef] [PubMed]

Article

Unlicensed Spectrum Allocation for LTE and Wi-Fi Coexistence with HAP

Wei Kuang Lai [1], Chin-Shiuh Shieh [2,*], Yuh-Chung Lin [3], Chun-Yi Tsai [4] and Yu-Dai Yan [1]

[1] Department of Computer Science and Engineering, National Sun Yat-Sen University, Kaohsiung 80424, Taiwan
[2] Department of Electronic Engineering, National Kaohsiung University of Science and Technology, Kaohsiung 807618, Taiwan
[3] School of Information Science and Technology, Sanda University, Shanghai 201029, China
[4] Department of Computer Science and Information Engineering, National Taitung University, Taitung 95092, Taiwan
* Correspondence: csshieh@nkust.edu.tw; Tel.: +886-937-316833

Citation: Lai, W.K.; Shieh, C.-S.; Lin, Y.-C.; Tsai, C.-Y.; Yan, Y.-D. Unlicensed Spectrum Allocation for LTE and Wi-Fi Coexistence with HAP. *Symmetry* **2022**, *14*, 1650. https://doi.org/10.3390/sym14081650

Academic Editors: Pingping Chen, Long Shi and Yi Fang

Received: 17 July 2022
Accepted: 6 August 2022
Published: 10 August 2022

Publisher's Note: MDPI stays neutral with regard to jurisdictional claims in published maps and institutional affiliations.

Copyright: © 2022 by the authors. Licensee MDPI, Basel, Switzerland. This article is an open access article distributed under the terms and conditions of the Creative Commons Attribution (CC BY) license (https://creativecommons.org/licenses/by/4.0/).

Abstract: In order to accommodate the ever-increasing traffic demands, numerous approaches have been developed to improve spectrum utilization. Among others, the coexistence of LTE (Long-Term Evolution) and Wi-Fi, addressed by the 3GPP (3rd Generation Partnership Project) with hyper access points (HAPs) as bridges, is well recognized as a promising candidate solution. Aimed at improving the spectrum utilization of the unlicensed bands by following LTE-Unlicensed (LTE-U), this article contributes to the determination of the optimal time ratio, δ, for the time-division multiplexing of LTE and Wi-Fi over unlicensed bands. Symmetric allocation with a duty cycle of 50% cannot be an optimal option. Asymmetric allocation according to the quality of service (QoS) requirements and traffic demands should be considered. The problem is formulated as an optimization problem optimizing the total throughput. The lower and upper bounds of δ are obtained according to the QoS requirements of Wi-Fi and the admission control requirements of LTE. The detailed procedure for finding an adequate δ is developed and presented. A series of simulations are conducted to demonstrate the feasibility and effectiveness of the proposed approach. Simulation results show that the proposed approach improves the total throughput without compromising the fairness of Wi-Fi, as intended. Ten percent of improvement in throughput compared with LTE-U can be achieved.

Keywords: Long-Term Evolution (LTE); Wi-Fi; LTE-Unlicensed (LTE-U); Hyper-AP (HAP)

1. Introduction

Wireless communication is a continuing trend with the growing number of wireless devices. A wide variety of devices and applications have been introduced as the technology is getting mature and popularized. As a consequence, traffic conveyed over the wireless networks grows explosively. Technology to accommodate the ever-increasing traffic is a pressing yet challenging issue. Unlike wired networks, the radio spectrum for wireless communication is inherently scarce and expensive. Many approaches are studied. One possible solution to ameliorate spectrum utilization is advanced modulation and coding technology. Another exciting alternative is the introduction of novel designs to radio apparatus, such as the work by Mahmud et al. [1]. Based solely on resonators, their two-element filtering antenna array design had achieved improved transceiving efficiency. However, there are physical limitations to the modulation and coding technology, as well as new radio apparatus designs.

As a prospective mechanism, the coexistence of LTE (Long-Term Evolution) and Wi-Fi (wireless fidelity) has received considerable attention for its potential to achieve better spectrum utilization. This study advances the same philosophy and contributes to determining an optimal time ratio for the time-division multiplexing between the LTE and Wi-Fi networks. Symmetric allocation with a duty cycle of 50% cannot be an optimal option. Asymmetric allocation according to the quality of service (QoS) requirements and traffic demands should be considered. As a de facto standard, LTE is an all-IP system with a higher data rate, high-level security, improved spectrum efficiency, lower latency, QoS support, and so forth. LTE was initially designed to operate in the licensed band. To accommodate more traffic, a promising alternative is to allow the LTE to cooperate in the unlicensed band with the Wi-Fi networks.

However, there is a fundamental obstacle to this approach. The transmission mechanism of Wi-Fi is intrinsically different from that of LTE. The unlicensed band is already occupied by numerous wireless systems, particularly the Wi-Fi system. LTE adopts a non-contention MAC (media access control) protocol to avoid packet collision among users. It uses the scheduling mechanism in centralized control units, such as eNBs (evolved Node B). The eNBs decide how to allocate resources to users. Each user can utilize the allocated resources to transmit data. On the other hand, Wi-Fi employs the carrier sense multiple access with collision avoidance (CSMA/CA) mechanism to resolve the packet collision problem. CSMA/CA is intrinsically a contention-based MAC protocol for shared, broadcast-based media. In Wi-Fi, when a node has data to transmit, it detects the channel status. If the channel is idle, the node is allowed to transmit data. Otherwise, it will exercise a back-off algorithm waiting for other opportunities to transmit data.

Our contributions are threefold.

1. A utility function is defined, and an optimization problem is formulated for the time-division multiplexing between Wi-Fi stations and LTE networks. Then a new scheme is proposed for adequate allocations of spectrum resources utilizing HAPs as bridges. This scheme is peculiarly beneficial to LTE-U (LTE-Unlicensed) systems that plan to maintain the QoS requirements of Wi-Fi users. The proposed scheme can further preserve the access right of Wi-Fi QoS stations (QSTAs).
2. The disadvantages to Wi-Fi users due to the inclusion of LTE users in the unlicensed band for LTE-U can be minimized. It is argued that the Wi-Fi networks would be less advantageous when LTE and Wi-Fi coexist in the same unlicensed band. In recognition of these problems, this study conducts an analytical analysis to determine an optimal ratio for the time-division multiplexing between LTE and Wi-Fi networks, seeking to maximize the total throughput and maintain fairness in the coexistence of Wi-Fi and LTE-U.
3. Simulation results confirm that the scheme would have better throughput while keeping fair access between LTE and Wi-Fi stations in either heavily or lightly loaded Wi-Fi environments. By adequately assigning weights to the utility function, when loads of Wi-Fi stations are high, our scheme favors Wi-Fi stations to preserve the access right of Wi-Fi stations. On the other hand, when loads of Wi-Fi stations are light, the remaining resources are allocated to LTE stations for maximal bandwidth efficiency.

The rest of the paper is organized as follows. Section 2 presents related works. In Section 3, we define the system model and the formulated optimization problem for the time-division multiplexing between LTE and Wi-Fi networks. The proposed method is described in detail in Section 4. Section 5 presents the simulation settings and shows the numerical results accompanied by analysis and discussion. Finally, we draw some conclusions in Section 6.

2. Related Technology and Works

The concept of unlicensed LTE was first introduced in the 3rd Generation Partnership Project (3GPP) Release 10. Years of advancement led to three main variants, namely LTE-U, Licensed Assisted Access (AAC), and MulteFire [2–4].

2.1. LTE-Unlicensed (LTE-U)

LTE-U [2] and Wi-Fi share the same unlicensed spectrum in a time-division manner. A certain portion of individual repeated cycles is allocated to LTE, and the rest is allocated to Wi-Fi. LTE-U is favorable in that no PHY/MAC layer change is required. Carrier sense adaptive transmission (CSAT) [5] is a medium access procedure proposed by Qualcomm. Based on modifications of the carrier aggregation [6], CSAT enables the coexistence of LTE and Wi-Fi. The CSAT technique calculates the most appropriate coexistence period, ensuring that Wi-Fi is minimally affected. First, the LTE-U eNB performs CSAT to detect and analyze channel conditions of the unlicensed band, including the number of adjacent LTE-U eNBs, Wi-Fi APs, the types and lengths of packets, and so on. Next, according to the measurements, the adaptive duty cycle (ADC) will be divided into the on/off cycle, which defines the access periods of LTE-U eNB and Wi-Fi. The percentage of allocation (the duty cycle of the ADC) is a critical parameter for system performance. An informed choice of the allocation percentage is traffic dependent. It strongly affects the total system throughput and the fairness between the LTE and Wi-Fi networks. This issue is precisely the primary concern of this study.

2.2. Licensed Assisted Access (AAC)

Another mechanism proposed to exploit the unlicensed band is the Licensed-Assisted Access (LAA) [3] drafted in 3GPP Release 13. The core concept of LAA is Listen-Before-Talk (LBT). To reduce the interference to the Wi-Fi system while accessing the unlicensed band, four mechanisms are specified in LAA, namely carrier selection (CS), listen-before-talk (LBT), discontinuous transmission (DTX), and transmit power control (TPC) [7]. LBT can be regarded as the LTE version of the carrier sense multiple access (CSMA) schemes. Unlike the CSAT scheme, it operates in a distributed manner rather than a centralized one. It provides a flexible and adaptive coexistence solution among heterogeneous networks through quick channel sensing and dynamic spectrum access. The LBT scheme gives all the contending nodes equal spectral access opportunities in the long term. However, it sacrifices spectral utilization in exchange for reducing the probability of collision.

2.3. MulteFire

MulteFire [4] is a standalone LTE system designed to operate entirely in the unlicensed band, in which both the control signal and data transmission are delivered in the unlicensed band. It is distinguished for improving LTE performance and simplifying LTE deployment in the unlicensed band. Basically, the MulteFire builds on 3GPP standards and utilizes the LBT mechanism to coexist with Wi-Fi or LAA users. One of the most important application areas of MulteFire is industrial IoT, which demands fast transmission and broad bandwidth for collecting a large volume of data to support intelligent industrial operations using advanced data analysis tools. Due to the use of LTE technology, MulteFire enjoys certain advantages, including high capacity, better coverage, seamless mobility, industrial-grade reliability, and LTE-based security. In [8], the challenges and solutions of deploying the MulteFire in the unlicensed band are discussed.

2.4. Related Works on the Coexistence of LTE and Wi-Fi

Many studies are devoted to the coexistence of LTE and Wi-Fi in the unlicensed band. The following is a brief survey of existing approaches.

In [9], Alsenwi et al. proposed a novel Hopfield neural network-based mechanism as an efficient and fair coexistence mechanism in the unlicensed bands for an LTE-U base station alongside Wi-Fi access points (APs). The coexistence problem was modeled as an optimization problem, in which both the LTE-U data rate and the QoS of the Wi-Fi network are considered for fairness. Another scheme, named mLTE-U, was proposed in [10]. The proposed approach adopts an adaptive LBT scheme. After a variable transmission opportunity (TXOP), mLTE-U has a variable muting period, which the Wi-Fi networks can exploit to gain access to the media. A Q-learning technique is employed to achieve fair coexistence between mLTE-U and Wi-Fi networks. The proposed scheme can decide on an appropriate mixture of TXOP and muting period for fair coexistence. In [11], Mosleh et al. address issues neglected in previous works, such as the uncertainties in LAA-based coexistence systems. It could be that only partial or no information on MAC and physical layer protocol are available in the systems. The lack of such accurate information may inaccurately estimate the key performance indicators. A novel machine learning mechanism that combines a neural network with a logistic regression algorithm is proposed in the paper. It can track and estimate key performance indicators (KPIs) and probability of coexistence (PoC) of LTE-LAA and Wi-Fi networks without the information of MAC and physical layer parameters. A reinforcement learning-based sub-channel selection technique is introduced in [12] for a coexistence scenario with multiple LAA and Wi-Fi competing for channel access in an unlicensed band. The proposed scheme allows access points and eNBs to select the best sub-channel by the MAC protocol considering the physical layer's parameters.

In [13], a novel proportional fair allocation scheme was proposed to guarantee fair coexistence between LTE-U and Wi-Fi networks. It allocates the channel access time in a proportional-fair manner to each entity without message-passing between LTE-U and Wi-Fi networks. In [14], a cross-layer proportional-fairness-based framework is proposed to achieve throughput-oriented proportional fairness between the LTE-U and Wi-Fi networks. When LTE-U eNBs operate with the LBT scheme to access the channel, the interactions between the LTE-U and Wi-Fi networks can be modeled by two interactive Markov chains. He et al. analyzed the throughput of LTE-U and Wi-Fi and formulated a utility function of throughput, transforming the problem into an optimization problem. The architecture with Hyper-AP (HAP) is proposed in [15]. In [16], the operation of HAP is divided into a contention-free period and a contention period for LTE-U and Wi-Fi users, respectively. To improve system throughput and user fairness, Chen et al. take the resource allocation and user association into consideration to maximize the network utility based on the Nash bargaining solution (NBS). To decide what percentage of a repeated cycle in the time domain should be allotted to the LTE users, the NBS (Nash bargaining solution) algorithm is utilized to solve the allocation of limited resources among many contestants. We would refer to the scheme as NBS. Any competitor in the game would like to obtain a maximum benefit. When one of the participants receives profits, it will cause others to lose some profits. After the bargaining process, the distributions of resources will achieve a balance status among contestants. In [17], Al-Khansa and Artail propose a semi-distributed LTE-Unlicensed scheme in which the Wi-Fi-like carrier sense, back-off, and QoS mechanism are equipped in the LTE base station. The proposed scheme also uses the almost blank sub-frame (ABS) to control the interference. For performance evaluation, it uses the ns3 to simulate LAA and Wi-Fi coexistence scenarios. The results show that it can achieve fairness between LTE-U and Wi-Fi users in a small cell environment. In [3], the four main functionalities of LAA, i.e., CS, LBT, DTX, and TPC, are investigated. Q-learning mechanisms are used for carrier selection that takes DTX or both DTX and TPC into account to provide an efficient coexistence scheme. Using the Markov model, Qin et al. [18] model and analyze the coexistence of LTE and Wi-Fi, including throughput, access probability, and collision probability. Our study and [18] share the observation of the change in throughput as the number of STA varies. In [19], an optimal detector for detecting Wi-Fi APs is designed based on second-order statistics (SOS) of orthogonal frequency-division multiplexing (OFDM) signals and using the singular value decomposition (SVD) method. Theoretical expressions are derived for the detection and the false alarm probabilities. The flexible carrier sensing adaptive transmission (CSAT) framework and algorithm are designed for spectrum access and sharing. In [20], a coexistence model of LTE and Wi-Fi with two virtual zones is suggested. The inner zone is the secondary zone, which represents Wi-Fi with an unlicensed spectrum and the outer zone is the primary zone, which represents LTE with a licensed spectrum. The numerical solution of the model is presented using MOSEL-2 simulation and the mathematical solution is derived to validate the model. A threshold minimum bit rate established the user admission. Samy et al. [21] address the detection of selfish behaviors in Wi-Fi/LTE coexistence environments, such as the tamping of the back-off mechanism, traffic class parameters, the clear channel access (CCA) threshold, and others. Their approach applies correlation-based signal detection to accurately infer the operational parameters of LTE transmissions without decoding. The researches mentioned above have their contributions. However, many of the proposed mechanisms sacrifice Wi-Fi users when facing a dilemma in improving fairness or increasing the throughput.

3. The Time-Division Multiplexing Problem

Aimed at improving the spectrum utilization of the unlicensed bands by following LTE-Unlicensed (LTE-U), this article contributes to the determination of the optimal time ratio, δ, for the time-division multiplexing of LTE and Wi-Fi over unlicensed bands. We explain the typical environments this study intended and formulate the finding of the optimal δ value as a one-dimensional mixed integer programming problem.

3.1. System Model

HAP is equipped with both LTE and Wi-Fi communication interfaces, as shown in Figure 1. The HAP is an eNB capable of the function of Wi-Fi AP. Thus, the HAP can coordinate the spectrum allocation and manage the switching of interfaces between Wi-Fi and LTE. The Wi-Fi interface of HAP can only access the unlicensed band. In contrast, the LTE interface of the HAP can access both licensed and unlicensed bands through carrier aggregation technology.

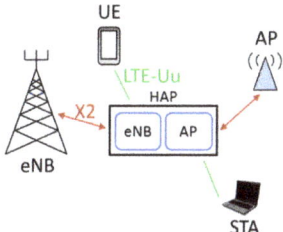

Figure 1. Hyper access point (HAP) architecture.

The scenario for the coexistence of Wi-Fi and LTE in an indoor environment is shown in Figure 2. In this scenario, there is one LTE eNB, N_{UE} LTE users, N_{HAP} hyper-APs, N_{AP} access points, and N_{STA} Wi-Fi stations. We employ a new wireless AP architecture called Hyper-AP (HAP) [15,16]. There are two types of Wi-Fi stations, namely QSTA and non-QoS STA, depending on whether they have QoS support. Among the N_{STA} Wi-Fi stations, there are N_{QSTA} QSTAs.

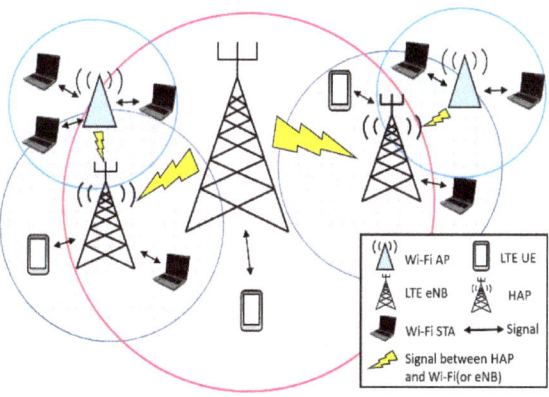

Figure 2. A scenario of a coexistence environment.

To be consistent with the LTE-U standard, this paper adopts the concept of carrier sense adaptive transmission (CSAT) to control the time-division multiplexing between LTE and Wi-Fi. The LTE-U standard, proposed by Qualcomm, enables LTE users and Wi-Fi stations to effectively and fairly access the unlicensed band. An unlicensed band can be divided into repeated Repetition Intervals in the time domain. Each repetition interval can be further divided into a contention period (CP) and a contention-free period (CFP), as shown in Figure 3. LTE users are allowed to access the unlicensed band during the contention-free period with the point coordination function (PCF) mechanism. On the other hand, Wi-Fi stations can transmit data using the traditional CSMA/CA mechanism during the contention period. The length of the repetition interval is denoted by L in Figure 3. We denote the ratio of the CP to the repetition interval by δ. That is, $\delta = CP/L$. The ratio for the contention-free period is then $(1 - \delta) = CFP/L$.

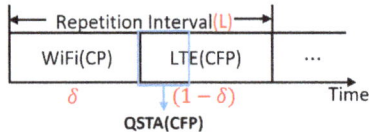

Figure 3. Repetition interval.

3.2. Problem Formulation

The objective of this study is to achieve good throughput performance without compromising the fairness between LTE users and Wi-Fi stations. Therefore, the utility function is defined as the sum of the weighted throughputs of Wi-Fi and LTE subject to constraints that both Wi-Fi and LTE can meet their QoS requirements. The optimization problem is formulated as follows:

$$\max_{\delta} U(\delta) = \mathbb{E}\{\alpha \cdot Throughput_{WiFi} + (1-\alpha) \cdot Throughput_{LTE}\} \quad (1a)$$

Subject to the following constraints:

$$Throughput_i^{WiFi} \geq Throughput_{th}^{WiFi}, \forall \text{ Wi-Fi station } i \quad (1b)$$

$$T_j^{LTE} \cdot \mathbb{E}\left(s_j^{LTE}\right) \geq s_{th}^{LTE}, \forall \text{ LTE user } j \quad (1c)$$

$$P(d < D | N_{STA}) \geq P_{th} \quad (1d)$$

$$0 \leq \alpha, \delta \leq 1 \quad (1e)$$

where $Throughput_{WiFi}$ is the throughput of all Wi-Fi stations; $Throughput_{LTE}$ is the throughput of all LTE users; $Throughput_i^{WiFi}$ denotes the throughput of Wi-Fi station i; $Throughput_{th}^{WiFi}$ refers to the throughput threshold of Wi-Fi station; T_j^{LTE} means the duration that LTE user j can access the unlicensed band; $\mathbb{E}\left(s_j^{LTE}\right)$ represents the expected throughput of LTE user j; s_{th}^{LTE} symbolizes the throughput threshold of LTE users; $P(d < D | N_{STA})$ is the probability that a Wi-Fi station transmits successfully with a transmission delay d less than a maximum saturation delay D when the number of stations is N_{STA}; P_{th} represents the threshold of successful transmission probability of Wi-Fi stations; α is the weight assigned to Wi-Fi throughput.

The constraint (1b) assures that the throughput of Wi-Fi station i must be above a certain threshold $Throughput_{th}^{WiFi}$. The throughput of Wi-Fi station i is defined as (2).

$$Throughput_i^{WiFi} = \delta \cdot L \cdot P\Big(d < D | N_{STA}\Big) \cdot \mathbb{E}\left(s_i^{WiFi}\right) \quad (2)$$

where $\mathbb{E}\left(s_i^{WiFi}\right)$ is the expected throughput of Wi-Fi station i. Constraint (1c) assures that the throughput of LTE user j must be larger than a certain threshold s_{th}^{LTE}. Constraint (1d) guarantees that the successful transmission probability of Wi-Fi stations must be above a certain threshold. Constraint (1e) represents that the value of α and δ is between 0 and 1.

4. The Proposed Scheme

In our approach, we improve the concept of carrier sense adaptive transmission (CSAT), which performs time-division multiplexing between LTE and Wi-Fi to share the same unlicensed spectrum. More specifically, we evaluate the upper and lower bounds of the time ratio, δ, of the multiplexing according to the traffic demands of LTE and Wi-Fi. We can then decide on an optimal δ value by optimizing a utility function considering both Wi-Fi's minimal QoS requirements and the total throughput.

The contention-free period (CFP) is exploited and modified compared to the LTE-U standard to support the Wi-Fi system's QoS provisioning and resolve the bias problem of the CSAT mechanism towards LTE networks. It is not solely reserved for LTE users but is further divided into two sub-intervals. The first subinterval is to provide a contention-free operation for Wi-Fi QSTAs. During the first sub-interval, QSTAs can access the unlicensed band by a PCF polling mechanism. The second CFP subinterval is LTE users' turn to access the unlicensed band. If no LTE users would like to access the resource, Wi-Fi stations can access the resource during the entire repetition interval. Therefore, the adjustment of the lengths of CP and CFP is the core issue of this study. For example, assuming that the transmission time for a polled QSTA is T_{QSTA}, the duration that N_{QSTA} of QSTAs would need $T_{QSTA} \cdot N_{QSTA}$ in the CFP sub-interval if we want to guarantee that all QSTAs can be served as in Figure 3.

The procedure for LTE eNB to utilize the unlicensed band is as follows. If the eNB wants to deliver packets using the unlicensed band, firstly, it performs channel detection to select the least utilized channel. The nearby HAP informs the Wi-Fi AP using the selected channel. Then, based on the QoS requirement of Wi-Fi and the traffic demands of LTE, the Wi-Fi AP calculates an adequate δ to maximize the total throughput and maintain fairness in the meantime. The δ value will be passed back to the LTE eNB through HAP. As the eNB receives the δ information, it can decide the start and end time of the CFP duration to access the unlicensed band.

Figure 4 shows the procedure for finding the optimal δ in our approach. First, we define the utility function and some constraints which need to be satisfied. We calculate the transmission probability and throughput threshold of Wi-Fi stations. Next, the lower bound of δ can be obtained using the constraints and threshold of Wi-Fi stations. The upper bound of δ can be obtained by exercising the user filtering mechanism. By substituting all feasible solutions into the utility function, the solution maximizing the utility function is the optimal value of δ. In the following, we explain successful access probability, threshold adjustment, lower and upper bounds of δ, user filtering mechanism, and time complexity in detail.

4.1. Successful Access Probability of Wi-Fi Stations

In the subsection, we examine the successful access probability of Wi-Fi stations. In Wi-Fi systems, stations compete with each other for the channel access opportunity to transmit packets. The station will invoke a back-off mechanism if the channel is busy or a transmission collision occurs. The back-off process will continue until the station successfully sends a packet or reaches the maximal number of retransmissions.

The above situation is called the saturation back-off mechanism, as shown in Figure 5. Assume that a station's packet transmission experiences a back-off delay d smaller than the maximal saturation back-off, D. We denote the probability as $P(d < D)$, where d is the back-off delay [22]. After this interval, the packet can be successfully transmitted. Therefore, the Wi-Fi successful transmission probability can be defined as the probability that $d < D$, as indicated in (3).

$$P(d< D \mid N_{STA}) = \sum_{i=0}^{Ry} \sum_{j=0}^{W_i} P(d < D \mid i\, col,\, j\, slots) \cdot P(j\, slots \mid i\, col) \cdot P(i\, col) \qquad (3)$$

where Ry is the retry limit and $W_i = \sum_{k=0}^{i}(CW_k - 1)$ is the accumulated size of the contention window for the i-th retransmission.

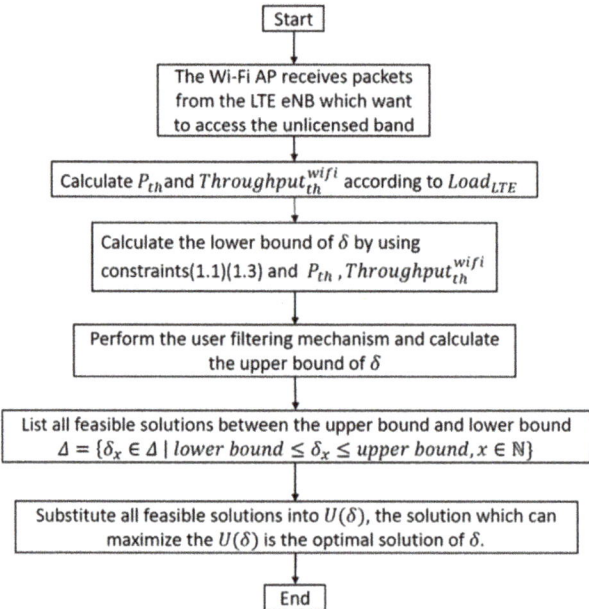

Figure 4. Flow chart for the evaluation of an optimal δ.

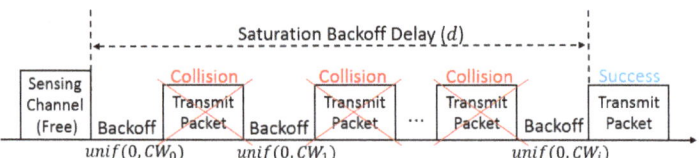

Figure 5. The saturation back-off delay.

During the saturation back-off delay d, collisions may happen i times. The whole backoff procedure may take the total number of j slots which is the sum of the number of slots for each backoff before succeeded transmission. As a result, the probability of the successful transmission of Wi-Fi in (3) can be divided into three parts. $P(i\, col)$ represents the probability of i collision. $P(j\, slots \mid i\, col)$ represents the probability that the sum-up numbers of back-off slots are equal to j when there are i collisions. $P(d < D \mid i\, col,\, j\, slots)$ is the probability of $d < D$ with i collisions and j back-off slots [11]. The detailed derivation and evaluation of these terms are given in Appendix A.

The probability given in (3) serves as an important indicator regarding the loading of the Wi-Fi system. It will be used to decide on an adequate δ value to optimize the time-division multiplexing between LTE and Wi-Fi.

4.2. Wi-Fi Threshold Adjustment

To make the coexistence of LTE and Wi-Fi more flexible, we dynamically adjust the P_{th} and $Throughput_{th}^{WiFi}$, as shown in Figure 6. When the LTE eNB is heavily loaded, we would like to improve LTE users' opportunity to access the unlicensed band. Therefore, we examine if we can relax the restrictions on P_{th} and $Throughput_{th}^{WiFi}$. Conversely, if the loading of the LTE eNB is not heavy, there is no need to lower the thresholds. However, the premise of the above adjustment is that the Wi-Fi AP is not heavily loaded, such that the QoS requirements of the Wi-Fi system can be ensured.

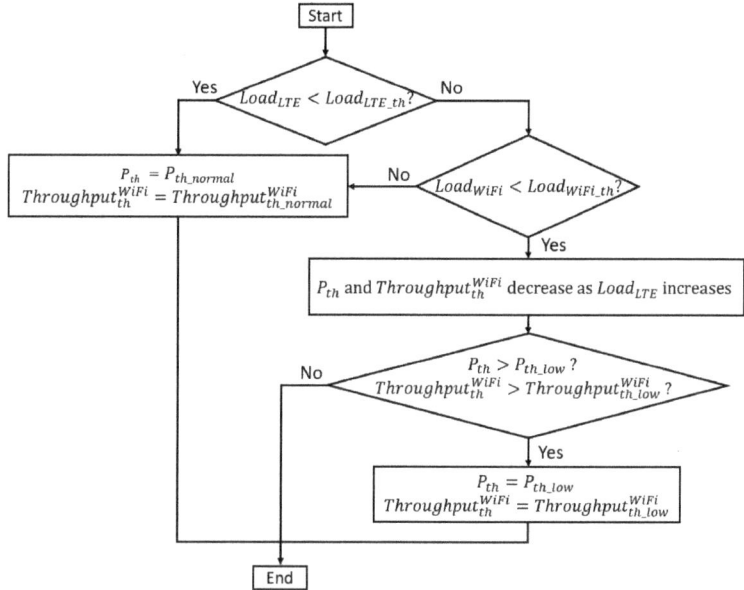

Figure 6. Evaluation of the threshold of time-division.

The load of LTE eNB is denoted as ρ_n, which is defined as the ratio of the number of resource blocks (RBs) requested by users to the total number of RBs available from eNB n, as shown in (4).

$$\rho_n = \frac{1}{N_{PRB}} \sum_{x=1}^{N_{UE}} \frac{D_x}{R(SINR_x)} \quad (4)$$

where N_{PRB} means the total number of RBs in eNB n; N_{UE} is the number of LET users; D_x represents the number of RBs requested by user x; $R(SINR_x)$ denotes the transmission rate per RB for user x.

When the load of LTE eNB is not high, the threshold of P_{th}, and $Throughput_{th}^{WiFi}$ are set to normal, i.e., $P_{th} = P_{th\_normal}$ and $Throughput_{th}^{WiFi} = Throughput_{th\_normal}^{WiFi}$. P_{th_normal} and $Throughput_{th\_normal}^{WiFi}$ are the normal threshold of successful transmission probability and the normal throughput threshold of Wi-Fi AP when the load of Wi-Fi AP is not highly. If the load of LTE exceeds the threshold, we would examine the load of Wi-Fi. If the Wi-Fi is not heavily loaded, the Wi-Fi threshold can be dynamically adjusted according to the overloading of LTE, as in (5) and (6).

$$P_{th} = P_{th\_normal} \times \left(1 - \left(Load_{LTE} - Load_{LTE_{normal}}\right)\right) \quad (5)$$

$$Throughput_{th}^{WiFi} = Throughput_{th\_normal}^{WiFi} \times \left(1 - \left(Load_{LTE} - Load_{LTE_{normal}}\right)\right) \quad (6)$$

In the dynamic adaptation of the P_{th} and $Throughput_{th}^{WiFi}$, the minimum allowed values are P_{th_low} and $Throughput_{th\_low}^{WiFi}$, which represent the lowest threshold of successful transmission probability and the lowest throughput threshold of WiFi, respectively.

4.3. Lower Bound and Upper Bound of δ

According to the utility function $U(\delta)$ defined in (1), we would like to find the lower and upper bounds of δ, which is the ratio of transmission duration for WiFi stations and LTE users. As described in the previous sub-section, we can get the $Throughput_{th}^{WiFi}$ dynamically in response to the loading change of LTE. After the threshold is obtained, the lower bound of δ will be calculated.

First, considering the constraints (1b) and (2), we can substitute (2) into the constraint (1b) and obtain one of the lower bound conditions of δ, as in (7), which is deduced as follows:

$$Throughput_i^{WiFi} = \delta \cdot L \cdot P(d < D | N_{STA}) \cdot \mathbb{E}(s_i^{WiFi}) \geq Throughput_{th}^{WiFi}$$
$$\Rightarrow \delta \geq \frac{Throughput_{th}^{WiFi}}{L \cdot P(d < D | N_{STA}) \cdot \mathbb{E}(s_i^{WiFi})} \tag{7}$$

According to the explanation in Appendix A, we can get a D^*, which is the minimum duration satisfying the successful transmission constraint (1d). That is, the contention period, $D = \delta \times L$, must be greater than or equal to D^* to satisfy the threshold of successful transmission probability. We now have the following second bound:

$$\delta \geq \frac{D^*}{L} \tag{8}$$

Moreover, $0 \leq \delta \leq 1$, we finally have the lower bound of δ, given in (9).

$$\delta \geq \min\left\{1, \max\left\{\frac{Throughput_{th}^{WiFi}}{L \cdot P(d < D | N_{STA}) \cdot \mathbb{E}(s_i^{WiFi})}, \frac{D^*}{L}\right\}\right\} \tag{9}$$

Under the same concept, the upper bound of the time interval ratio δ can be derived. The constraint on LTE throughput is given in (1c), that is, $T_j^{LTE} \geq \frac{s_{th}^{LTE}}{\mathbb{E}(s_j^{LTE})}$. During the contention-free period of a repetition interval, the sub-period at the front is for the QoS-STAs (QSTAs) to access the channel resources. Assume that there are N_{QSTA} QSTAs in the environment. The sum of the polling time for each QSTA plus the longest transmission time is T_{QSTA}. Therefore, $T_{QSTA} \cdot N_{QSTA}$ is the longest duration that the channel is occupied by the Wi-Fi PCF mechanism. In each repetition interval, for all LTE users, the total time to access the unlicensed band is the competition-free period subtracted by the time interval occupied by the PCF mechanism, as follows:

$$\sum_{j=1}^{N_{UE}} T_j^{LTE} = (1 - \delta) \cdot L - T_{QSTA} \cdot N_{QSTA} \tag{10}$$

The upper bound of δ can be obtained by using (10) and satisfying (1c) as shown in (11).

$$\delta \leq 1 - \left(\sum_{j=1}^{N_{UE}} \frac{s_{th}^{LTE}}{\mathbb{E}(s_j^{LTE})} + T_{QSTA} \cdot N_{QSTA}\right) \times \frac{1}{L} \tag{11}$$

Since the upper bound of δ varies with the number of LTE users, the LTE user filtering mechanism described in the following subsection is used to limit the number of LTE users. Finally, we can combine the calculated upper and lower bound of δ, i.e., Equations (9) and (11), to obtain the interval of the feasible solution of the time ratio δ, as shown in (12).

$$\min\left\{1, \max\left\{\frac{Throughput_{th}^{WiFi}}{L \cdot P(d<D|N_{STA}) \cdot \mathbb{E}(s_i^{WiFi})}, \frac{D^*}{L}\right\}\right\} \leq \delta$$
$$\leq 1 - \left(\sum_{j=1}^{N_{UE}} \frac{s_{th}^{LTE}}{\mathbb{E}(s_j^{LTE})} + T_{QSTA} \cdot N_{QSTA}\right) \times \frac{1}{L} \quad (12)$$

In the previous subsection, we calculated the lower bound of δ by using Wi-Fi stations' successful transmission probability and throughput requirement. Therefore, the length of CFP in a repetition interval should not be less than this limit. We also use the minimum demands of QSTA users to calculate the upper bound of δ. However, the minimum resource requirement of LTE is based on the sum of the minimum requirements of each LTE user who uses the unlicensed band as in constraint (1c). When the LTE demand is too high, the upper bound of δ in (11) may be lower than the lower bound in (9). Therefore, we propose a filtering mechanism to prevent this situation. After calculating the upper and lower bounds of δ in each round, if the upper bound is less than the lower bound, the user filtering mechanism will be invoked to confine the number of LTE users who can access the unlicensed band in each round. Then the best time ratio δ can be found by the utility function. The concept is illustrated in Figure 7.

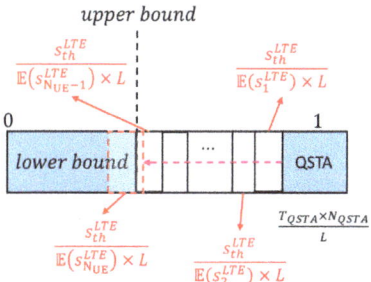

Figure 7. The occupation time proportion for user filtering mechanism.

4.4. User Filtering Mechanism

To screen LTE users for admission control of the unlicensed band, it is necessary to sort the LTE users by their access priority. The LTE users who need to transmit timing-sensitive packets, such as voice over IP (VoIP), are assigned the highest priority. The next priority is for LTE users located at the cell's edge or with an inferior signal to interference plus noise ratio (SINR). According to the above priority classification, all LTE users are roughly classified into different classes. and we assume there are C priority classes. Then in each class, the priority of each user will be ordered by its minimum bandwidth requirement. After the LTE user precedence is settled, the upper bound of δ can be adjusted accordingly.

Firstly, the upper bound of δ is initialized to 1. In the contention-free period, the Wi-Fi QSTAs have the highest priority to access the channel. Therefore, before considering the LTE users, the upper bound of δ should be subtracted by $\frac{T_{QSTA} \cdot N_{QSTA}}{L}$, which is the ratio occupied by Wi-Fi QSTAs. After that, for each additional LTE user j, the upper bound of δ must be recalculated by subtracting $\frac{s_{th}^{LTE}}{\mathbb{E}(s_j^{LTE}) \cdot L}$, which is the resource quota used by LTE user j. If the value of the upper bound is not less than the value of the lower bound, the user can access the unlicensed band and continue the filtering scheme to find the next user in the same class. As illustrated in Figure 8, when considering the LTE users by the priority order one by one, the upper bound of δ will approach the lower bound. If no other users are allowed to access the unlicensed band in the class, then we switch to the next priority category and continue the filtering process. If all categories have been filtered, no additional LTE users can be selected. The remaining LTE users are not allowed to access the unlicensed band, and the upper bound of the δ is obtained.

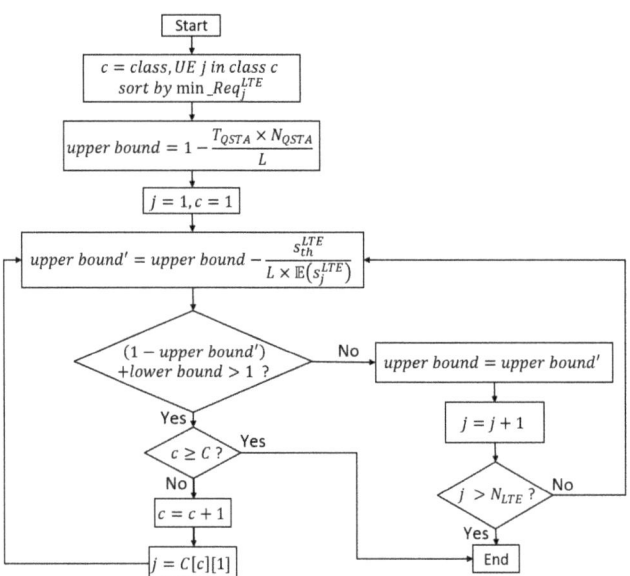

Figure 8. User filtering mechanism flow chart.

4.5. Determination of the Optimal δ

Next, we will explain how to find out the optimal solution of δ. The physical resource block (PRB) is the minimum time unit that an LTE device can use. It is 180 kHz wide in frequency and 0.5 ms long (1 slot) in time. The contention-free period, during which LTE users can access the unlicensed band, must be a multiple of T_{slot}, as follows:

$$(1-\delta) \cdot L = x \cdot T_{slot}, \ x \in \mathbb{N} \tag{13}$$

In (12), we can obtain the upper and lower bounds of δ which limits the possible solution of δ. According to (13), a feasible solution is a set of points within δ's upper and lower bounds. We denoted this set by Δ. We examine the utility values for all points in Δ. The optimal δ maximizing the utility function can be found by comparing all the calculated values. This is essential for a one-dimensional mixed integer programming problem. The process for finding the optimal δ is given in Algorithm 1.

Algorithm 1: Determination of the Optimal δ

1:                                //List all feasible solutions between the upper and lower limits
2:     $\Delta = \{\delta_x \in \Delta \mid lower\ bound \leq \delta_x \leq upper\ bound, x \in \mathbb{N}\}$
3:     **Initial**: $U = 0$
4:     **for** $x = 1; x \leq \text{sizeof}(\Delta); x$++ **do**
5:         $U' = U(\delta_x)$
6:         **if** $U' > U$ **then**
7:             $U = U'$
8:             $opt = x$
9:         **end if**
10:    **end for**
11:    δ_{opt} is the optimal solution.

$$\min\left\{1, \max\left\{\frac{Throughput_{th}^{WiFi}}{L \cdot P(d<D|N_{STA}) \cdot \mathbb{E}(s_i^{WiFi})}, \frac{D^*}{L}\right\}\right\} \leq \delta$$
$$\leq 1 - \left(\sum_{j=1}^{N_{UE}} \frac{s_{th}^{LTE}}{\mathbb{E}(s_j^{LTE})} + T_{QSTA} \cdot N_{QSTA}\right) \times \frac{1}{L} \quad (12)$$

In the previous subsection, we calculated the lower bound of δ by using Wi-Fi stations' successful transmission probability and throughput requirement. Therefore, the length of CFP in a repetition interval should not be less than this limit. We also use the minimum demands of QSTA users to calculate the upper bound of δ. However, the minimum resource requirement of LTE is based on the sum of the minimum requirements of each LTE user who uses the unlicensed band as in constraint (1c). When the LTE demand is too high, the upper bound of δ in (11) may be lower than the lower bound in (9). Therefore, we propose a filtering mechanism to prevent this situation. After calculating the upper and lower bounds of δ in each round, if the upper bound is less than the lower bound, the user filtering mechanism will be invoked to confine the number of LTE users who can access the unlicensed band in each round. Then the best time ratio δ can be found by the utility function. The concept is illustrated in Figure 7.

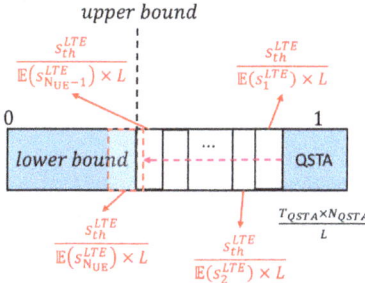

Figure 7. The occupation time proportion for user filtering mechanism.

4.4. User Filtering Mechanism

To screen LTE users for admission control of the unlicensed band, it is necessary to sort the LTE users by their access priority. The LTE users who need to transmit timing-sensitive packets, such as voice over IP (VoIP), are assigned the highest priority. The next priority is for LTE users located at the cell's edge or with an inferior signal to interference plus noise ratio (SINR). According to the above priority classification, all LTE users are roughly classified into different classes. and we assume there are C priority classes. Then in each class, the priority of each user will be ordered by its minimum bandwidth requirement. After the LTE user precedence is settled, the upper bound of δ can be adjusted accordingly.

Firstly, the upper bound of δ is initialized to 1. In the contention-free period, the Wi-Fi QSTAs have the highest priority to access the channel. Therefore, before considering the LTE users, the upper bound of δ should be subtracted by $\frac{T_{QSTA} \cdot N_{QSTA}}{L}$, which is the ratio occupied by Wi-Fi QSTAs. After that, for each additional LTE user j, the upper bound of δ must be recalculated by subtracting $\frac{s_{th}^{LTE}}{\mathbb{E}(s_j^{LTE}) \cdot L}$, which is the resource quota used by LTE user j. If the value of the upper bound is not less than the value of the lower bound, the user can access the unlicensed band and continue the filtering scheme to find the next user in the same class. As illustrated in Figure 8, when considering the LTE users by the priority order one by one, the upper bound of δ will approach the lower bound. If no other users are allowed to access the unlicensed band in the class, then we switch to the next priority category and continue the filtering process. If all categories have been filtered, no additional LTE users can be selected. The remaining LTE users are not allowed to access the unlicensed band, and the upper bound of the δ is obtained.

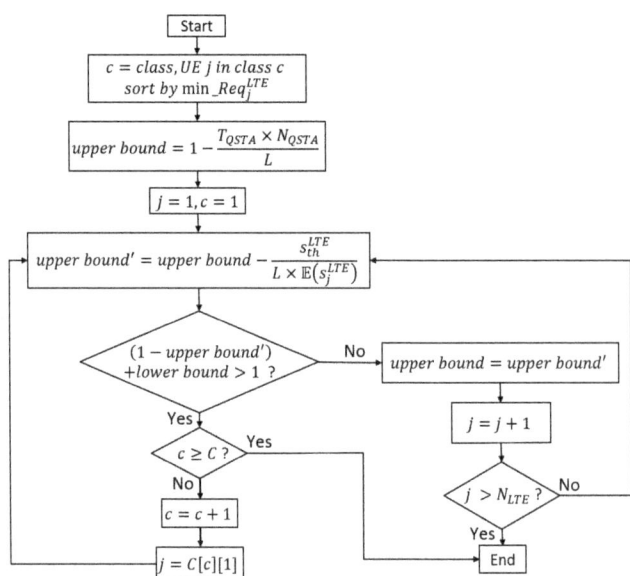

Figure 8. User filtering mechanism flow chart.

4.5. Determination of the Optimal δ

Next, we will explain how to find out the optimal solution of δ. The physical resource block (PRB) is the minimum time unit that an LTE device can use. It is 180 kHz wide in frequency and 0.5 ms long (1 slot) in time. The contention-free period, during which LTE users can access the unlicensed band, must be a multiple of T_{slot}, as follows:

$$(1-\delta) \cdot L = x \cdot T_{slot}, \; x \in \mathbb{N} \tag{13}$$

In (12), we can obtain the upper and lower bounds of δ which limits the possible solution of δ. According to (13), a feasible solution is a set of points within δ's upper and lower bounds. We denoted this set by Δ. We examine the utility values for all points in Δ. The optimal δ maximizing the utility function can be found by comparing all the calculated values. This is essential for a one-dimensional mixed integer programming problem. The process for finding the optimal δ is given in Algorithm 1.

Algorithm 1: Determination of the Optimal δ

1: //List all feasible solutions between the upper and lower limits
2: $\Delta = \{\delta_x \in \Delta \,|\, lower\ bound \leq \delta_x \leq upper\ bound,\ x \in \mathbb{N}\}$
3: Initial: $U = 0$
4: for $x = 1; x \leq sizeof(\Delta); x$++ do
5:      $U' = U(\delta_x)$
6:      if $U' > U$ then
7:          $U = U'$
8:          $opt = x$
9:      end if
10: end for
11: δ_{opt} is the optimal solution.

$$\min\left\{1, \max\left\{\frac{Throughput_{th}^{WiFi}}{L \cdot P(d<D|N_{STA}) \cdot \mathbb{E}(s_i^{WiFi})}, \frac{D^*}{L}\right\}\right\} \leq \delta$$
$$\leq 1 - \left(\sum_{j=1}^{N_{UE}} \frac{s_{th}^{LTE}}{\mathbb{E}(s_j^{LTE})} + T_{QSTA} \cdot N_{QSTA}\right) \times \frac{1}{L} \quad (12)$$

In the previous subsection, we calculated the lower bound of δ by using Wi-Fi stations' successful transmission probability and throughput requirement. Therefore, the length of CFP in a repetition interval should not be less than this limit. We also use the minimum demands of QSTA users to calculate the upper bound of δ. However, the minimum resource requirement of LTE is based on the sum of the minimum requirements of each LTE user who uses the unlicensed band as in constraint (1c). When the LTE demand is too high, the upper bound of δ in (11) may be lower than the lower bound in (9). Therefore, we propose a filtering mechanism to prevent this situation. After calculating the upper and lower bounds of δ in each round, if the upper bound is less than the lower bound, the user filtering mechanism will be invoked to confine the number of LTE users who can access the unlicensed band in each round. Then the best time ratio δ can be found by the utility function. The concept is illustrated in Figure 7.

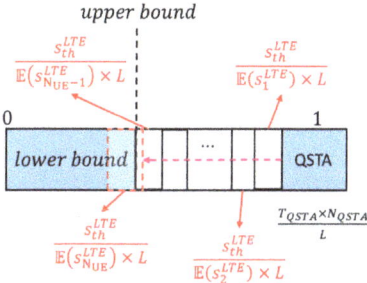

Figure 7. The occupation time proportion for user filtering mechanism.

4.4. User Filtering Mechanism

To screen LTE users for admission control of the unlicensed band, it is necessary to sort the LTE users by their access priority. The LTE users who need to transmit timing-sensitive packets, such as voice over IP (VoIP), are assigned the highest priority. The next priority is for LTE users located at the cell's edge or with an inferior signal to interference plus noise ratio (SINR). According to the above priority classification, all LTE users are roughly classified into different classes. and we assume there are C priority classes. Then in each class, the priority of each user will be ordered by its minimum bandwidth requirement. After the LTE user precedence is settled, the upper bound of δ can be adjusted accordingly.

Firstly, the upper bound of δ is initialized to 1. In the contention-free period, the Wi-Fi QSTAs have the highest priority to access the channel. Therefore, before considering the LTE users, the upper bound of δ should be subtracted by $\frac{T_{QSTA} \cdot N_{QSTA}}{L}$, which is the ratio occupied by Wi-Fi QSTAs. After that, for each additional LTE user j, the upper bound of δ must be recalculated by subtracting $\frac{s_{th}^{LTE}}{\mathbb{E}(s_j^{LTE}) \cdot L}$, which is the resource quota used by LTE user j. If the value of the upper bound is not less than the value of the lower bound, the user can access the unlicensed band and continue the filtering scheme to find the next user in the same class. As illustrated in Figure 8, when considering the LTE users by the priority order one by one, the upper bound of δ will approach the lower bound. If no other users are allowed to access the unlicensed band in the class, then we switch to the next priority category and continue the filtering process. If all categories have been filtered, no additional LTE users can be selected. The remaining LTE users are not allowed to access the unlicensed band, and the upper bound of the δ is obtained.

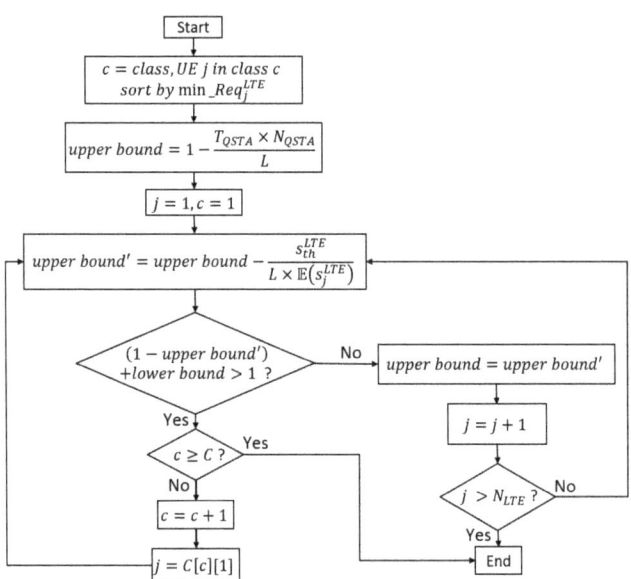

Figure 8. User filtering mechanism flow chart.

4.5. Determination of the Optimal δ

Next, we will explain how to find out the optimal solution of δ. The physical resource block (PRB) is the minimum time unit that an LTE device can use. It is 180 kHz wide in frequency and 0.5 ms long (1 slot) in time. The contention-free period, during which LTE users can access the unlicensed band, must be a multiple of T_{slot}, as follows:

$$(1-\delta) \cdot L = x \cdot T_{slot}, \ x \in \mathbb{N} \tag{13}$$

In (12), we can obtain the upper and lower bounds of δ which limits the possible solution of δ. According to (13), a feasible solution is a set of points within δ's upper and lower bounds. We denoted this set by Δ. We examine the utility values for all points in Δ. The optimal δ maximizing the utility function can be found by comparing all the calculated values. This is essential for a one-dimensional mixed integer programming problem. The process for finding the optimal δ is given in Algorithm 1.

Algorithm 1: Determination of the Optimal δ

1:     //List all feasible solutions between the upper and lower limits
2:     $\Delta = \{\delta_x \in \Delta \,|\, lower\ bound \leq \delta_x \leq upper\ bound, \ x \in \mathbb{N}\}$
3:     **Initial**: $U = 0$
4:     **for** $x = 1; x \leq \text{sizeof}(\Delta); x++$ **do**
5:         $U' = U(\delta_x)$
6:         **if** $U' > U$ **then**
7:             $U = U'$
8:             $opt = x$
9:         **end if**
10:    **end for**
11:    δ_{opt} is the optimal solution.

4.6. Time Complexity

We analyze the time complexity of the coexistence mechanism proposed in this paper. According to the optimization process for δ, as shown in Figure 5, we list the time complexity of each step.

First, we will determine the throughput threshold P_{th} and transmission probability threshold $Throughput_{th}^{WiFi}$ of Wi-Fi based on the load of LTE eNB and Wi-Fi AP. Assuming that there are n LTE users in the environment, the time complexity of calculating the load of LTE eNB is $O(n)$, and the time complexity of determining the threshold of Wi-Fi stations is $O(1)$. Therefore, the time complexity of the step is $O(n)$. The next step is to compute the lower bound of δ according to the throughput threshold P_{th} of Wi-Fi. To do this, we need to calculate the successful transmission probability of Wi-Fi stations, $P(d < D \mid N_{STA})$. Suppose that the maximum retry limit is R and the number of STA is m, the loop that calculates the successful transmission probability will execute $\sum_{i=0}^{R}\sum_{j=0}^{CW_0*(2^{i+1}-1)}\sum_{l=0}^{c}\sum_{k=0}^{i} 1$ times, where CW_0 represents the initial size of the contention window, and c denotes a constant count for sampling the probability in (5). The complexity of calculating the lower bound of δ is equal to the complexity of calculating the successful transmission probability of Wi-Fi stations. In computing $P(d < D \mid N_{STA})$ of (3), the time complexity is $O(R2^R)$ as in (5).

The procedure of finding out the upper bound of δ is to sum up the throughput of all LTE users. Therefore, the complexity of this part is $O(n)$. On the other hand, when considering the user filtering mechanism, there are two parts to the procedure. The first part is to sort all the LTE users according to their assigned priorities using the Quicksort algorithm. Therefore, the complexity is $O(n \log n)$. The second part is simply filtering the sorted users in which the complexity is $O(n)$. Thus, the complexity of performing the user filtering mechanism is $O(n \log n)$.

Finally, we can get the list of all feasible solutions between the upper and lower bounds. All these feasible solutions will be substituted into the utility function and find out the optimal δ which maximizes the utility function. The complexity of finding the optimal δ is $O(n)$.

According to the above analysis, the most time-consuming procedure is the calculation of the successful transmission probability of Wi-Fi stations and performing the LTE user filtering mechanism. Therefore, the time complexity of the coexistence mechanism proposed in this paper is $\max\{O(R2^R), O(n \log n)\}$.

5. Performance Evaluation

In this paper, we use MATLAB to simulate the performance of the proposed mechanism. We will compare our approach with NBS, LAA, and LTE-U. The simulation environment and the setting of parameters refer to [3,16,23] for NBS, LAA, and LTE-U, respectively. Table 1 lists related parameter settings in our simulations. In the LAA simulation, the four functions of LAA are fully emulated. We simply set the carrier sense adaptive transmission (CSAT) period for the LTE-U simulation to the repeating interval.

The repetition interval is set according to [16]. Regardless of the value of δ, the longer the repetition interval is, the longer the contention period (CP) and the contention-free period (CFP) are. The length of the repetition interval will not have a critical impact on LTE users because the licensed band is available for the LTE users during the contention-free period. However, the Wi-Fi stations can only access the resource on the unlicensed band. Therefore, when the contention-free period (CFP) increases, the packet transmission delay will also increase accordingly for the Wi-Fi stations. On the contrary, if the repetition interval is too short, the coexistence mechanism will be performed frequently, leading to high overhead. In our simulation, the repetition interval is set to 100 ms [16].

Table 1. Simulation parameters.

Parameter	Value
Number of eNBs	1
Number of HAPs	10
Number of Wi-Fi APs	10
Radius of eNB	120 m
Radius of HAP	60 m
Radius of AP	30 m
Transmit power on licensed band	30 dBm
Transmit power on unlicensed band	24 dBm
The bandwidth of licensed band	10 MHz
The bandwidth of unlicensed band	20 MHz
Path loss model	LTE : $140.7 + 36.7 \times \log_{10} d$ WiFi: ITU InH [13]
Number of LET users	20–60
Number of Wi-Fi stations	5–25
Min. contention window	16
Max. contention window	1024
α	0.5
$P_{th\_normal}^{WiFi}$	0.8
$Throughput_{th\_normal}$	2 Mbps
Repetition Interval	100 ms

Previously, we defined a utility function with which the weighting factor α decides the relative weightings of the throughputs of Wi-Fi and LTE systems. The setting of α will affect the individual throughput of Wi-Fi and LTE systems. Intuitively, the optimal value of δ is also affected by the settings of α. We would like to know the impact of the setting of α on the resulted δ. Therefore, we simulate the following scenario to figure out the relationship between α and δ. In the scenario, there are 15 Wi-Fi stations and 50 LTE users. Generally speaking, if α is larger, the communication system is friendlier to Wi-Fi stations. LTE users get more resources if α is smaller. As shown in Figure 9, the relationship between α and δ is almost linear. When α is small, the throughput contribution of Wi-Fi stations in the utility function is also small. Therefore, the duration of accessing the unlicensed band for LTE users will be longer such that the optimal value of δ is smaller. In our scheme, the throughput thresholds will be set to meet the basic requirements for Wi-Fi and LTE systems. When we change the value of α from 0.1 to 0.9, the value of δ by the calculation mechanism is from 0.43 to 0.6, respectively. α will be set to 0.5 in subsequent experiments.

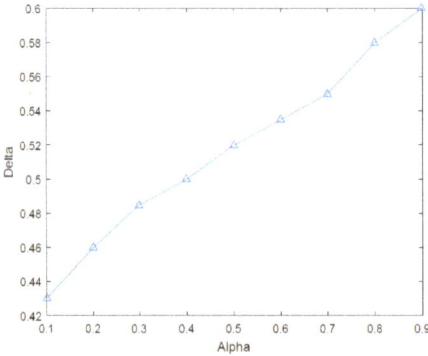

Figure 9. The δ versus weight value α.

A typical scenario in Figure 10 is used to examine the feasibility and effectiveness of the proposed scheme. In the simulation scenario, there is one LTE eNB, which is a small base station. Moreover, multiple Wi-Fi APs are deployed, and we suppose there is a HAP located between each AP and eNB serving as a bridge. We compare our approach with other well-known schemes. The overall throughput will be compared under different loading situations. To be more realistic, we change the number of LTE users and Wi-Fi stations in different experiments to observe the performance variation in typical environments. We compare the proposed scheme with other coexistence mechanisms, including the original scheme without a coexistence mechanism (denoted as original), NBS (Nash bargaining solution) [16], LAA (Licensed Assisted Access) [24,25], and LTE-U (LTE-Unlicensed) [2,5,6]. Overall throughput is the primary performance index for the comparative study.

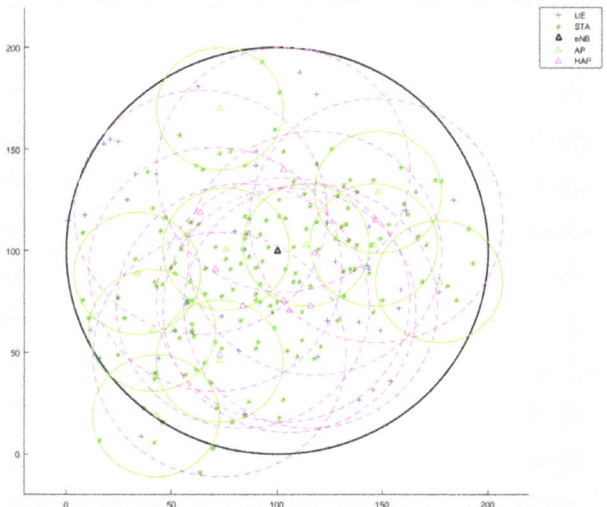

Figure 10. Simulation scenario.

Figure 11 shows the throughput of Wi-Fi and LTE using different mechanisms in a lightly loaded environment. Because of the low load environment, the throughput of the original scheme between Wi-Fi and LTE is much closer in the absence of a coexistence mechanism. When the coexistence mechanism is adopted, the throughput of Wi-Fi degrades because some resources of the unlicensed band are allocated to LTE users. On the other hand, LTE can utilize the license-free band to improve throughput. Therefore, the throughput of LTE increases significantly. Our proposed scheme is based on the utilization function to adjust the time ratio for time-division multiplexing between the Wi-Fi and LTE to maximize the overall throughput. However, the LTE performance of NBS is a little better than our proposed scheme since NBS sacrifices Wi-Fi performance. The proposed solution provides a fairer access method for Wi-Fi and LTE. Interestingly, the technology of LAA makes Wi-Fi and LTE have the same priority to access the unlicensed band. Compared with the proposed scheme, it can give more access opportunities to Wi-Fi stations in a lightly loaded situation. As a result, the throughput of Wi-Fi is better than those of other schemes. Due to the LBT mechanism, LTE users with LAA will compete with Wi-Fi stations to access the unlicensed band, which wastes bandwidth resources. Therefore, the throughput of LTE decreases dramatically. On the other end, instead of using the LBT mechanism to prevent LTE from interfering with Wi-Fi stations, NBS and our proposed scheme integrated the HAP to coordinate LTE users and Wi-Fi stations to access the unlicensed band. Doing so can avoid interference between LTE and Wi-Fi. Differently, LTE-U is based on the CSAT scheme, which can calculate a suitable duty cycle according to channel status. But without HAP to coordinate LTE users and Wi-Fi stations, Wi-Fi stations cannot know when LTE users will utilize the unlicensed band. Therefore, it will increase the collision rate in the unlicensed band, decreasing the throughput of Wi-Fi. We have a similar observation when Wi-Fi is heavily loaded.

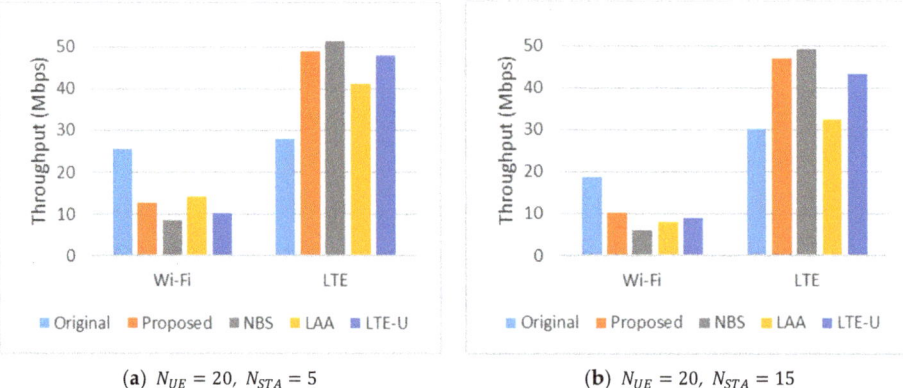

(a) $N_{UE} = 20$, $N_{STA} = 5$

(b) $N_{UE} = 20$, $N_{STA} = 15$

Figure 11. The throughput of Wi-Fi and LTE.

Table 2 presents the same experiment results from a different perspective. It is evident that the proposed scheme possesses the highest total throughput compared with other approaches, as intended. Notice that NBS has a secondary total throughput close to the proposed approach. However, NBS's fairness is inferior to the proposed scheme, as we shall see in later experiments.

Table 2. Total throughput (Mbps).

	$N_{UE} = 20$, $N_{STA} = 5$			$N_{UE} = 20$, $N_{STA} = 15$		
	Wi-Fi	LTE	Total	Wi-Fi	LTE	Total
Original	25.7	28.1	53.8	18.8	30.1	48.8
Proposed	12.7	49.0	**61.7**	10.1	47.1	**57.2**
NBS	8.6	51.4	60.0	6.1	49.1	55.2
LAA	14.1	41.1	55.2	8.1	32.4	40.5
LTE-U	10.3	48.0	58.3	9.0	43.4	52.3

To understand the effect of the number of Wi-Fi stations on the overall throughput, the number of STAs gradually increased without changing the number of LTE users. Figure 12a shows the change in the overall Wi-Fi throughput. Under the original mechanism without a coexistence mechanism, the throughput dropped rapidly with the increase in STAs. Because LAA utilizes the pure contention-based mechanism named LBT, the Wi-Fi throughput also dropped significantly due to the increment of the number of STAs. LTE-U adopts the CSAT mechanism to coexist with Wi-Fi, which can detect and analyze the number of neighboring base stations, including LTE-U base stations and Wi-Fi APs. Based on the observation, the access time will be divided into several adaptive duty cycles in which LTE users and Wi-Fi stations operate in a time-division manner such that the neighboring base stations can equally share resources. Therefore, the increase of STAs does not significantly impact the overall Wi-Fi throughput. Like LTE-U, the proposed method also finds an adequate δ value to dynamically adjust the resources that Wi-Fi can obtain. The adjustment of δ is closer to the optimal resource allocation, so it performs better than LTE-U. The NBS algorithm also calculates the period that LTE users can use the unlicensed band. The LTE users obtain more resources according to the time ratio calculated by NBS, so the Wi-Fi system's throughput performance is slightly worse.

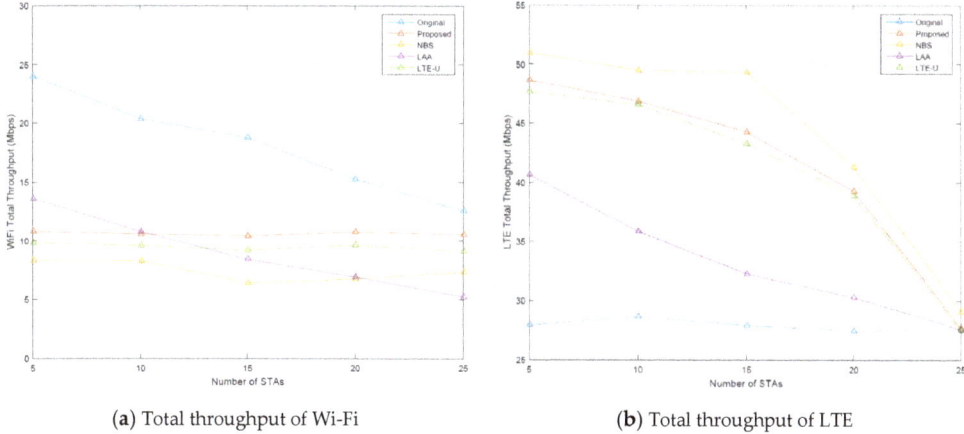

(a) Total throughput of Wi-Fi

(b) Total throughput of LTE

Figure 12. Total throughput under a different number of stations with 20 LTE users.

We also examine the performance of each scheme with heavily loaded LTE in Figure 12b. The number of LTE users is set to 50. When the LTE load is greater than the threshold $Load_{LTE\_th}$, the Wi-Fi thresholds, P_{th} and $Throughput_{th}^{WiFi}$, will be adjusted according to (5) and (6). As the load of LTE increases, the thresholds decrease to relax the conditions for LTE to use unlicensed bands. However, when the load of Wi-Fi is also very high, the Wi-Fi thresholds need to be adjusted back to normal values to protect Wi-Fi. We have results that resemble the patterns in Figure 11.

In the next experiment, the Wi-Fi load is maintained at a low level, and the LTE load varies from low to high. As can be seen from Figure 13, since the mechanism proposed in this paper focuses on fairness, it will maximize the overall throughput while meeting the minimum Wi-Fi and LTE QoS requirements. Therefore, the decline in Wi-Fi throughput will be lower than that in NBS. The throughput will decline as the number of LTE users increases until the LTE load exceeds the threshold. In this scenario, the Wi-Fi load is very low, and the number of STAs is only 5. LTE users will benefit from accessing the unlicensed band. The proposed scheme will dynamically adjust the time ratio δ when the LTE load exceeds the threshold to maximize the overall throughput. Therefore, the period for LTE to access the unlicensed band will increase, as well as the LTE throughput.

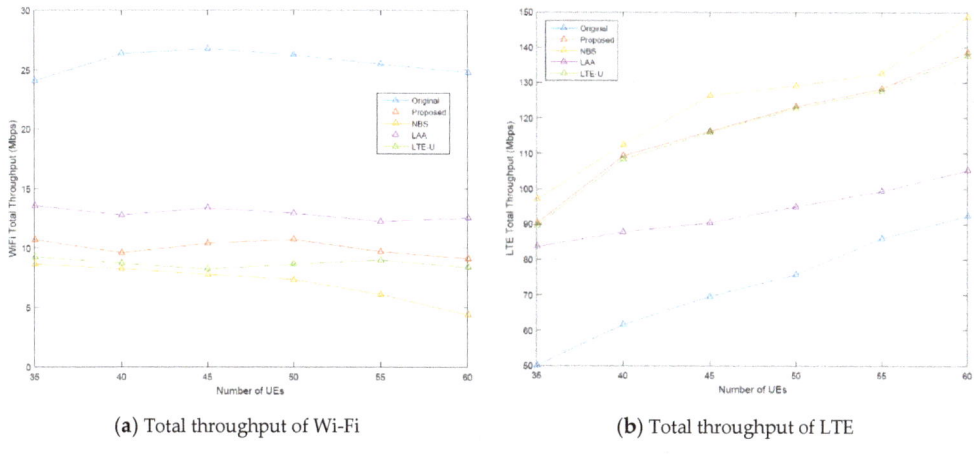

(a) Total throughput of Wi-Fi

(b) Total throughput of LTE

Figure 13. Total throughput under a different number of LTE users with 5 Wi-Fi stations.

Next, we would like to assess how friendly the coexistence mechanisms are to Wi-Fi. The fairness indices for different schemes are examined [26]. Jain's fairness index [27,28] is employed for the evaluation. The fairness index equation is given in (14).

$$F = \frac{(\sum_{i=1}^{n} x_i)^2}{n \times \sum_{i=1}^{n} x_i^2} \quad (14)$$

$$x_i = \frac{Throughput_i}{Throughput_i^{opt}} \quad (15)$$

where x_i represents the throughput proportion of entity i, which can be expressed as the user throughput divided by the optimal user throughput in the network and n is the number of LTE users and Wi-Fi stations. For Jain's fairness index, the value of this fairness index is between 0 and 1, and the larger the value is, the fairer it is.

There are 20 LTE users in this simulation, and the number of Wi-Fi stations increases from 5 to 25. The result is shown in Figure 14a. As shown in the figure, as the number of users increases, both our proposed scheme and NBS can improve the fairness index. When the number of Wi-Fi stations is small, Wi-Fi is in a light load condition. Wi-Fi stations do not need too many resources. Therefore, the thresholds of Wi-Fi remained at a relatively low level. LTE can then allocate more resources to the unlicensed band. It can significantly improve the throughput. When the Wi-Fi is lightly loaded, the difference in throughput between LTE and Wi-Fi will be significant, resulting in relatively poor fairness. As the number of Wi-Fi stations increases, Wi-Fi will ask for more resources in the unlicensed bands. The Wi-Fi throughput and the fairness index of both schemes will also improve. Our proposed scheme pays more attention to the issue of fairness. Hence, the fairness index is higher than that of NBS.

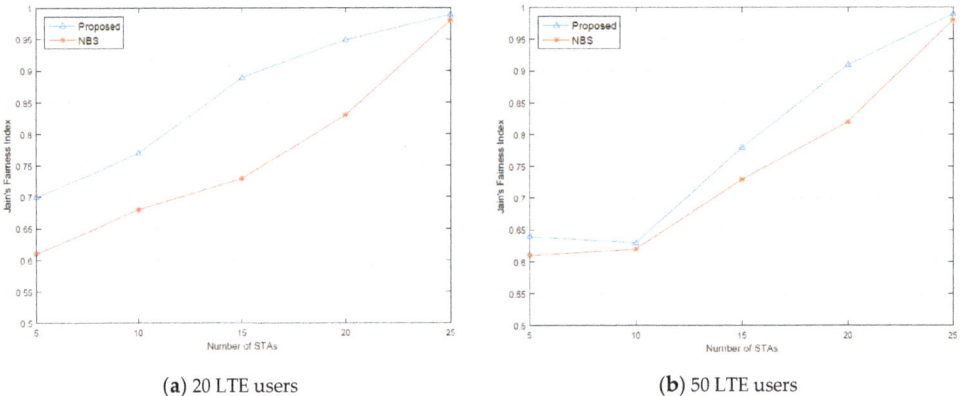

(a) 20 LTE users (b) 50 LTE users

Figure 14. Jain's Fairness Index under a different number of stations with 20 LTE users.

Figure 14b shows the change in the fairness index when the LTE is heavily loaded. There are 50 LTE users, and the number of Wi-Fi stations increased from 5 to 25. When the Wi-Fi load is light, and the LTE load is heavy, LTE will get more resources and result in a lower fairness index to maximize the overall throughput. Figure 14b shows that if the number of Wi-Fi stations is 10, the fairness index is dropped slightly in our proposed scheme compared to when the number of Wi-Fi stations is 5. The reason is that the Wi-Fi load is still not too heavy to adjust the time ratio δ to give Wi-Fi more resources. Therefore, LTE obtains more resources to maximize the overall throughput and causes a lower fairness value in this situation. As the Wi-Fi load increases, Wi-Fi stations can have more sharing of the resources according to both schemes' adjustments. The fairness index is improved. The improvement of our proposed schemes is better than that of NBS, as shown in the figure.

6. Conclusions

Due to the difference in radio access technologies, the introduction of LTE to the unlicensed band often degrades Wi-Fi performance. Moreover, the lack of communication between LTE and Wi-Fi systems is even more detrimental to the two systems' coexistence. Therefore, this study uses HAP as a relay point between LTE and Wi-Fi. Integrating the two interfaces can communicate with these two different systems. Wi-Fi can be informed when LTE wants to use the unlicensed band. Transmission abortion due to interference can be avoided. In the proposed scheme, we formalize the utility function for the overall throughput and propose an algorithm to adjust the time ratio δ of the contention period (CP) and the contention-free period (CFP) in a repetition interval such that the maximization of overall throughput can be achieved.

We simulated several scenarios to examine the proposed scheme's performance and compare it with other methods. The simulation results show that the proposed scheme outperforms others in overall throughput. When the Wi-Fi load is low, the LTE throughput can be significantly improved by utilizing the unlicensed band. Another critical issue is how friendly the coexistence mechanism is to Wi-Fi. Most previous schemes can enhance the performance of LTE while sacrificing the performance of Wi-Fi in the unlicensed band. The proposed scheme has considered the fairness issue in the coexistence of Wi-Fi and LTE. Therefore, in the last two simulations, the results show that the proposed scheme's fairness index is better than NBS by adjusting the accessing periods of Wi-Fi and LTE. We show that the proposed scheme can improve the LTE throughput and consider the fairness of the resource allocation in the unlicensed band in the coexistence of Wi-Fi and LTE.

Author Contributions: Conceptualization, W.K.L. and Y.-D.Y.; methodology, W.K.L.; software, Y.-D.Y.; validation, C.-S.S. and C.-Y.T.; formal analysis, C.-Y.T.; investigation, Y.-C.L.; resources, C.-S.S.; data curation, Y.-D.Y.; writing—original draft preparation, Y.-C.L.; writing—review and editing, C.-S.S.; visualization, C.-S.S.; supervision, W.K.L.; project administration, W.K.L.; funding acquisition, C.-S.S. All authors have read and agreed to the published version of the manuscript.

Funding: This research was partly funded by the Ministry of Science and Technology, Taiwan under the grant numbers MOST 111-2221-E-110-025 and MOST 111-2221-E-992-066.

Data Availability Statement: Not applicable.

Conflicts of Interest: The authors declare no conflict of interest.

Appendix A

$P(i\ col)$ is the probability of i collision. After the i-th collision, Wi-Fi stations can transmit the packets successfully at the $(i+1)$-th retransmission. Therefore, $P(i\ col)$ can be expressed as the probability of i collision multiplied by the probability of no collision. That is, it is the probability of the successful transmission.

$$P(i\ col) = \left(1 - (1-\tau)^{N_{STA}-1}\right)^i (1-\tau)^{N_{STA}-1} \tag{A1}$$

where τ is the probability of a Wi-Fi station transmitting packets. It can be obtained using the Markov chain [29].

$P(j\ slots\ |\ i\ col)$ represents the probability that the sum-up numbers of back-off slots are equal to j when there are i collisions [22].

$$P(j\ slots\ |\ i\ col) = P(\sum_{k=0}^{i} unif(0, CW_k - 1) = j) \tag{A2}$$

where $unif(0, CW_k - 1)$ stands for a discrete random variable uniformly distributed in the range $\{0, 1, ., CW_k - 1\}$, and CW_k represents the size of the contention window for the k-th back-off.

$P(d < D \mid i \, col, j \, slots)$ is the probability of $d < D$ with i collisions and j back-off slots [11].

$$P(d < D \mid i \, col, j \, slots) = \begin{cases} 0.5 + 0.5 \cdot \text{erf}\left(\frac{D-m_{ij}}{\sqrt{2}\sigma_{ij}}\right), & \frac{D-m_{ij}}{\sigma_{ij}} \geq 0 \\ 0.5 \cdot \text{erfc}\left(\frac{D-m_{ij}}{\sqrt{2}\sigma_{ij}}\right), & \frac{D-m_{ij}}{\sigma_{ij}} < 0 \end{cases} \quad (A3)$$

where m_{ij} is the sum of the average duration of all slot times in d_{ij}, as shown below:

$$m_{ij} = jm_n + iT_c + T_s \quad (A4)$$

where m_n is the average duration within which the Wi-Fi station does not transmit a packet, T_c is the duration of a collision and T_s is the duration of a successful transmission.

With the assumption of independence between different slot times, the standard deviation σ_{ij} can be computed according to (A5).

$$\sigma_{ij}^2 = j\delta_n^2 \quad (A5)$$

where σ_n is the standard deviation of the duration within which the Wi-Fi station does not transmit packets.

References

1. Mahmuda, R.H.; Awl, H.N.; Abdulkarim, Y.I.; Karaaslan, M.; Lancaster, M.J. Filtering two-element waveguide antenna array based on solely resonators. *Int. J. Electron. Commun. (AEÜ)* **2020**, *121*, 153232. [CrossRef]
2. Zhang, R.; Wang, M.; Cai, L.X.; Zheng, Z.; Shen, X.; Xie, L.-L. LTE-unlicensed: The future of spectrum aggregation for cellular networks. *IEEE Wirel. Commun.* **2015**, *22*, 150–159. [CrossRef]
3. Galanopoulos, A.; Foukalas, F.; Tsiftsis, T.A. Efficient Coexistence of LTE With WiFi in the Licensed and Unlicensed Spectrum Aggregation. *IEEE Trans. Cogn. Commun. Netw.* **2016**, *2*, 129–140. [CrossRef]
4. Branda, M. Introducing MulteFire: LTE-Like Performance with Wi-Fi-Like Simplicity I Qualcomm. Available online: https://www.qualcomm.com/news/onq/2015/06/introducing-multefire-lte-performance-wi-fi-simplicity (accessed on 12 July 2022).
5. Qualcomm-Making Best Use of Unlicensed Spectrum for 1000x. Qualcomm White Paper. 2015. Available online: https://gsacom.com/paper/making-best-use-of-unlicensed-spectrum-for-1000x/ (accessed on 12 July 2022).
6. Evolved Universal Terrestrial Radio Access (E-UTRA); Carrier Aggregation; Base Station (BS) Radio Transmission and Reception. 3GPP, TR 36.808. 2012. Available online: https://portal.3gpp.org/desktopmodules/Specifications/SpecificationDetails.aspx?specificationId=2487 (accessed on 12 July 2022).
7. Ericsson, Qualcomm, Huawei, and Alcatel-Lucent. Study on Licensed-Assisted Access Using LTE. RP-141664, 3GPP TSG RAN Meeting #65. 2014. Available online: https://www.3gpp.org/DynaReport/TDocExMtg--RP-65--30566.htm (accessed on 12 July 2022).
8. Rosa, C.; Kuusela, M.; Frederiksen, F.; Pedersen, K.I. Standalone LTE in Unlicensed Spectrum: Radio Challenges, Solutions, and Performance of MulteFire. *IEEE Commun. Mag.* **2018**, *56*, 170–177. [CrossRef]
9. Alsenwi, M.; Tun, Y.K.; Pandey, S.R.; Hong, C.S. A Hopfield Neural Networks Based Mechanism for Coexistence of LTE-U and WiFi Networks in Unlicensed Spectrum. In Proceedings of the 2019 20th Asia-Pacific Network Operations and Management Symposium (APNOMS), Matsue, Japan, 18–20 September 2019; pp. 1–6. [CrossRef]
10. Maglogiannis, V.; Naudts, D.; Shahid, A.; Moerman, I. A Q-Learning Scheme for Fair Coexistence Between LTE and Wi-Fi in Unlicensed Spectrum. *IEEE Access* **2018**, *6*, 27278–27293. [CrossRef]
11. Mosleh, S.; Ma, Y.; Rezac, J.D.; Coder, J.B. A Novel Machine Learning Approach to Estimating KPI and PoC for LTE-LAA-Based Spectrum Sharing. In Proceedings of the 2020 IEEE International Conference on Communications Workshops (ICC Workshops), Dublin, Ireland, 7–11 June 2020; pp. 1–6. [CrossRef]
12. Mosleh, S.; Ma, Y.; Rezac, J.D.; Coder, J.B. Dynamic Spectrum Access with Reinforcement Learning for Unlicensed Access in 5G and Beyond. In Proceedings of the 2020 IEEE 91st Vehicular Technology Conference (VTC2020-Spring), Antwerp, Belgium, 25–28 May 2020; pp. 1–7. [CrossRef]
13. Cano, C.; Leith, D.J. Coexistence of WiFi and LTE in unlicensed bands: A proportional fair allocation scheme. In Proceedings of the 2015 IEEE International Conference on Communication Workshop (ICCW), London, UK, 8–12 June 2015; pp. 2288–2293. [CrossRef]
14. He, H.; Shan, H.; Huang, A.; Cai, L.X.; Quek, T.Q.S. Proportional Fairness-Based Resource Allocation for LTE-U Coexisting with Wi-Fi. *IEEE Access* **2017**, *5*, 4720–4731. [CrossRef]
15. Chen, Q.; Yu, G.; Elmaghraby, H.M.; Hamalainen, J.; Ding, Z. Embedding LTE-U within Wi-Fi Bands for Spectrum Efficiency Improvement. *IEEE Netw.* **2017**, *31*, 72–79. [CrossRef]

16. Chen, Q.; Yu, G.; Ding, Z. Optimizing Unlicensed Spectrum Sharing for LTE-U and WiFi Network Coexistence. *IEEE J. Sel. Areas Commun.* **2016**, *34*, 2562–2574. [CrossRef]
17. Al-Khansa, R.; Artail, H. A semi-distributed LTE-WiFi system design for future LTE-unlicensed: Deployments in small-cell environments. In Proceedings of the 2015 IEEE 11th International Conference on Wireless and Mobile Computing, Networking and Communications (WiMob), Abu Dhabi, United Arab Emirates, 19–21 October 2015; pp. 43–50. [CrossRef]
18. Qin, Z.; Li, A.; Wang, H. Modeling and performance analysis of LTE coexisting with Wi-Fi. In Proceedings of the 2020 IEEE 8th International Conference on Information, Communication and Networks (ICICN), Xi'an, China, 22–25 August 2020; pp. 43–50. [CrossRef]
19. Ahmed, F.; Arslan, H. Signal statistics based multiple AP detection for smart spectrum sharing in LTE-U/Wi-Fi coexistence. In Proceedings of the 2021 IEEE 93rd Vehicular Technology Conference (VTC2021-Spring), Helsinki, Finland, 25–28 April 2021; pp. 1–5. [CrossRef]
20. Zreikat, A.I.; Alabed, S. Performance Modeling and Analysis of LTE/Wi-Fi Coexistence. *Electronics* **2022**, *11*, 1035. [CrossRef]
21. Samy, I.; Han, X.; Lazos, L.; Li, M.; Xiao, Y.; Krunz, M. Misbehavior Detection in Wi-Fi/LTE Coexistence over Unlicensed Bands. In *IEEE Transactions on Mobile Computing*; IEEE: Piscataway, NJ, USA, 2022. [CrossRef]
22. Banchs, A.; Serrano, P.; Azcorra, A. End-to-end delay analysis and admission control in 802.11 DCF WLANs. *Comput. Commun.* **2006**, *29*, 842–854. [CrossRef]
23. Alcatel-Lucent, Ericsson, Qualcomm Technologies Inc., Samsung Electronics, Verizon. LTE-U Technical Report—LTE. Technical Report. 2015. Available online: https://studylib.net/doc/18297695/lte-u-technical-report---lte (accessed on 12 July 2022).
24. *IEEE Std 802.11b-1999*; IEEE Standard for Information Technology—Telecommunications and Information Exchange between Systems—Local and Metropolitan Networks—Specific Requirements—Part 11: Wireless LAN Medium Access Control (MAC) and Physical Layer (PHY) Specifications: Higher Speed Physical Layer (PHY) Extension in the 2.4 GHz Band. IEEE: Piscataway, NJ, USA, 2000; pp. 1–96. [CrossRef]
25. Qualcomm Technologies, Inc. LTE in Unlicensed Spectrum: Harmonious Coexistence with WiFi. White Paper. 2014. Available online: https://www.qualcomm.com/content/dam/qcomm-martech/dm-assets/documents/lte-unlicensed-coexistence-whitepaper_june2014.pdf (accessed on 12 July 2022).
26. Shi, H.; Prasad, R.V.; Onur, E.; Niemegeers, I.G.M.M. Fairness in Wireless Networks: Issues, Measures and Challenges. *IEEE Commun. Surv. Tutor.* **2014**, *16*, 5–24. [CrossRef]
27. Jain, R.K.; Chiu, D.-M.W.; Hawe, W.R. A Quantitative Measure of Fairness and Discrimination for Resource Allocation in Shared Computer System. Technical Report. Volume 38. No. Digital Equipment Corporation. 1984. Available online: https://www.cs.wustl.edu/~jain/papers/ftp/fairness.pdf (accessed on 12 July 2022).
28. Jain, R.; Durresi, A.; Babic, G. *Throughput Fairness Index: An Explanation*; Technical Report; Department of CIS, The Ohio State University: Columbus, OH, USA, 1999. Available online: https://www.cse.wustl.edu/~jain/atmf/ftp/af_fair.pdf (accessed on 12 July 2022).
29. Wu, H.; Peng, Y.; Long, K.; Cheng, S.; Ma, J. Performance of reliable transport protocol over IEEE 802.11 wireless LAN: Analysis and enhancement. In Proceedings of the Twenty-First Annual Joint Conference of the IEEE Computer and Communications Societies, New York, NY, USA, 23–27 June 2002; Volume 2, pp. 599–607. [CrossRef]

Article

New Unequal Error Protection Strategy for Image Transmission Based on Bilayer-Lengthened PLDPC Code in Half-Duplex Relay System

Tian Gao [1], Min Xiao [1,*], Pingping Chen [2,*] and Diyan Gao [3]

1. School of OPTO-Electronic and Communication Engineering, Xiamen University of Technology, Xiamen 361005, China
2. School of Physics and Information Engineering, Fuzhou University, Fuzhou 350108, China
3. Maynooth International School of Engineering, Fuzhou University, Fuzhou 350108, China
* Correspondence: xiaomin_ced@xmut.edu.cn (M.X.); ppchen.xm@gmail.com (P.C.)

Abstract: To reduce the waste of energy in communications, unequal error protection (UEP) is used to provide asymmetric protection for messages with different levels of importance. This paper proposes new efficient strategies of UEP based on bilayer protograph-based low-density parity check (PLDPC) codes in decoding-and-forward (DF) relay systems. In particular, we jointly utilize source coding and channel coding to design UEP strategies and then save transmission energy. According to the different levels of importance of discrete cosine transform (DCT) coefficients of image and variance statistical characteristics of image sub-blocks, bilayer-lengthened PLDPC codes are exploited to protect the transmitted image information with different importance levels at the half-duplex relay system. In the end, the simulation result shows that the proposed UEP schemes achieve excellent performance gains compared to conventional equal error protection (EEP) scheme. Additionally, the complexity analysis of the UEP strategies is given.

Keywords: bilayer PLDPC; unequal error protection; joint source-channel coding; image segment

1. Introduction

In recent years, many research activities both on the coding and decoding of co-operative communication schemes have attracted a lot of attention [1–3]. Relay co-operative communication has won increasingly broad applications for its high ability of anti-fading in wireless multi-path channels, improving the reliability of information transmission [4,5]. Since the wireless co-operation communications utilize additional relay nodes, the cost of energy increases accordingly. Thus, improving the energy efficiency is one of the important issues in this co-operation system. Reference [6] considered the joint utility-based uplink power and rate allocation to raise the efficiency of energy in communication, and reference [7,8] studied the performance of resource allocation in non-orthogonal multiple access- (NOMA) based networks to solve the efficiency maximization problem of the downlink NOMA-based, massive multiple-input-multiple-output (MIMO) system.

As information is becoming more diversified and complicated, distinguishing information of different importance levels and providing asymmetric protection is essential to cater to the requirements of high performance and low transmission power nowadays. Reference [9] proposed a concept of unequal error protection (UEP) for channel coding that reduces energy consumption by providing different levels of protection for information with different levels of importance. Reference [10] presented rate allocation optimization algorithms based on rate-compatible codes for embedded image bit streams transmitted over noisy channels under UEP. Reference [11] proposed a UEP scheme by tracing the mapping between the important information data and the elite bits of an irregular LDPC code.

Reference [12] proposed a good tradeoff UEP-scheme between reliability and spectrum efficiency by using sixteen quadrature amplitude modulation (QAM) mapping. Reference [13] realized UEP by classifying the bit-channel type based on the delayed bit-interleaved coded modulation (DBICM). Reference [14] took advantage of the adaptive segmentation and weight-increase parity check (WIPC) LDPC code to achieve UEP for image sources. A UEP scheme based on the Luby transform (LT) codes was proposed in [15] for image transmission over multiple-input-multiple-output (MIMO) channels. Reference [16] presented a novel autoencoder-based approach for designing codes that provide UEP capabilities, and reference [17] proposed a type-aware coding approach to achieve UEPs for multiple classes of messages.

In this paper, we design two UEP strategies based on bilayer protograph-based LDPC (PLDPC) codes in a half-duplex relay system. PLDPC code is a subclass of LDPC codes [18,19], which benefit from simple structures and desirable performance in wireless applications [20–25]. Bilayer PLDPC code was put forward in decoding-and-forward (DF) relay systems. It is an especially useful class of structured LDPC codes and more general multi-layer codes and allows decoding of the same codeword with two (or more) different decoders [26–28]. We find that most existing UEP strategies focused on the implementation of channel coding without considering the characteristics of the source, and the optimization methods of these UEP-based codes are relatively complex. Thus, to address this issue, we exploit lengthened bilayer-lengthened PLDPC codes in UEP to transmit the information of different source characteristics. Bilayer PLDPC code can perform remarkably in this case due to its advantages, such as low encoding complexity, modular structure for easy design, and rate compatibility. Moreover, bilayer PLDPC code under the UEP scheme in relay systems can match a set of channel conditions without extensive re-optimization. Based on this, we propose two new UEP strategies with excellent performance. The main contributions of this work are summarized as follows:

(1) This paper proposes the concept that the integer and decimal parts of DCT coefficients have different levels of importance instead of considering high-frequency and low-frequency components of DCT coefficients with different levels of importance traditionally. Based on this, a joint source-channel coding UEP scheme (UEP-1) is designed based on bilayer-lengthened PLDPC code in half-duplex relay systems.

(2) This paper further proposes an elaborate UEP scheme (UEP-2) with excellent performance. We can realize UEP for image sub-blocks information with different levels of importance by variable rates and only need to store one bilayer protograph base matrix without extensive re-optimization. It reduces the required cache space for practical applications greatly. In the UEP-2 scheme, image sub-blocks are assigned to the corresponding class according to the classification map generated by K-means clustering.

At last, the simulation results show that the proposed UEP-1 scheme has 0.8 dB and 0.3 dB gains, and the proposed UEP-2 scheme has 1.6 d B and 1.1 d B gains compared to EEP and the traditional UEP scheme in low and high SNR regions, respectively. Compared to the traditional UEP scheme, both UEP-1 and UEP-2 schemes can achieve better performance. Moreover, we compare the FSIM between the recovered image and the original image under different SNRs, which shows that the performance of proposed UEP scheme is superior to that of EEP scheme. The complexity analysis of UEP strategies is given by discussing the usage of modules and computing the average number of decoding iterations.

2. Preliminaries and Notations

The table of notations in this section is shown in Table 1.

Table 1. Notations in Section 2.

Section 2.1	
B	Protograph base matrix
H	Protograph LDPC matrix
v	Variable node
c	Check node
Z	Lifting factor from protograph base matrix to protograph LDPC matrix
N_p	The number of variable nodes in the protograph base matrix
N	The number of variable nodes in the protograph LDPC matrix
M_p	The number of check nodes in the protograph base matrix
M	The number of check nodes in the protograph LDPC matrix
K	The number of information bits in the protograph LDPC code
Section 2.2	
B_{sd}	Bilayer-lengthened protograph base matrix with a lower rate
B_e	Extension base matrix
B_{sr}	Bilayer-lengthened protograph base matrix with high rate extended by B_{sd}
Section 2.3	
X_1	The broadcasted signal from the source during time slot one
X_2	The broadcasted signal from the source during time slot two
Y_1	Received signal in the destination during time slot one
Y_2	Received signal in the destination during time slot two
V_1	Received signal in the relay during time slot one
L_2	The transmitted signal from the relay to the destination during time slot two
Z_{sr}	Additive Gaussian noise received by the relay
Z_{d1}	Additive Gaussian noise received by destination during time slot one
Z_{d2}	Additive Gaussian noise received by destination during time slot two
P_{s_1}	The power constraint of the source during time slot one
P_{s_2}	The power constraint of the source during time slot two
P_{R_2}	The power constraint of the relay during time slot two
SNR_{ij}	Signal-to-noise ratio between node i and node j

2.1. Protograph LDPC Code

Protograph LDPC codes define a subclass of multi-edge type LDPC (MET-LDPC) codes, which allow extending a base matrix or graph prototype (base graph) to a complete matrix or graph [28]. A well-designed protograph LDPC code can achieve better performance and is suitable for an efficient encoding/decoding implementation [29,30]. A protograph $B = (\mathcal{V}, \mathcal{C}, \mathcal{E})$ can be represented by a tanner graph with a relatively small number of nodes, which consists of three sets, $\mathcal{V}, \mathcal{C}$ and $\mathcal{E}$, corresponding to N_p variable nodes (VNs), M_p check nodes (CNs), and the connecting edges, respectively. Each edge $e_{i,j} \in \mathcal{E}$ connects a VN $v_j \in \mathcal{V}$ to a CN $c_i \in \mathcal{C}$. A graphical example of generating the derived graph is shown in Figure 1. An (N, K) protograph code (an equivalent LDPC code) is derived by using a process known as *lifting*, where N and $N - K$ equals the number of VNs and CNS in the derived tanner graph corresponding to the base protograph graph, respectively. The *lifting* process utilizes the copy-and-permutation operation. The number of copy times is decided by the lifting factor $Z = N/N_p = M/M_p$, where $M = N - K$.

2.2. Bilayer-Lengthened PLDPC Code

Graph Structure: Geometrically, the variable nodes are divided into two layers: *layer-1* and *layer-2*, and the check nodes are all in one set in a bilayer-lengthened protograph [27]. Figure 2 shows that the edges of the base graph are connected in the first layer of variable nodes with the set of check nodes forming a base graph with a lower rate. The entire edges and nodes constitute a base graph with a high rate. The rate of bilayer-lengthened PLDPC code can be increased by adding the number of variable nodes in *layer-2*.

The entire protograph base matrix has the form

$$B_{sr} = [B_{sd}|B_e] \tag{1}$$

where B_{sd} is the protograph base matrix with a lower rate corresponding to *layer-1*, and B_e is the extension base matrix corresponding to *layer-2* in the tanner graph.

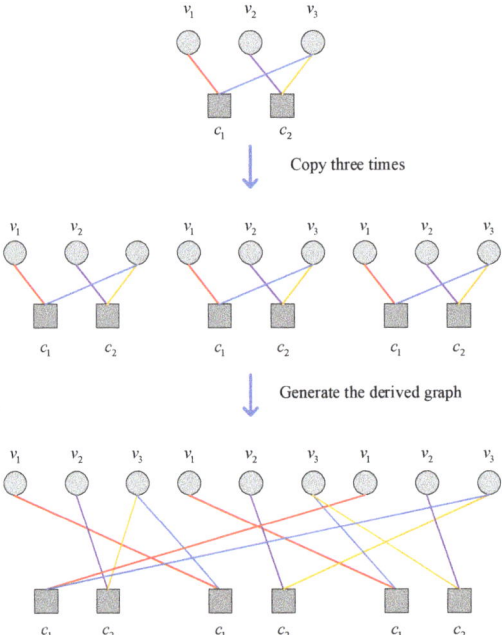

Figure 1. A graphical example of generating the derived graph.

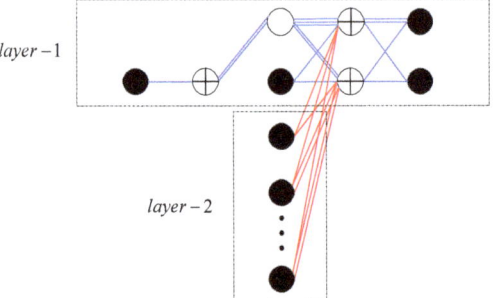

Figure 2. A tanner graph of bilayer-lengthened photograph. Black circles and circles with plus represent VNs and CNs, respectively, and the blank circle denotes the VNs which have been punctured.

2.3. Half-Duplex Relay System

According to the classic work of Cover and El Gamal [31], DF protocol describes that the relay completely decodes the transmitted message from the source and partially forwards the decoded message to the destination. In the destination, the receiver recovers the message by processing the signals transmitted by the source and relay. Half-duplex relay system is widely studied system in practice. This paper exploits the novel UEP scheme for the half-duplex relay system, where the relay can communicate with only one node in a time slot. According to [31] and Figure 3, the received signal in a half-duplex relay channel can be given by

$$V_1 = h_2 X_1 + Z_{sr} \qquad (2)$$

$$Y_1 = h_1 X_1 + Z_{d1} \qquad (3)$$

$$Y_2 = h_1 X_2 + h_3 L_2 + Z_{d2} \qquad (4)$$

where X_1, Y_1, and V_1 denote the transmitted signal from a source (**S**), the received signal in the destination (**D**), and the relay (**R**) during time slot one (a fraction t_1 of the transmission interval), respectively. X_2, L_2, and Y_2 denote the transmitted signals from source, relay, and the received signals in the destination during time slot two (a fraction $t_2 = 1 - t_1$), respectively. h_1, h_2, and h_3 are **S**-to-**D**, **S**-to-**R**, and **R**-to-**D** channel coefficients, respectively. $Z_{sr} \sim N(0, \sigma_{sr})$, $Z_{d1} \sim N(0, \sigma_{sd})$, and $Z_{d2} \sim N(0, \sigma_{sr} + \sigma_{rd})$ denote additive Gaussian noises at the relay and at destination for time slot one and time slot two, respectively. In time slots one and two, the communication channel can be seen as a broadcast channel and a multi-access channel, respectively. The source has power constraint $P_{S_1} = E(X_1^2)$ in time slot one and power constraint P_{S_2} in time slot two. P_{R_2} represents relay power constraint in time slot two. Thus, signal-to-noise ratios (SNR) SNR_{SR}, SNR_{SD}, and SNR_{RD} can be defined at the relay and destination at time slot one and at the destination at time slot two, respectively.

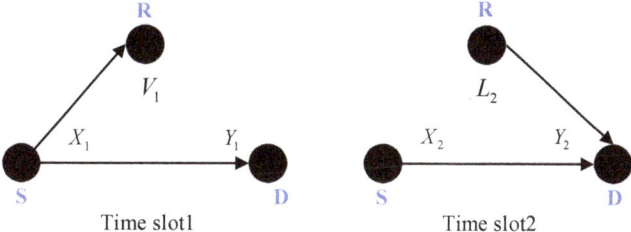

Figure 3. Half-duplex relay channel.

3. New UEP Strategy

3.1. UEP System Model

For practical purposes, we consider gray images as research objects for the UEP strategy in this paper. A new UEP scheme (UEP-1) system model in a half-duplex relay system is shown in Figure 4. After block discrete cosine transform (DCT) [32,33] processing of the input image, we found that each DCT coefficient Q can be divided into two parts—the integer part Q_i and the decimal part Q_d, where Q_d is approximated by retaining the binary number of k bits. The recovery performance of the image is dependent on the size of k. The degradation coefficients Q' can be represented as

$$Q' = \begin{cases} Q_i + Q_d, & \text{if } Q \geq 0 \\ Q_i - Q_d, & \text{if } Q < 0 \end{cases} \qquad (5)$$

where if $Q \geq 0$, $Q_i = \lfloor Q \rfloor$ and $Q_d = Q - Q_i$; else $Q_i = \lceil Q \rceil$ and $Q_d = Q_i - Q$. This step not only conserves transmission quality significantly, but also facilitates the combination of image transmission and UEP strategy. Q_i and Q_d have different attribution to Q'. In binary, Q' has a deviation of 2^i when an error happens in the i-th bit of Q_i. In contrast, only $\left(\frac{1}{2}\right)^i$ deviation in Q' when an error happens in the i-th bit of Q_d. Thus, the proposed UEP strategy provides two transmission paths for Q_i and Q_d. For Q_d with less attribution to Q', a traditional point-to-point channel (S-D link) coding and decoding mode is adopted. For Q_i with much attribution to Q', the relay transmits additional mutual information to help the destination decode the source message. In the destination, estimated information $\widetilde{Q}_i$ and $\widetilde{Q}_d$ are decoded, and the estimated DCT coefficient $\widetilde{Q}$ can be estimated by

$$\widetilde{Q} = \begin{cases} \widetilde{Q}_i + \widetilde{Q}_d, & \text{if } \widetilde{Q}_i \geq 0 \\ \widetilde{Q}_i - \widetilde{Q}_d, & \text{if } \widetilde{Q}_i < 0 \end{cases} \qquad (6)$$

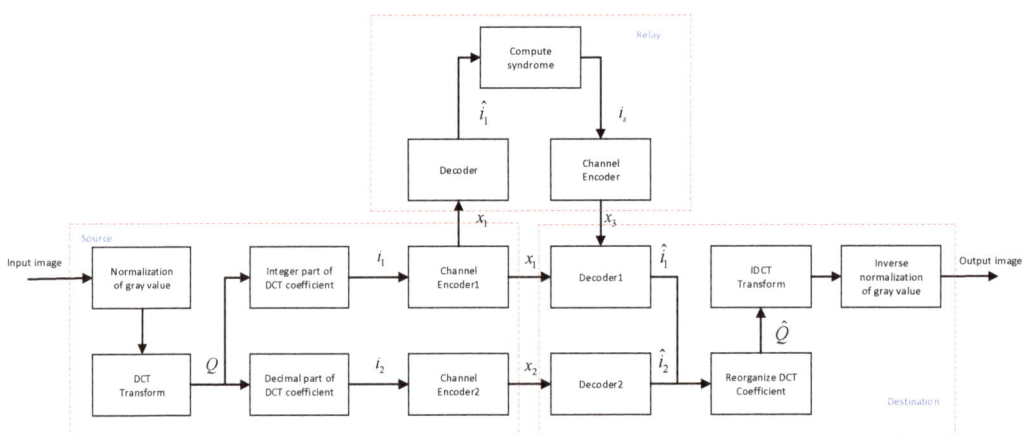

Figure 4. An UEP system model based on half-duplex relay system.

At last, the image can be restored by two steps, such as inverse discrete cosine transform (IDCT) and inverse normalization.

Encoding/Decoding of UEP System

The encoding of the UEP strategy only needs to store the bilayer protograph base matrix B_{sr}, extending by a lower-rate bilayer protograph base matrix B_{sd}, $B_{sr} = [B_{sd}|B_e]$. The signal i_1 of integer parts and the signal i_2 of decimal parts are encoded by H_{sr} (lift from B_{sr}) to generate the codewords x_1 and x_2 by encoder1 and encoder2, respectively. Encoder2 sends the codeword $x_2 = G_{sr}^T i_2$ to the destination, and encoder1 broadcasts the codeword $x_1 = G_{sr}^T i_1$ to relay and destination. G_{sr} is the generating matrix of parity check matrix H_{sr}. The relay encodes the syndrome i_s and transmits codeword x_3 to the destination by

$$x_3 = G_{sd}^T i_s \qquad (7)$$

where $i_s = \widetilde{i}'_1 H_{sd}^T$, and $\widetilde{i}'_1$ is the estimated information corresponding to variable nodes in *layer-2*, which is extracted from the estimated information $\widetilde{i}_1$. Estimated information $\widetilde{i}_1$ have been decoded from x_1 at the relay. H_{sd} is lifted from the base matrix B_{sd}.

Figure 5a,b show the iterative decoding factor graphs in decoder1 and decoder2. In Figure 5a, the variable nodes in *layer-2* are checked by the parity check matrix H_{sr}. The additional Log-Likelihood Ratio (LLR) of variable nodes in *layer-2* provide help for decoding the variable nodes in *layer-1*. We can see that the message from the j-th check node to the i-th variable node is

$$L(r_{ji}) = 2\tanh^{-1}\left(\prod_{i' \in R(j)/i} \tanh\left(L\left(q_{i'j}\right)/2 \right) \right) \qquad (8)$$

where $q_{i'j}$ is the message from i'-th variable node to j-th check node, and i' belongs to set $R(j)/i$. The elements in $R(j)/i$ can be divided into two parts corresponding to *layer-1* and *layer-2*. Compared to decoder2 in Figure 5b, decoder1 has a much more reliable message from the variables nodes that are connected to the syndrome in *layer-2*. It suggests a more reliable LLR $L(q_i)$ for the i-th variable node, computed by

$$L(q_i) = L(P_i) + \sum_{j \in C(i)} L(r_{ji}) \qquad (9)$$

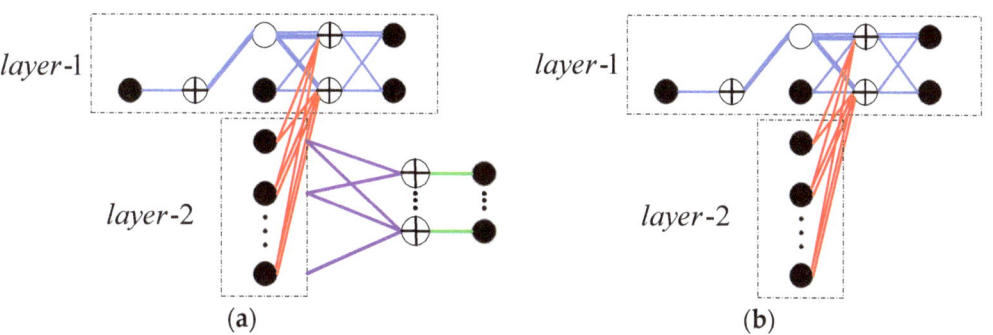

Figure 5. (**a**) Factor graph for decoder1. (**b**) Factor graph for decoder2.

3.2. Image Segmentation UEP Strategy

The image segmentation UEP strategy is illustrated in Figure 6. In this diagram, the classification map is generated by K-means clustering. In the source, the classification map is used to order sub-blocks of an input image and choose bilayer matrix with different rates for sub-blocks in different classes. Integer parts of DCT coefficients are encoded by bilayer PLDPC code with a fixed rate. Decimal parts of DCT coefficients are encoded by bilayer PLDPC code with a certain rate that is chosen from the classification map. Transmission message $x_s = [x_1, x_2]$ is broadcasted to the relay and the destination in time slot 1, respectively. The relay sends the message $x_3 = G_{sd}^T i_s$ to destination after decoding the message x_s and computing syndrome i_s. DCT coefficients can be recovered after decoding $\hat{x}_s$ in destination. A recovery image is obtained by reordering the sub-blocks with a classification map known at the receiver. We describe the main two steps of the UEP scheme (UEP-2) in this section, such as the image segmentation and the encoding procedure.

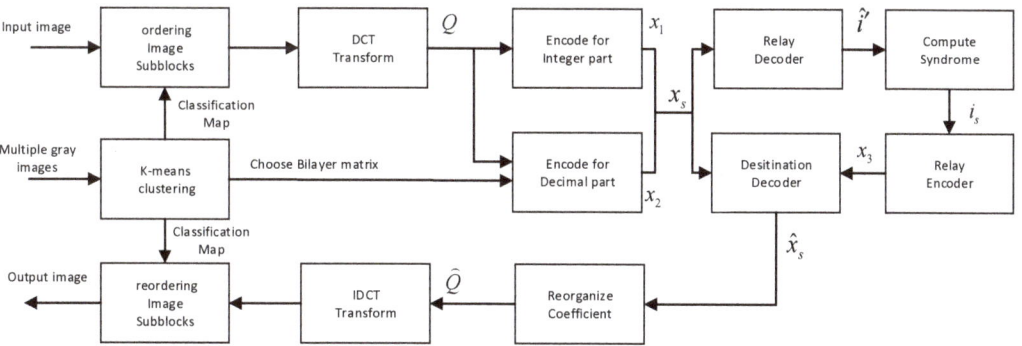

Figure 6. The frame diagram of the image segmentation UEP scheme.

3.2.1. Image Segmentation

To segment the original image of size (M, N) and distinguish sub-blocks of different levels of importance from all sub-blocks, we can discover the intensity of the pixel of sub-blocks change by defining the variance σ of the sub-blocks,

$$\sigma = \frac{\sum_{i=1}^{m}\sum_{j=1}^{n}(x_{i,j} - \overline{x})^2}{m \times n} \tag{10}$$

$$\overline{x} = \frac{\sum_{i=1}^{m}\sum_{j=1}^{n} x_{i,j}}{m \times n} \tag{11}$$

where $x_{i,j}$ represents the value of the pixel of the sub-blocks, and m and n are the size of the sub-blocks. An original image can be segmented into $z = M/m = N/n$ sub-blocks, and an array of variances $\sigma = [\sigma_1, \sigma_2, \ldots, \sigma_z]$ can be computed corresponding to z sub-blocks. Then, the variance matrix of sub-blocks of k images can be represented by

$$\begin{pmatrix} s_1 & \cdots & s_z \end{pmatrix} = \begin{pmatrix} \sigma_{1,1} & \cdots & \sigma_{1,z} \\ & \ddots & \\ \sigma_{k,1} & \cdots & \sigma_{k,z} \end{pmatrix} \tag{12}$$

where $\sigma_{i,j}$ denotes the variance of the j-th sub-block in the i-th image, and column vector s_j represents the variances of the j-th sub-block of all the images. The classes are developed by K-means clustering [34] to classify sub-blocks from multiple images (except for the images waiting for transmission).

3.2.2. Encoding of Image Segmentation UEP Strategy

Assuming that sub-blocks of the input image are divided into four groups by classification map, for sorted sub-blocks of the input image, we match the integer parts signal i_1 of DCT coefficients with a fixed lower-rate bilayer PLDPC code $H_{sr,1}$ and decimal parts signal i_2 of DCT coefficients with diverse rates bilayer-lengthened code $H_{sr,i}$, $i \in [1,2,3,4]$, by

$$x_1 = G_{sr,1}^T i_1 \tag{13}$$

$$x_{2,i} = G_{sr,i}^T i_{2,i} \tag{14}$$

where $i_2 = [i_{2,1}, i_{2,2}, i_{2,3}, i_{2,4}]$ are the decimal parts of DCT coefficients after ordering all of the image sub-blocks, and $i_{2,i}$ corresponds to the i-th group that decimal parts of sub-blocks belong to. The source broadcasts codeword $x_s = [x_1, x_2]$ to the relay and destination, where $x_2 = [x_{2,1}, x_{2,2}, x_{2,3}, x_{2,4}]$. $G_{sr,i}$ denotes the generator matrix of the parity check matrix $H_{sr,i}$, lifting from $B_{sr,i}$. $B_{sr,i}$ is a sub-protograph base matrix with a higher rate extended by

$$B_{sr,1} = [B_{sd}|B_e] \tag{15}$$

$$B_{sr,2} = [B_{sr,1}|B_{e,1}] \tag{16}$$

$$B_{sr,i} = [B_{sr,i-1}|B_{e,i-1}] \tag{17}$$

As can be seen in Equations (15)–(17), diverse rates can be achieved for the decimal parts of DCT coefficients of sub-blocks with different levels of importance by the matrix expansion method, and only one base matrix $B_{sr,i}$ needs to be stored. $B_{sr,i-1}$ and $B_{e,i-1}$ corresponding to *layer-1* and *layer-2* are combined to create a capacity-approaching code for image transmission.

Relay decodes the codeword x_s and extracts the second layer information $\hat{i}_1''$ and $\hat{i}_2''$ from x_1 and x_2 and then computes syndrome $i_s = [i_{s1}|i_{s2}]$, $i_{s1} = \hat{i}_1'' H_{sd}^T$, and $i_{s2} = \hat{i}_2'' H_{sd}^T$, respectively. As shown in Figure 6, codeword $x_3 = G_{sd}^T i_s$ is decoded at the destination, and the syndrome i_s is recovered during the second time slot. With the recovered syndrome, we have bilayer PLDPC codes $H_{sr,1}$ and $H_{sr,i}$, as shown in Figure 7. The check relationship between *layer-2* variables nodes and syndrome nodes helps the destination with forming lower rate codes to decode the codeword x_s from the source.

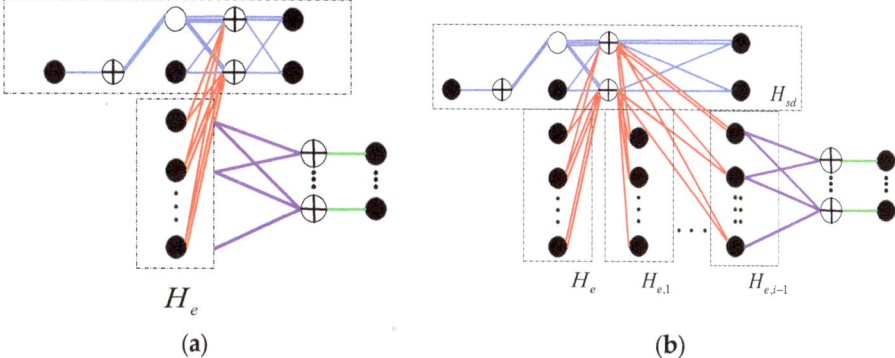

Figure 7. The tanner graph of bilayer PLDPC codes with the syndrome. (**a**) Bilayer PLDPC codes $H_{sr,1}$ with the syndrome; (**b**) Bilayer PLDPC codes $H_{sr,i}$ with the syndrome.

4. Results

4.1. Simulation Result

This part demonstrates the simulation performance of the proposed UEP schemes. The software and hardware platforms of simulation are C++, Matlab, Intel i7, and Nvidia 3060, respectively. The preset parameters are shown in Table 2; we compared three strategies, and the length of codes was 1296 in simulation. The first strategy (EEP) protected the integer and decimal parts of DCT coefficients of the image by the classical AR3A code with a 3/4 rate equally in the point-to-point channel (S-D link). The second strategy (UEP-1) provided UEP for the integer and decimal parts of DCT coefficients of the image. The integer and decimal parts were encoded by bilayer-PLDPC code H_{sr} with a 3/4 rate. The integer parts were transmitted in the relay channel while decimal parts were transmitted in the point-to-point channel (S-D link). The third strategy (UEP-2) utilizesd the image segmentation scheme and applied diverse rates (2/3, 3/4, 4/5, 5/6) of bilayer PLDPC codes for the decimal parts of DCT coefficients in four groups (classified by K-means clustering 40 images). The integer parts were encoded with a 2/3 rate bilayer PLDPC coded and were transmitted together with decimal parts in the half-duplex relay channel. The protograph base matrix $H_{1/2}$ and the corresponding extended sub-protograph base matrices $H_{2/3}$, $H_{3/4}$, $H_{4/5}$, and $H_{5/6}$ were opitimized by protograph extrinsic infromation transfer (PEXIT) alogrithm [28] as

$$H_{1/2} = \begin{pmatrix} 1 & 2 & 0 & 0 & 0 & 1 & 0 \\ 0 & 3 & 1 & 1 & 1 & 1 & 0 \\ 0 & 1 & 2 & 2 & 2 & 1 & 1 \\ 0 & 2 & 0 & 0 & 0 & 0 & 2 \end{pmatrix} \tag{18}$$

$$H_{2/3} = \left(H_{1/2} \left| \begin{array}{ccc} 0 & 1 & 1 \\ 1 & 1 & 1 \\ 2 & 1 & 2 \\ 0 & 1 & 0 \end{array} \right. \right), \quad H_{3/4} = \left(H_{2/3} \left| \begin{array}{ccc} 0 & 0 & 2 \\ 2 & 2 & 0 \\ 1 & 1 & 2 \\ 0 & 0 & 1 \end{array} \right. \right)$$

$$H_{4/5} = \left(H_{3/4} \left| \begin{array}{ccc} 0 & 1 & 2 \\ 1 & 2 & 2 \\ 2 & 1 & 1 \\ 0 & 0 & 0 \end{array} \right. \right), \quad H_{5/6} = \left(H_{4/5} \left| \begin{array}{ccc} 0 & 0 & 1 \\ 2 & 2 & 0 \\ 1 & 1 & 2 \\ 0 & 0 & 2 \end{array} \right. \right) \tag{19}$$

where $H_{2/3}$, $H_{3/4}$, $H_{4/5}$, and $H_{5/6}$ were lifted 216, 144, 108, and 87 times to achieve the 1296 code length corresponding to bilayer-PLDPC full matrices $H_{sr,1}$, $H_{sr,2}$, $H_{sr,3}$, and $H_{sr,4}$ respectively. The end-to-end relay channel error can be presented as a function of the three SNRs (SNR_{sd}, SNR_{sr}, and SNR_{rd}) of its constituent channels, represented by

$$SNR_{SR} = SNR_{SD} + a, \ SNR_{RD} = SNR_{SD} + b \quad (20)$$

where a and b are variable parameters [28].

Table 2. Simulation parameter setting.

Parameters	EEP	UEP-1	UEP-2
Code length	1296	1296	1296
Code rate	3/4	3/4	2/3, 3/4, 4/5, 5/6
a (dB)	no relay	1.4	1.4
b (dB)	no relay	1.6	1.6

Figure 8 shows the end-to-end performance comparison of different bilayer PLDPC code and the conventional AR3A code in half-duplex relay system. It is observed that the bilayer PLDPC codes had performance gains of 0.3 dB and 0.2 dB over the AR3A code at rates of 2/3 and 3/4, respectively.

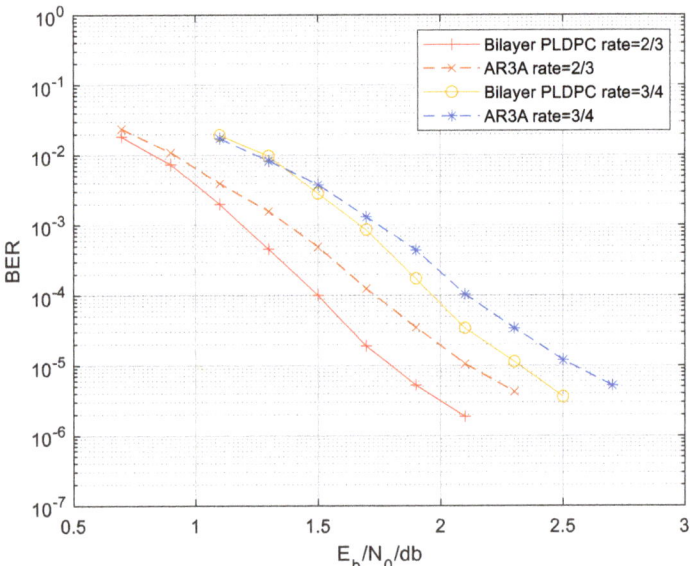

Figure 8. The end-to-end performance comparison of bilayer-lengthened PLDPC code and AR3A code in in half-duplex relay system.

Figure 9 shows the performance of recovery image of the three strategies with $SNR_{SD} = 1.3, 1.9, 2.1$ dB, $a = 1.4$, and $b = 1.6$. We can see that the recovery image qualities of the UEP-1 and UEP-2 strategies were significantly better than that of the EEP strategy under different SNRs. The UEP-1 and UEP-2 strategies achieved 19 dB and 31 dB peak signal-to-noise ratio (PSNR) gain over the EEP scheme for image 'Pepper' at $SNR_{SD} = 2.5$ dB, respectively.

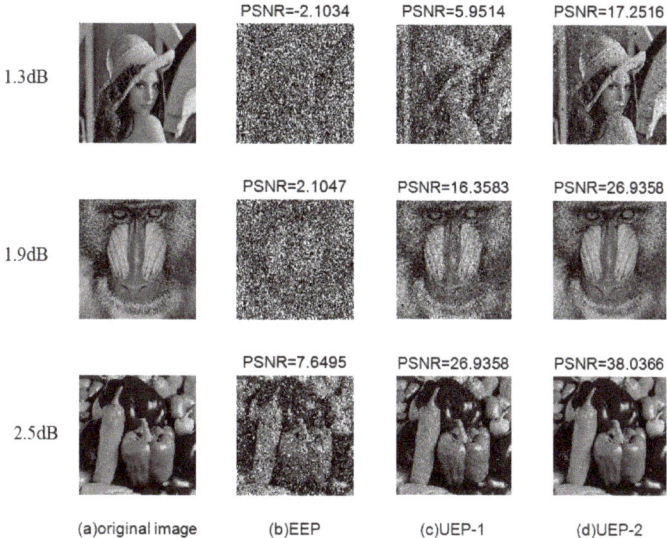

Figure 9. The comparison of recovery images in 3 strategies.

Figure 10 demonstrates the comparison of the PSNR of recovered images in four schemes under different SNRs. The AR3A code with a threshold at 3.1 dB was utilized for both integer and decimal parts of DCT coefficients in the EEP scheme. The UEP-0 scheme is the mainstream UEP method in joint source-channel coding system, which provides UEP for the high and low frequency of DCT coefficients [14]. The UEP-1 and UEP-2 schemes were designed in Sections 3.1 and 3.2, respectively. As can be seen in Figure 10, the 'Lena' image can be recovered at 3.1 dB and 3 dB by EEP and UEP-0 schemes, respectively. Compared to EEP and UEP-0 schemes, the UEP-1 scheme can achieve 0.3 dB and 0.2 dB gains, and the gains are higher in the low SNR region, reaching 0.8 dB and 0.6 dB, respectively. The UEP-2 scheme provides a delicate UEP strategy for decimal parts of DCT coefficients by image segmentation. As shown in Figure 10, UEP-2 had 0.8 dB and 0.7 dB gains in high SNR regions and 1.3 dB and 1.1 dB gains in the low SNR region, in contrast to the EEP and UEP-0 schemes, respectively.

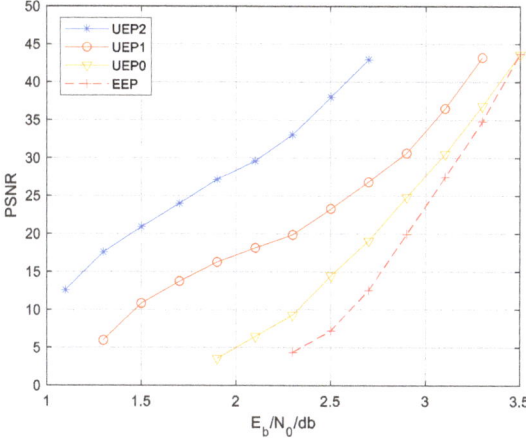

Figure 10. The PSNR comparison of 'Lena's recovery image in 4 protection strategies.

Furthermore, Figure 11 shows the comparison of the feature similarity index measure (FSIM) between the recovery image and original image in three schemes under different SNRs. We can see the FSIM achieved 0.99 at 1.5 dB in the UEP-2 scheme, which is superior to those of UEP-1 and EEP of 1 dB and 1.3 dB, respectively. Moreover, it is interesting to note that the FSIM goes up to the top very quickly in the EEP scheme, compared to the proposed UEP schemes. This is due to that the decimal part of the DCT coefficients focuses on describing the details of the image, and this part of information can be recovered at high the SNR region in the proposed UEP schemes.

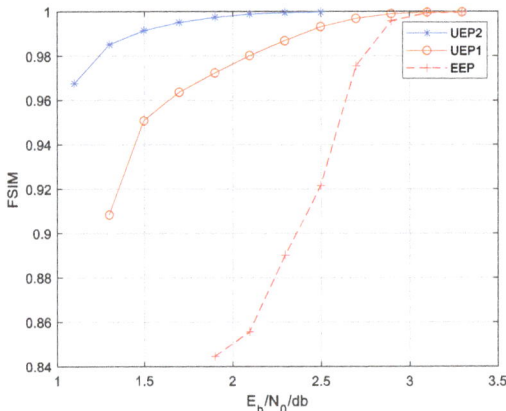

Figure 11. The FSIM comparison of 'Lena's recovery image in 3 protection strategies.

4.2. Complexity Analysis

The complexity of proposed joint source-channel coding frameworks is discussed in this section. As shown in Table 3, we tracked the usage of different modules in three strategies. In UEP-2, the module of reordering image sub-block is needed as compared to EEP and UEP-1. Since K-means clustering classifies the image sub-blocks into p groups, additional p times reordering operations are required. Moreover, both UEP-1 and UEP-2 strategies require the module to distinguish image source and additional l rounding operations and $2l$ addition operations for telling the integer and decimal source apart, where l is the number of the transmitted DCT coefficients. Furthermore, we considered the complexity of channel decoding in the three strategies. As shown in Table 3, both UEP-1 and UEP-2 strategies required the relay decoding and the joint decoding modules at the destination.

Table 3. The usage of modules in three transmission strategies.

Strategy	Modules in Three Strategies			
	Reordering Image Sub-Block	Distinguish Image Source	Relay Decoding	Destination Joint Decoding
EEP	no	no	no	no
UEP-1	no	yes	yes	yes
UEP-2	yes	yes	yes	yes

Morever, we show the convergence of the BP decodings by calculating the average number of decoding iterations, as given in Figure 12. It can be observed that UEP-1 had about two more iterations in comparison to EEP, even if extra decoders were added in the relay and the desitination. While UEP-2 had significantly higher iterations than EEP, the main reason is that the relay and the destination need to use more decoding resources to decode the encoding message of the decimal part.

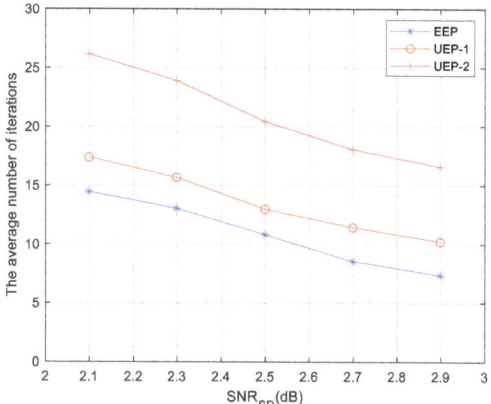

Figure 12. The average number of decoding iterations comparison in three strategies.

5. Discussion and Conclusions

A novel joint source-channel coding scheme is introduced into the half-duplex relay system to design a UEP strategy for image transmission in this paper. According to the different levels of importance of image DCT coefficients and variance statistical characteristics of image sub-blocks, two kinds of image non-symmetric protection strategies were proposed and realized based on a family of bilayer-lengthened PLDPC codes. The first UEP scheme is designed for different parts of DCT coefficients with different transmission strategies. The second UEP scheme provides non-symmetric protection for image sub-blocks with different levels of importance that are segmented from the original image. The simulation results show that the proposed UEP schemes both have excellent performance compared to the conventional EEP and UEP scheme in the half-duplex relay systems. In the end, some prospects are put forward. Note that it is hard to achieve the optimal image segmentation technique for UEP strategy. More excellent UEP strategy needs to be studied, such as the joint design of the image feature extraction technique [35–38] and channel coding technique. It is expected that the unequal error protection for the integers and decimals can be applied to various occasions, in addition to image transmission, when applying source-channel coding methods. Additionally, note that the optimization design for source structures and the bilayer PLDPC codes in UEP strategy deserves our further study.

Author Contributions: Conceptualization, T.G. and M.X.; methodology, T.G.; software, T.G.; validation, M.X., P.C. and D.G.; formal analysis, D.G.; investigation, T.G.; resources, M.X.; data curation, T.G.; writing—original draft preparation, T.G.; writing—review and editing, T.G. and P.C.; visualization, D.G. and P.C.; supervision, M.X.; project administration, M.X.; funding acquisition, M.X. All authors have read and agreed to the published version of the manuscript.

Funding: This research was supported the by Natural Science Foundation of Fujian Province, China under Grant no 2018J01569.

Institutional Review Board Statement: Not applicable.

Informed Consent Statement: Not applicable.

Data Availability Statement: Not applicable.

Conflicts of Interest: The authors declare no conflict of interest.

References

1. Li, Q.; Yu, M.; Pandharipande, A.; Ge, X. Outage Analysis of Co-Operative Two-Path Relay Channels. *IEEE Trans. Wirel. Commun.* **2016**, *15*, 3157–3169. [CrossRef]
2. Chen, P.; Xie, Z.; Fang, Y.; Chen, Z.; Mumtaz, S.; Rodrigues, J.J.P.C. Physical-Layer Network Coding: An Efficient Technique for Wireless Communications. *IEEE Netw.* **2020**, *34*, 270–276. [CrossRef]
3. Chen, P.; Liew, S.C.; Shi, L. Bandwidth-Efficient Coded Modulation Schemes for Physical-Layer Network Coding with High-Order Modulations. *IEEE Trans. Commun.* **2017**, *65*, 147–160. [CrossRef]
4. Hunter, T.E.; Nosratinia, A. Diversity through Coded Cooperation. *IEEE Trans. Wirel. Commun.* **2006**, *5*, 283–289. [CrossRef]
5. Rossetto, F.; Zorzi, M. Mixing Network Coding and Cooperation for Reliable Wireless Communications. *IEEE Wirel. Commun.* **2011**, *18*, 15–21. [CrossRef]
6. Tsiropoulou, E.E.; Vamvakas, P.; Papavassiliou, S. Joint Utility-Based Uplink Power and Rate Allocation in Wireless Networks: A non-cooperative game theoretic framework. *Phys. Commun.* **2013**, *9*, 299–307. [CrossRef]
7. El-ghorab, M.A.; El-meligy, M.R.; Ibrahim, M.M.; Newagy, F. Energy-Efficient User Pairing for Downlink NOMA in Massive MIMO Networks. *Appl. Sci.* **2022**, *12*, 5421. [CrossRef]
8. Ali, Z.J.; Noordin, N.K.; Sali, A.; Hashim, F.; Balfaqih, M. Novel Resource Allocation Techniques for Downlink Non-Orthogonal Multiple Access Systems. *Appl. Sci.* **2020**, *10*, 5892. [CrossRef]
9. Zhao, M.; Akansu, A.N. UEP of progressive images in wireless channels. In Proceedings of the Vehicular Technology Conference Fall 2000, Boston, MA, USA, 24–28 September 2000.
10. Zhao, M.; Akansu, A.N. Optimization of dynamic UEP schemes for embedded image sources in noisy channels. In Proceedings of the International Conference on Image Processing (ICIP), Vancouver, BC, Canada, 10–13 September 2000.
11. Yang, X.; Yuan, D.; Ma, P.; Jiang, M. New research on unequal error protection (UEP) property of irregular LDPC codes. In Proceedings of the First IEEE Consumer Communications and Networking Conference (CCNC), Las Vegas, NV, USA, 5–8 January 2004.
12. Ma, P.; Kwak, K.S. Modulation-assisted UEP-LDPC codes in image transmission. In Proceedings of the 9th International Symposium on Communications and Information Technology (ISCIT), Icheon, Korea, 28–30 September 2009.
13. Liao, Y.; Qiu, M.; Yuan, J. Design and Analysis of Delayed Bit-Interleaved Coded Modulation with LDPC Codes. *IEEE Trans. Commun.* **2021**, *69*, 3556–3571. [CrossRef]
14. Xu, B.; Zhang, Z.M.; Zhang, E.Y.; He, Y.L. Research on Unequal Error Protection with Irregular LDPC and Application on Image Transmission. In Proceedings of the 2nd International Congress on Image and Signal Processing (ICISP), Tianjin, China, 17–19 October 2009.
15. Zhang, W.; Jing, X.; Zhang, Z.; Chen, Q. Image transmission with UEP-LT over MIMO channels. In Proceedings of the 22nd Wireless and Optical Communication Conference (WOCC), Chongqing, China, 16–18 May 2013.
16. Ninkovic, V.; Vukobratovic, D.; Häger, C.; Wymeersch, H.; Graell i Amat, A. Autoencoder-Based Unequal Error Protection Code. *IEEE Commun. Lett.* **2021**, *25*, 3575–3579. [CrossRef]
17. Yao, X.; Wan, H.; Ma, X. A type-aware coding approach for unequal message protection. *Phys. Commun.* **2022**, *53*, 101721. [CrossRef]
18. Chung, S.-Y.; Forney, G.D.; Richardson, T.J.; Urbanke, R. On the Design of Low-density Parity-check Codes within 0.0045 dB of the Shannon Limit. *IEEE Commun. Lett.* **2001**, *5*, 58–60. [CrossRef]
19. Fossorier, M.P.C. Iterative reliability-based decoding of low-density parity check codes. *IEEE J. Sel. Areas Commun.* **2001**, *5*, 908–917. [CrossRef]
20. Dai, L.; Fang, Y.; Yang, Z.; Chen, P.; Li, Y. Protograph LDPC-Coded BICM-ID With Irregular CSK Mapping in Visible Light Communication Systems. *IEEE Trans. Veh. Technol.* **2021**, *70*, 11033–11038. [CrossRef]
21. Chen, P.; Wang, L.; Lau, F.C.M. One Analog STBC-DCSK Transmission Scheme not Requiring Channel State Information. *IEEE Trans. Circuits Syst. I Regul. Pap.* **2013**, *60*, 1027–1037. [CrossRef]
22. Chen, P.; Cai, K.; Zheng, S. Rate-Adaptive Protograph LDPC Codes for Multi-Level-Cell NAND Flash Memory. *IEEE Commun. Lett.* **2018**, *22*, 1112–1115. [CrossRef]
23. Chen, L.; Chen, P.; Lin, Z. Artificial Intelligence in Education: A Review. *IEEE Access* **2020**, *8*, 75264–75278. [CrossRef]
24. Chen, C.; Xiang, J.; Ye, Z.; Yan, W.; Wang, S.; Wang, Z.; Chen, P.; Xiao, M. Deep Learning-Based Energy Optimization for Edge Device in UAV-Aided Communications. *Drones* **2022**, *6*, 139. [CrossRef]
25. Fang, Y.; Bu, Y.; Chen, P.; Lau, F.C.M.; Otaibi, S.A. Irregular-Mapped Protograph LDPC-Coded Modulation: A Bandwidth-Efficient Solution for 6G-Enabled Mobile Networks. *IEEE Trans. Intell. Transp. Syst.* **2021**. early access. [CrossRef]
26. Razaghi, P.; Yu, W. Bilayer Low-density Parity-check Codes for Decode-and-Forward in Relay Channels. *IEEE Trans. Inf. Theory* **2007**, *53*, 3723–3739. [CrossRef]
27. Vahabzadeh, O.; Salehi, M. Design of bilayer lengthened LDPC codes for Rayleigh fading relay channels. In Proceedings of the 45th Annual Conference on Information Sciences and Systems, Baltimore, MD, USA, 23–25 March 2011.
28. Van Nguyen, T.; Nosratinia, A.; Divsalar, D. Bilayer protograph codes for half-duplex relay channels. *IEEE Trans. Wirel. Commun.* **2013**, *12*, 1969–1977. [CrossRef]
29. Fang, Y.; Bi, G.; Guan, Y.L.; Lau, F.C. A survey on protograph LDPC codes and their applications. *IEEE Commun. Surv. Tutor.* **2015**, *17*, 1989–2016. [CrossRef]

30. Dai, J.; Tan, K.; Si, Z.; Niu, K.; Chen, M.; Poor, H.V.; Cui, S. Learning to decode protograph LDPC codes. *IEEE J. Sel. Areas Commun.* **2021**, *39*, 1983–1999. [CrossRef]
31. Cover, T.; Gamal, A.E. Capacity theorems for the relay channel. *IEEE Trans. Inf. Theory* **1979**, *25*, 572–584. [CrossRef]
32. Lengwehasatit, K.; Ortega, A. Scalable Variable Complexity Approximate forward DCT. *IEEE Trans. Circuits Syst. Video Technol.* **2004**, *14*, 1236–1248. [CrossRef]
33. Triantafyllidis, G.A.; Tzovaras, D.; Strintzis, M.G. Blocking Artifact Detection and Reduction in Compressed Data. *IEEE Trans. Circuits Syst. Video Technol.* **2002**, *12*, 877–890. [CrossRef]
34. Banerjee, S.; Choudhary, A.; Pal, S. Empirical Evaluation of K-Means, Bisecting K-Means, Fuzzy C-Means and Genetic K-Means Clustering Algorithms. In Proceedings of the IEEE International WIE Conference on Electrical and Computer Engineering (WIECON-ECE), Pune, India, 19–21 December 2016.
35. Singh, U.P.; Chouhan, S.S.; Jain, S. Images as Graphical Password: Verification and analysis using non-regular low-density parity check coding. *Int. J. Inf. Technol.* **2020**, *1*, 41. [CrossRef]
36. Chouhan, S.S.; Koul, A.; Singh, U.P. Image Segmentation Using Computational Intelligence Techniques: Review. *Arch. Comput. Methods Eng.* **2018**, *64*, 533–596. [CrossRef]
37. Chouhan, S.S.; Koul, A.; Singh, U.P. Soft computing approaches for image segmentation: A survey. *Multimed. Tools Appl.* **2018**, *77*, 28483–28537. [CrossRef]
38. Chouhan, S.S.; Koul, A.; Singh, U.P. Image segmentation using fuzzy competitive learning based counter propagation network. *Multimed. Tools Appl.* **2019**, *5*, 35263–35287. [CrossRef]

MDPI
St. Alban-Anlage 66
4052 Basel
Switzerland
Tel. +41 61 683 77 34
Fax +41 61 302 89 18
www.mdpi.com

Symmetry Editorial Office
E-mail: symmetry@mdpi.com
www.mdpi.com/journal/symmetry

www.ingramcontent.com/pod-product-compliance
Lightning Source LLC
LaVergne TN
LVHW070043120526
838202LV00101B/419